Teaching Talent

Teaching Talent

A Visionary Framework
for Human Capital in Education

Edited by Rachel E. Curtis and Judy Wurtzel

HARVARD EDUCATION PRESS
CAMBRIDGE, MA

Library of Congress Control Number 2009942747

Paperback ISBN 978-1-934742-49-5
Library Edition ISBN 978-1-934742-50-1

Published by Harvard Education Press,
an imprint of the Harvard Education Publishing Group

Harvard Education Press
8 Story Street
Cambridge, MA 02138

Cover Design: Billy Boardman

The typefaces used in this book are Adobe Garamond Pro and Formata.

*For the superintendents who participate in the
Aspen Institute's Urban Superintendents Network:
their thoughtfulness, strategic thinking, courage,
tenacity, and profound commitment create
opportunities for millions of children every day.*

Contents

Acknowledgments

The blue sky and snowcapped mountains of Aspen, Colorado, are a source of great inspiration. The idea for this book grew out of the 2007 summer workshop of the Aspen Institute's Education and Society Program, when we began to explore human capital management in public education and introduced the earliest draft of this book's culminating vision. The participants' energy and ideas made it clear we were onto something important and inspired us to dig deeper. We thank Tammy Battaglino, Richard Clarke, Darryl Cobb, David Coleman, Robert Gordon, Tom Kane, Tim Knowles, Renee Moore, Stefanie Sanford, Steve Seleznow, Gretchen Crosby Sims, Shivam Mallick Shah, Harry Spence, LaVerne Srinivasan, David Vitale, and Susan Zelman for their participation in the workshop. Their willingness to imagine what might be possible if American education focused on improving teaching quality, the vision they developed, and their willingness to wrestle with ideas that were simultaneously messy and promising set the direction for this book.

By summer 2008, we had refined our thinking and had the opportunity to focus workshop participants on what the key human capital innovations would be in schools and school systems. We are grateful to Barbara Adams and Carol Johnson of the Boston Public Schools, Kathy Augustine and Millicent Few of the Atlanta Public Schools, and Brad Jupp and Shayne Spalten of the Denver Public Schools, who helped us map vision to current reality and build bridges from one to the other. The Ajax Mountain Team members—Andy Rotherham, Ruth Wattenberg, Charlotte Danielson, Ross Wiener, Sandra Licon, Carol Johnson, and Mindy Hernandez—provided the framing for chapter 5. Bob Schwartz, the cofacilitator of the Aspen Education and Society Program and the facilitator of Ajax team thanks them while absolving them of any responsibility for the final chapter. Fred Frelow, Heather Harding, Ben Levin, Sandra Licon, and Vince Riveroll brought a wealth of experience, expertise, passion, and perspective to the workshop that informed the chapters related to second-stage teachers and the role of principals as human capital managers. Mike O'Keefe joined Bob Schwartz in guiding both summer workshops masterfully. They knew when to drop anchor and look beneath the surface and when to take advantage of the wind generated by participants' thinking to move the conversations and work forward.

Over the last two and a half years, the superintendents in the Aspen Urban Superintendents Network dug deeply into the ideas generated in the summer workshops. We give a special thanks to the participating superintendents—Andres Alonso, Bill Andrekopoulos, Michael Bennet, Tom Boasberg, Arne Duncan, John Deasy, Bill Hite, Maria Goodloe-Johnson, Pete Gorman, Beverly Hall, Carol Johnson, Mark Roosevelt, and Abe Saavedra—for their partnership. They served as our critical friends, adding to and burnishing the ideas reflected in this book, making them better able to stand up to the reality of the work of school systems and their partners and to drive improvement. They kept us honest, pushed our thinking, and experimented with human capital innovations, teaching us all along the way. Bob Schwartz's and Warren Simmons' skillful facilitation of the group and the critical role that Tony Bryk, Jennifer O'Day, Tom Payzant, and Uri Treisman played as Aspen Advisers helped build and sustain the group's momentum.

Using all the grist for the mill generated at the workshops and by the superintendents, the contributing authors created this book. They deftly honed a jumble of promising ideas and early experiments into a vision bolstered by concrete images of the work and its impact on children's learning.

Another group of people demonstrated their commitment to human capital management through their willingness to participate at multiple levels. Betsy Arons, Karolyn Belcher, Tony Bryk, Tim Daly, Jane Hannaway, Brad Jupp, Francine Lawrence, Andy Rotherham, Bob Schwartz, Shayne Spalten, Larry Stanton, Sandra Stein, and Ross Wiener each did double or triple duty as workshop participants, manuscript reviewers, and in some cases, chapter authors. Their tireless good humor and willingness to continually talk about and hone the ideas reflected in this volume was a great gift for which we are thankful.

The evolution of this book from an idea born under blue sky and amid snowcapped mountains to that which you are reading would not have been possible without the help of many people who served as thought partners, technical experts, and reviewers of chapters. Martha Piper and Susan Colby provided insights on how to "frame" a framework. Michelle Boyers, Susan Moore Johnson, John Luczak, Karen Miles, Andy Moffitt, Lynn Olson, Monica Rosen, Susan Sclafani, Regis Shields, and Lee Teitel provided close, critical reads and nudged us in the right direction when we had lost our way.

Noel Danforth gets a special nod for her curiosity, artistry, and patience as she helped us create the right graphic image to accompany the framework.

The staff at the Aspen Institute's Education and Society Program brought together these various networks and communities of learning. It is an indefatigable group led by the long-standing program director Nancy Pelz-Paget, who used her vast network and powers of partnership to bring the right people together to explore the issues. Mindy Hernandez was an important thought partner and facilitated the collaborative work required on several chapters. Katrin Thomas lent her unflappable style and incredible attention to detail to the effort, never letting us stray far. Jane Ngo joined this work midstream and stepped right, in providing quiet leadership, clarity, and incredible research. Sylvie Thomas appeared on the scene at the last minute and worked wonders in organizing the research that undergirds this book in ways that every reader will appreciate. The program's new leader, Ross Wiener, first joined us at the 2008 summer workshop and quickly moved from that circle to the center of the Venn diagram as the new executive director of the Aspen Institute's Education and Society Program.

We must thank the two people who shepherded us through the process of compiling this volume. Robert Rothman's stellar editing brought clarity and coherence within and across chapters. Caroline Chauncey at the Harvard Education Press offered sage counsel, grace, and never-ending faith, all of which made working with her both a blessing and a delight.

Finally, all the work described was made possible through the generous support of the Bill and Melinda Gates Foundation, the William and Flora Hewlett Foundation, the Spencer Foundation, and the Stupski Foundation. Each foundation entrusted us to move the human capital conversation forward and provide ideas and images that can drive action in school systems on behalf of students' learning. We hope we have done them justice. We could not have done this work without them. That said, we are responsible for the content of the book; it does not necessarily reflect the views of the foundations.

Foreword

A Profession's Progress

Michael F. Bennet, Senator from Colorado

"In a global economy where the greatest job qualification isn't what you can do but what you know, our teachers are the key to our nation's success; to whether America will lead the world in the discoveries and the innovations and economic prosperity of this new century."

—*President Barack Obama, at National and State Teachers of the Year event, April 28, 2009*

Our schools are fundamentally human efforts. The improvement we make as a system is achieved school-by-school, classroom-by-classroom, teacher-by-teacher, and student-by-student. It is impossible to imagine the fall to spring cycle of the school year, and the longer journey from kindergarten to graduation, without teachers at the center. It is not surprising, then, that nearly twenty years ago, researchers as different in their methods and perspectives as statisticians and economists concluded that the single most important factor in improving student learning is the teacher. It is just as unsurprising that in schools where we see the achievement gap closing, we see teams of like-minded teachers working together to close those gaps.

What is surprising is that we are still largely reliant on policies, systems, and practices designed in the middle of the last century. Times have changed tremendously since then. In 1960 a gallon of gas cost 30 cents, Elvis and the Everly Brothers were atop the charts, a first year lawyer earned about the same as a first year teacher, and women basically had two professional choices: becoming a nurse or going into the classroom. In 2009, as nation after nation moves past us in educational achievement, we're kidding ourselves if we think methods of preparing, recruiting, compensating, and retaining teachers that came in when the hula hoop went out are a serious response to America's current needs.

This paradox—between the singular importance of each individual member of our teaching corps on the one hand, and antiquated policies and practices that shape the teaching career on the other—has grim consequences for our teachers and students, especially for those students on the wrong side of the achievement gap. As long as we rely on such out of date means to develop, attract, retain, and reward the teachers in our classrooms, our nation's students will continue to fall behind those of other nations. More and more will find themselves in growing company on the wrong side of a global economic opportunity gap.

When I began as superintendent of the Denver Public Schools in 2005, I knew the work that was cut out for us. Of the seventy-five-thousand students in the district, only thirty-three African American students and sixty-one Latino students, fewer than four classrooms, scored proficient on the tenth grade math test, a test that measures a junior high standard of proficiency in Europe. This was failure by any measure.

I also had an abstract understanding of the work that needed to be done to update the teaching career if we were to reverse the trend. It was clear that the teacher was the force animating the academic success of the students in her class. During my time in office, it became clearer and clearer that the regulations, systems, and job expectations placed before her were woefully out of synch with what we expected her to accomplish in this new era of higher expectations for our students. If we had the opportunity to sit down and design a career in teaching from scratch, it would look very little like the career we offer today.

We made some progress, but not by doing things as they had been done before. We worked backwards from the idea that every student who enters Denver Public Schools would graduate ready for college. With a team of teachers, principals and administrators, we developed a roadmap for reform, which we called "The Denver Plan." Following that roadmap, we initiated a number of reforms we hoped would not only make the job in teaching a better one, but also that would drive improved student performance.

We implemented the Professional Compensation System for Teachers, or ProComp, a groundbreaking pay system that rewards teachers who improve student performance and provides incentives for teachers to go to the neediest schools. We accomplished this change by working with our union, the Denver Classroom Teachers Association. It took a lot of effort, and we had a lot of disagreements, but we made progress because of a fundamental commitment to get the job done on behalf of children, not just score points in a political debate.

We began collaborations with both Teach for America and The New Teacher Project. They are now partners in our annual recruiting effort, serving as a combined source of more than 125 teachers per year. Those partnerships taught us a great deal about how to match high-quality sources of teaching talent with the demand for teachers. Inspired in part by our success with them, as well as by the challenge of having to hire more than four-hundred teachers per year, we went one step further. We developed our own teacher preparation program, modeled after a medical residency, in partnership with the University of Denver. As that program matures, it will be a source for as many as one-hundred teachers per year, all committed to work a minimum of four years in Denver Public Schools in exchange for the extraordinary preparation they receive in that program.

We developed measures of student growth that helped us assess more accurately the work of teachers individually and collectively. Prompted in part because ProComp called for incentives to be awarded to teachers and faculties, we began measuring the difference in student performance from one year to the next. This study had two consequences. First, it pushed us to develop more robust data systems to make more precise connections between teachers and students. Second, it served as a cornerstone in a set of measures that we called the School Performance Framework, a multiple measure system we use to assess school progress in our school improvement planning process. We are also using that same growth measure, along with observed teacher performance, to assess the performance of incoming teachers, and to use that information to assess the institution that prepared those teachers.

Now, my successor Tom Boasberg and his team and the teacher union are beginning tough talks about how to improve our teacher evaluation system so that it can inform critical career milestone decisions, including tenure and advancement. Just as with ProComp, this will be hard work, and there will be disagreements. But if everyone involved can be guided by the reality that well-executed classroom practices advance student learning, then this effort will be a breakthrough, too.

We will never claim that our work in this area is perfect, or that we are close to being finished. However, insofar as we placed the work of teaching at the center of our view of effective schools, we are headed in the right direction. Nearly five years after beginning reform in Denver Public Schools, I now have a very concrete understanding not only of what is possible, but also of how much work there is to be done, if we are going to update the job of teaching.

Teaching Talent is a significant contribution to the broader and grow-ing movement to move past the outdated regulations, systems, and prac-tices that still exert too much control over the job of teaching. It imagines teaching as if it were no longer held back by the weight of outmoded ways of working. Efficacy matters and is measured. School leadership and dis-trict systems place a premium on talent and results. Teachers are advanced to challenging new opportunities because of what they accomplish. This book is the practical advice I wish were in my hands and the hands of my staff five years ago.

The book lays out a simple, common-sense framework that serves to reorganize our thinking about the teaching career, one that consistently places premium on measured efficacy in every stage of the teaching career from preparation to on-boarding, from tenure to advancement. It persis-tently avoids false choices in its advice. For instance, the book recognizes that the art of measuring teacher effectiveness is only emerging, but it also recognizes that to deprive thoughtful professionals—teachers, princi-pals, and central office administrators—of meaningful information about teacher performance is foolish.

It pays proper focus to the early stages of the teaching career, when rates of turnover are highest and when it is possible for schools and districts to craft great faculties by investing in and advancing talent. This is breakthrough thinking. It has become commonplace to fault public school systems for treating teachers as replaceable parts, even though we know we cannot place a physics teacher in a kindergarten classroom and hope for success. When teachers are viewed as widgets, human resources departments work only to fill slots and take no responsibility for student success. This book imagines schools and districts as systems where teachers are treated as capable individ-uals, each with a personal record of hopes and accomplishments, who want to take on hard work, advance, and take on new challenges. It also imagines leaders and systems that work with passion to match teaching talent directly with academic needs in order to improve student performance.

In such a system, the leaders, especially principals, take on new im-portance. They become talent managers who must work with individual and collective potential, as well as lead efforts to support teachers who are struggling with their jobs. The book explores what this work looks like and the implications for the role of the principal and principal prepara-tion. It also acknowledges that all of this work happens most effectively in the context of a district that provides data to manage performance and inform decisions and has key structures and systems in place that drive teaching quality. Concrete examples of how data can be compiled, analyzed, and used to manage performance; the district infrastructure required to improve teaching quality; and high-leverage areas for district focus offer immediately useful guidance.

Teaching Talent is focused on its potential users—superintendents and union presidents, principals and human resource managers, teacher leaders, and state and local policy leaders. It is written as a toolkit, knowing that the field needs new work to be done. Just because the book is useful, however, does not mean that the work it calls for will be easy. Many of the issues the book raises—measuring teacher performance, advancing teachers on a basis other than years of service, creating data systems that connect student performance to teachers—have been the subject of decades of debate. This book aims to push the issues beyond the debate into the realm of action. As educators, we have debated modest and incremental reforms, instead of doing the hard work of identifying successful school structures and human capital strategies and taking them to scale. And we have been stuck debating whether teachers should be paid more based on merit, while roughly half of our teachers quit in the first five years of their career.

Narrow, small politics has allowed us to duck ever making real choices. And it has, failure after failure, shriveled our shared ambition for America's children. As long as we have these same conversations, today's nine-year-olds will see their younger brothers and sisters enter fourth grade with the same low odds of graduating from college they have—just as they saw their older brothers and sisters face the same odds.

The work ahead of us is clear. It is time for us to set aside systems of the past, just as it is time to set aside the ideologies of adults and attend to the needs of our kids and our teachers first. It is time for us to call for a profession's progress out of the depths of the last century and forward to the challenges of our times. When we succeed, we will better support our states and school districts in providing a public education that meets the challenges and possibilities of our time. When we succeed, we will see not only more students graduating from high school, but more of those graduates going on to complete college as well. We will not only see the achievement gap shrink, but we will see the United States once again lead the world in academic achievement.

Introduction

Education Is a People Business

Rachel E. Curtis

It was the end of the day, and Joyce, the superintendent, finally had a moment to catch her breath. She started her day welcoming this year's class of new teachers as they prepared for the first day of school. Later in the morning, she met with the head of human resources to review the system's teacher work force data. The data were startling: 30 percent of new teachers were leaving the school system by the end of their third year of teaching, but there were no data on who was leaving and why; fewer than half of the teachers who were supposed to be evaluated this year had evaluations on file; it was not clear what criteria were used to award tenure to the 175 teachers who received it last spring; and the system released only two teachers last year for poor performance. The head of HR also shared several anecdotes with Joyce that suggested that some of the system's strongest principals were growing restless and looking outside the system for career opportunities.

The focus for Joyce's afternoon meeting with her senior leadership team was the status of the system's key initiatives to improve student learning. The review of the end-of-year student achievement data suggested that the system isn't realizing student achievement gains at the pace it expected and needs to ensure all students are working at grade level. The conversation ended up centering on the great variation in the talents of central office managers charged with driving this work and the number of central office vacancies. After that, Joyce interviewed three candidates for the chief academic officer role, a position that had been vacant for six months. Joyce had been searching high and low for strong candidates, and this third round of interviews still didn't produce a strong contender.

Leaning back in her chair, Joyce struggled to make sense of her day, saying to herself, "For an organization whose success is driven by its people, we're in serious trouble." She rubbed her temples as the symptoms of the problem that she had encountered all day raced through her head. Finally, she sat upright, asking the question, "How can we design a system that can meet the learning needs of all students by ensuring teaching competence, recognizing and rewarding talent, making employment in the system dynamic and fulfilling, and building the system's capacity?"

Joyce's question is one every superintendent struggles with. Whether a district is large or small, urban, suburban, or rural, its success depends on its people and how effectively they improve student performance. Although the problem of ensuring effective teaching for every student has many dimensions and may vary in different settings, the core issue of how to recruit, develop, and retain effective teachers is the same, regardless of system size, demographics, or geography.

We have explored the dimensions of this problem over the last two and a half years with a group of urban superintendents. The conversation has been part of the Aspen Institute's Urban Superintendents Network, which convenes a small group of twelve to fifteen superintendents of large school systems as varied as Atlanta, Boston, Chicago, Denver, Charlotte-Mecklenburg, and Pittsburgh twice a year to discuss common issues of concern. The focus on this topic grew out of the challenges superintendents face in their efforts to staff their schools and systems with top talent in order to realize results for students and in their simultaneous desire and struggle to think about these issues systemically.

Judy Wurtzel and I facilitated this work. Judy brought her policy background to the conversation, drawing on her years of work in the U.S. Department of Education during the Clinton administration and her role as the leader of the Learning First Alliance, a network of twelve national education associations focused on improving public K–12 education. I brought experience from more than a decade of work in the Boston Public Schools, where I focused on issues of teacher and principal preparation and development. During my tenure in Boston, I started nationally recognized residency and induction programs for principals, assisted in the development of the Boston Teacher Residency, developed teaching standards and an induction program for new teachers, and oversaw the training of all teachers and principals.

The Aspen superintendents identified common challenges. Their districts consistently struggle to meet the learning needs of all students and ensure achievement at the rate required to provide all students with the opportunities they need to be successful. There is enormous variation in teaching quality that has been hard to address effectively. Annual teacher attrition rates exceed 15 percent. Poorly designed teacher deployment systems concentrate the most effective teachers in schools that serve their most affluent students, leaving the lowest-performing schools with the least effective teachers. In some urban systems, the teacher demographics are the inverse of student demographics, with a predominantly white teaching force serving students who are predominantly black and Hispanic. Across the board, there is a struggle to hire effective teachers for special needs students and English language learners. The scope of these problems is vast in large school systems that have thousands of teachers, hundreds of schools, and a diverse student population. In smaller districts, the problem looks less dramatic but is still troubling. Some of the issues are the same—finding teachers for high-needs areas—and others are different. Yet all of these systems struggle to define effective teaching and ensure every teacher meets the criteria. Teacher career opportunities are often limited. Superintendents search, often fruitlessly, for principals who are a good match for the demographic and programmatic profiles of their schools.

In the midst of all these challenges, there are promising developments. Districts are trying to define teaching quality and make it measurable. Some are learning how to link teacher effectiveness to student achievement and then to pay. Others are employing strategies to better address the needs of the lowest-performing schools by creating teams of high-performing teachers and principals and providing freedom from some human resource constraints. Some are working to identify talent early and cultivating it with the goal of preparing school leaders and critical central office leaders. National organizations such as The New Teacher Project, Teach For America, the New Teacher Center, the Teacher Advancement Program, and the National Board for Professional Teaching Standards are critical partners that have been created to help school districts recruit talented teachers, nurture their early years in the classroom, and support their ongoing development, career opportunities, performance management, and compensation.

Human Capital: What Is It and Why Does It Matter?

The challenges framed are all things that are described, in other sectors, as human capital issues. In chapter 3, Milanowski and Kimball define human capital as:

> the productive skills and technical knowledge of workers. It includes individuals' knowledge, skills, and abilities and the values and motivation they have to apply their skills to the organization's goals. Economists and businesspeople call these individual characteristics *human capital* in order to emphasize the importance of employee skills and abilities and the need for organizations to invest in their people, just as they do in physical capital, in order to succeed.

Our school systems are essentially human enterprises— that is, they rely heavily on people to accomplish their goals. Eighty percent of the budget of most school systems is devoted to people—their salaries and benefits. Two-thirds of that investment in made in teachers. Given that tremendous investment, Joyce's human capital question becomes paramount: *How can we design a system that can meet the learning needs of all students by ensuring teaching competence, recognizing and rewarding talent, making employment in the system dynamic and fulfilling, and building the system's capacity?*

While parents may never use the words *human capital*, they deeply understand its importance. They know that some teachers are better than others, and they know how important it is for their children to have an effective teacher. Any parent who has suffered through a year when an ineffective teacher taught his or her child has a visceral memory of its cost in terms of both the child's learning and overall enthusiasm for learning and school. Research quantifies what parents observe, finding that "teachers near the top of the quality distribution can get an entire year's worth of additional learning out of their students compared to those near the bottom."[1] The cumulative impact of teaching quality is profound, with research showing that if a child has an ineffective teacher three years in a row, the student performs as much as 50 percentile points lower in mathematics than students assigned to three highly effective teachers.[2] The research is clear. The best way school systems can accelerate student learning is to ensure that every teacher in every classroom is effective.

Historically, school systems have been, at best, passive managers of their human capital. Systems set the goal of having a teacher in every classroom by the first day of school, but there was little thought given to how to ensure all the teachers were effective or what strategy to employ to meet hiring needs and ensure quality in high-needs areas. Similarly, the conversation about performance management and teaching effectiveness has been reduced to a conversation about a small percentage of chronically low-performing teachers rather than about how to implement a performance management system that holds all teachers to high expectations and supports their growth and development. Passivity on this issue has limited systems' ability to discern the talents of teachers more carefully, differentiate their treatment accordingly, and leverage talent to support student learning and school improvement.

The standards movement and then the high-stakes accountability of the federal No Child Left Behind Act brought the issue of teaching quality into view. Testing and the reporting of results made apparent what educators had always known but seldom discussed: there is great variance in teachers' effectiveness in facilitating student learning. It is becoming clear that as community leaders and policy makers have raised the stakes for academic success, this passive approach to human capital management is no longer acceptable.

Early Efforts in Human Capital Management

School systems that have begun to think about intentionally improving teaching effectiveness have approached this issue in different ways. Some focus on recruiting teachers who have the greatest likelihood of being effective. Others provide intensive support to teachers in their first few years on the job to build their effectiveness. Raising the overall quality of teaching by targeting low-performing teachers for support and—if improvement isn't realized—dismissal is an approach some systems have pursued. And others have decided to identify their most talented teachers and direct resources and support to build their talents and create roles where those talents can be used to support student learning, school improvement, and/or system reform.

All of these efforts have made two things clear. First, there are many different ways to begin the work of managing human capital. The needs and resources of each school system often determine the choice of a starting place. A school district that is losing 50 percent of its new teachers in their first three years in the classroom is likely to start to manage its human capital by better understanding the causes of attrition and addressing them.

Another system that draws the majority of its new teachers from a single preparation program and is concerned about the readiness of its newly hired teachers to teach literacy skills is likely to take a different tack. Partnering with the preparation program to build its graduates' understanding of literacy development and ability to teach literacy skills is likely a good place to start.

Second, the early work in human capital has made clear that regardless of where a school system begins its work, there is a set of key levers, all of which a system must ultimately pull to build a robust human capital management system that ensures teaching quality. Whatever lever a system starts with, once it has been pulled, another lever will require attention. Providing strong teacher-induction support leads a system to think about how to measure new teacher effectiveness. Defining measures of teacher effectiveness then leads to aligning teacher supervision and evaluation and the tenure review process to those measures. Similarly, recruiting top talent creates the need to provide the support, opportunities, and challenges required to retain high fliers. Human capital management is a bit like tuning an instrument. Each initiative pursued—like the tightening of a violin string—improves the system and the education it provides students. It also magnifies the remaining cacophony, pointing out other areas in need of attention. When all of the elements of human capital management are designed and brought together, the system is well tuned and able to address any human capital need that may arise.

Vision for Human Capital Management

Vision is about moving beyond current reality to imagine what is possible. Imagine for a moment what you would most want a robust human capital management system to look like and accomplish. What are the goals of the system? What are the top priorities you want to address? What barriers—structure, policy, capacity, and culture—do you most want to eliminate? What would you want a career in education to look like? Would it look the same for everyone? Having thought about this issue for quite a while, let us share our vision. It has grown out of the most promising human capital work in school systems and other sectors that have been focused on this issue for much longer than those of us in education. The research about the most important things to focus on to improve teaching quality and thereby student achievement drives this vision to ensure it addresses our greatest need: a great teacher for every child.

In the vision, there are multiple pathways into teaching, and preparation is tightly tied to the reality of the classroom and school experiences of teachers. Graduates of these preparation programs are truly ready for the rigors of classroom teaching. The programs are driven by school systems' needs. They produce teachers in high-needs areas at the level required, and teach teachers strategies to meet the needs of all students. The traditional sequence of preparing, recruiting, and hiring teachers is reconsidered, as some people are recruited and hired to teach and then trained, while others follow the more traditional process of preparation before hiring. Either way, the recruitment and hiring process is focused on quality of candidates over quantity. The recruitment, screening, and hiring processes are efficient and user-friendly and demonstrate that the system respects and values its employees. Districts track and compare the effectiveness of teachers from different sources using both student outcomes and teacher observations and focus their recruitment and hiring on sources whose graduates have the best results.

In the vision, once hired, teachers are heavily supported to ensure both their effectiveness and job satisfaction. This support focuses on skill development, in-classroom support, and the building of a culture of collaboration and shared learning among teachers. With this support come expectations for performance, including student learning outcomes. There are standards to which the support is aligned, and teacher performance is measured against them regularly. New teachers receive a lot of feedback on their practice; there are performance benchmarks at key points in the first three years of teaching. Teachers are identified by their performance on these benchmarks as top performing, making steady progress, or low performing. Support is differentiated based on performance levels, and weak teachers who don't show signs of improvement are dismissed.

There is a watershed moment when teachers demonstrate their talent and join the teaching profession. This moment is determined by readiness rather than by the number of years they have spent in the classroom. The bar is high, as are the rewards for meeting the expectations. Everybody understands that the measure of teaching effectiveness is student achievement, and there are systems in place to assess and reward improvement. Meeting the performance measures for joining the profession is significant and celebrated and is the gateway to opportunities.

Having demonstrated excellence, teachers have opportunities to take on leadership roles, be they in the classroom, the school, or the system, if that interests them. This work can complement full or part-time teaching or can be a way to work outside the classroom for a few months or a few years or for the rest of a career. For teachers whose greatest passion is teaching, the structures and culture of school support their continuous learning and collaboration with colleagues. In all this opportunity, teachers can carve out career pathways for themselves that build on their interests and expertise and respond to the needs of students. Throughout a career in teaching, compensation and rewards are tied to impact on students and their learning, and the work that systems most need talented teachers to do is incentivized.

This vision is possible. School systems across the country are taking steps toward realizing it.

Overview of the Book

We have written this book to support school systems as they work to make this vision a reality. We do this by answering Joyce's question: *How can we design a system that can meet the learning needs of all students by ensuring teaching competence, recognizing and rewarding talent, making employment in the system dynamic and fulfilling, and building the system's capacity?* This book taps the wisdom of a variety of players in the work of human capital management in education to define what it looks like in school systems. We consider what it requires of school systems and principals, how systems build their capacity to do this work, and how innovations and new ways of thinking about human capital provide exciting opportunities to think expansively about both the problem and possible solutions. The book is organized into two parts: (1) making human capital management a priority, and (2) recruiting, retaining, and leveraging talent. These two sections build toward a framework for human capital management that fleshes out the vision introduced earlier, drawing from the ideas introduced throughout the book.

Making Human Capital Management a Priority

This section addresses the question: *What are the conditions required in districts and schools to support human capital management?* Districts' policies and practices and their allocation of resources signal their priorities. They create the context in which rigorous human capital work can thrive or perish. Chapters 1 and 2 focus on the role of the district in building human capital management systems. Chapter 1 defines the district infrastructure required to support human capital management as well as strategic ways school systems can drive it. Chapter 2 focuses on data, the mechanism by which school systems assess the scope of their human capital needs, measure progress, inform improvements, and build a culture that supports and signals the importance of this work. The chapter hones in on how to build districts' capacity to quantify, understand, and prioritize human capital issues for action and to measure the effectiveness of their efforts.

Chapters 3 and 4 shift attention from the district to the schools, focusing on the role of the principal in human capital management, acknowledging the influence principals have in the daily work of ensuring teaching quality at the school level. Chapter 3 mines the extensive work done in the private sector and early experiments in education to make middle managers true managers of human capital. Lessons learned and successes realized from this work are translated to provide concrete images of the work of principals in this realm. Chapter 4 builds on the idea of the principal as human capital manager and expands it, introducing the notion of principals as leaders of learning. It considers the work principals must do to create an environment in which teachers work together to solve the messiest problems of student learning, the knowledge and skills this requires, and the implications for principals' preparation and district support.

Recruiting, Retaining, and Leveraging Talent

With the foundation required for a systemic and systematic approach to human capital addressed in part I, this section considers the question, *How can the entry into teaching and a career in teaching be redesigned to recruit, retain, and leverage talent?* The three chapters in this section provide a mix of blue sky, thought pieces that offer and provoke new ways of thinking about the preparation, support, accountability, and career opportunities for teachers and an existence proof of a promising innovation underway. Chapter 5 proposes a new "bargain" for the first three years of teaching that couples high support for new teachers with high standards for performance and aligned compensation. The chapter provides a concrete vision of the elements of such a bargain and how it could be implemented to increase retention of effective teachers while eliminating poor performers at or before tenure. Building on chapter 5's emphasis on training new teachers by immersing them in the work of teaching and student learning, chapter 6 deeply explores urban teacher residencies, a new approach to teacher preparation designed on the medical residency model.

This chapter illustrates new kinds of partnerships between urban school systems, institutions of higher education, and community-based intermediary organizations in which district staffing needs drive the work, schools are the laboratories in which aspiring teachers learn, and theory is used to explicate practice.

The focus shifts in chapter 7 to the active management of teachers who are in the second stage of their careers, years four through ten—an issue that has heretofore received little attention from school districts. The chapter explains the demographics of this group, what motivates them, and key considerations in managing them. High-potential employees, the group of tenured teachers who demonstrated particular talent in modeling effective instruction, facilitating student learning, and working collaboratively for the greatest good of students, colleagues, and schools, get particular attention. The chapter considers the variety of ways these teachers' talents can be leveraged for the good of students, schools, and the system as a whole.

Chapter 8 combines the ideas of the previous chapters into a framework for teacher human capital management that incorporates the vision introduced earlier. The framework describes the elements of a robust human capital system and the interrelationships of the elements. Current conditions are compared to the vision, and the research base that undergirds the framework is introduced. Finally, the conclusion identifies questions, tensions, and trade-offs that need to be considered in managing human capital. The appendixes provide resources that include the research base for the framework and recommended reading.

Drumbeats and Silences

Here are some of our core beliefs that have guided the design and writing of the book.

- Teaching effectiveness is defined by a teacher's ability to help students learn. We appreciate that measuring teachers' effect on student learning is challenging, but we think it is essential.

- The purpose of developing and implementing a human capital strategy is to drive significant and lasting improvement to overall student achievement. To do so, we must improve the quality of teaching and reduce the variance in teaching quality. It is about both raising the quality of teaching overall and lessening the gap between the highest- and lowest-performing teachers.

- Improving the quality of teaching cannot focus solely on improving the quality of individual teachers working independently. It must be done in a way that changes the workplace context of teaching so that it facilitates teacher collaboration focused on continuous individual and schoolwide improvement.

Similarly, there are several themes repeated in the book that are worth highlighting now because they reflect our thinking on where the greatest potential lies to transform human capital in education. First, traditional teacher preparation, as it is most often approached in the United States, is profoundly broken, and there is opportunity for fundamental redesign. Second, the lack of clear standards for teaching practice and measures of teacher effectiveness creates an enormous lost opportunity. Third is the tremendous untapped talent that teachers in the second stage (and beyond) of their career offer, and the need to create a wide array of career opportunities to keep teachers in the profession and use their expertise. Fourth, unions and school systems share the responsibility for the current state of affairs in teaching quality and human capital management. They need to partner to solve the human capital problem. Unions have much to contribute to the solution, and their engagement is critical to ensuring their ongoing relevance in the larger policy conversation. Fifth, principals are pivotal players in ensuring teaching effectiveness and teachers' job satisfaction. Finally, school systems are responsible for driving this work by creating the conditions in which it will thrive and ensuring that all of the pieces are developed and put in place to ensure teaching quality.

While these beliefs and themes may strike a drumbeat as you read, there are other important issues related to human capital management in education about which we are largely silent. They are worth noting, as they are often written about and debated, and our light treatment of them might be surprising. Any superintendent will tell you that she faces tremendous challenges in ensuring a high level of talent and effectiveness in principals and key central office positions. Yet we have chosen to focus the book on teachers, because they make up the vast majority of the work force and have the greatest impact on student learning. In choosing that focus, we hope to provide an entry point and support successes that can inform and motivate systems' human capital efforts with principals, central office staff, and senior leaders. These are critical issues, and some of the ideas introduced in this volume can be translated into human capital strategies for these three populations. We know that school systems will not improve quickly enough for children, until they address the human capital issues related to all of their employees.

The issues of pay for performance and measuring teaching effectiveness using a value-added method are current hot topics. Although we support both, they are complicated, and executing them well requires close analysis and careful study of experiments under way. Given that such an analysis is not the focus of this volume, we have decided to leave that for others. We believe that pay for performance and the value-added measures it requires are critical elements of human capital management systems in public education and reference them as such throughout the book. They must be attended to with care to ensure fairness, equity, and overall improvement in teaching quality. They can be used to greatest effect to support the improvement of teachers collectively and recognize school progress. We are well advised to avoid using them in ways that create a new set of perverse incentives that leave teachers competing against one another, when research resoundingly reminds us that excellence in teaching is facilitated by teacher collaboration.[3]

We say very little about highly qualified teachers. Every superintendent, principal, and teacher is familiar with this designation, which was defined by the No Child Left Behind Act. Some might think that is a place to start the conversation about teaching quality. Yet we believe that the term is a misnomer because of the criteria used to determine the status. As such, it distracts from a meaningful discussion of teaching quality. Its reliance on teachers' completion of course work and their performance on tests like the Praxis Series emphasizes things teachers do outside the classroom rather than their ability to facilitate student learning in the classroom. Most school systems view the designation as a compliance issue rather than a meaningful contributor to teaching quality. Perhaps there is an opportunity to redefine this status to measure what most contributes to student achievement, but we have chosen not to focus on reframing something widely perceived as a distraction rather than a lever to improve teaching quality.

Teacher quality is another term we avoid using. We have chosen, instead, to focus on teaching quality, teacher effectiveness, and other specific characteristics of teachers who successfully support student learning and raise student achievement. So much of what makes the conversation about teaching quality difficult is its human side. It is easy to label teachers good or bad. But in doing so, we make the people indistinguishable from their practice, and the praise or critique becomes quite personal. We find that unproductive because it distracts us from the most important issue: the effect of the teaching on students and their learning. That is what matters most.

How to Use the Book

Building a robust human capital management system will require that every partner in the education sector—higher education, teachers' unions, philanthropic organizations, community-based groups, and state policy makers—reflects on its current contributions to human capital successes and challenges and rethinks its work, driven by the goal of ensuring all students have access to excellent teaching. This book is intended to spur conversations within and across these stakeholders about the best ways to ensure teaching quality. Our hope is that those conversations will lead to new ways of thinking and strategic action that create true human capital management systems in districts. Readers may choose to focus on the district infrastructure, on the principal as a key player, on entry into teaching or career pathways, on a district's work relative to the framework, a university's involvement, or state policy.

For districts thinking about how to organize themselves to better manage their human capital, chapters 1 through 4 provide ways to think about such a reorganization and the capacity required to bring it about. Others may be more interested in the invitation that chapters 5 and 7 offer to think expansively about teacher recruitment and development, unfettered by current practice. We hope that readers will build from the ideas framed in these chapters, adapting and enhancing them to bring them to life in ways that work in different local and state contexts. The existence proofs in chapters 4 and 6 provide real, concrete images on new human capital approaches. Readers who find these ideas compelling and a possible good fit for their context will learn more about them to support replication or adaptation.

The people engaged in these conversations and the range of stakeholders included will define the richness of the discussions. Remember that human capital management is not a human resource issue; discussion of the book can be a way to introduce and invite a broader audience within and outside districts into the conversation.

PART I

Making Human Capital Management a Priority

$$\overset{\curvearrowright}{1}$$

Managing Human Capital to Improve Student Achievement

Five Levers That Affect Teaching Quality

Rachel E. Curtis

In education, human capital management is about ensuring and directing the talents of teachers and principals in order to improve student learning. The goal is that every student achieves at a high level because he or she receives great instruction in every class. To achieve that goal, all teachers must be highly skilled and work collaboratively to ensure their schools serve all students well; there is a relentless focus on improving student performance, student and parent engagement, graduation rates, and college success. Accomplishing this requires the capacity to discern the different talents of every employee. Armed with this information, systems then strategically differentiate the support, accountability, and opportunities they provide employees to ensure quality, reward talent, and leverage it to drive student learning and school improvement.

Currently, very few school systems have achieved this goal. Human capital management is haphazard at best, resulting in the problems with which educators and policy makers are increasingly familiar: an overall inadequate supply of quality teaching and an inequitable distribution of talent.

This chapter examines how school systems can most effectively address human capital issues. We begin at the district level, because districts have the most powerful levers for improving teaching quality. Districts also have a unique responsibility to address human capital across all schools. This chapter answers the questions: *Who manages human capital in a school system?*

What are the most powerful levers districts can pull to influence teaching quality? How do districts decide where to focus their human capital efforts? What infrastructure is required to support this work? What is the role of principals as key players in human capital management? What is the role of data in guiding these efforts?

Ownership

The school system must broadly own human capital management in order to realize the goal of ensuring a high level of instruction in every classroom. First, virtually every strategic decision a school system makes has human capital implications that it must consider. Take, for example, implementing new student assessments. Of course, leaders need to work with testing experts to make sure the measures are technically sound and with curriculum specialists to ensure that they are aligned with what is taught. But there are a host of other issues to consider if the assessments are to be effective, such as: Who do we need to train? How will we do that to maximize results? Is there talent in the system that we can leverage to implement the assessments, or do we need to develop capacity? Who will lead the data management work at the school, and what skills does this require? Can we fashion this work into leadership opportunities for teachers? Will these leaders be specially trained and/or compensated? What are the implications of the assessments for teachers' and principals' expectations and evaluations? What data skills do we want new and aspiring teachers and principals to possess? Do we want to train them in those skills or ensure that they are part of their preparation? What is the system's vision for its use of data in three years and how can we build or deploy human capital now to support the realization of that vision?

These questions pertain to current and potential employees—both teachers and principals. They relate to training and development, compensation, and performance management. They have implications for teacher and principal preparation and induction. Without close attention to all these issues, even a seemingly technical issue like implementing new assessments is unlikely to be effective.

Second, the system needs to own human capital management, because individuals must actively participate at every level of the organization. All managers or senior leaders are managers of human capital. They are constantly assessing, supporting, and tracking their direct reports' performance, potential, and career aspirations, with a particular focus on high-potential employees. Whenever the system undertakes new work or rethinks existing work, managers are expected to think about their staff, who might be well positioned to support the system's new efforts, and how that work fits into employees' growth and development plans.

Finally, human capital management requires close collaboration of human resources, budget, information management, and teaching and learning, to name just a few key departments. Processes need to be established and cross-functional teams developed to ensure effective execution of human capital priorities.

Consider, again, new assessments. Their success depends on teachers, principals, principal supervisors, the chief academic officer, and many central office departments. Human resources is responsible for the recruitment, screening, and hiring of the teacher leaders. Some combination of research and evaluation and information services builds the technology infrastructure and access to student achievement data that people in those positions need to do their jobs effectively. Principals need guidance in how to most effectively support and supervise teacher leaders and in tapping available resources to do so. Principal supervisors need to support principals in this work and hold them accountable. The chief academic officer works with the department(s) that designed the initiative to ensure that the infrastructure is in place that the new data managers need to be effective and that principals need to lead this initiative. The people in the central office who provide this support are held accountable for meeting the needs of their "customers"—the people in the schools.

Broad ownership of human capital starts at the top. A successful urban superintendent estimates that he spends 50 percent of his time on human capital issues. This time includes the relentless effort he puts into outreach, recruitment, and screening for vacancies at his senior cabinet level, his supervision and evaluation of senior leaders, and succession planning. Collaborating with unions to negotiate agreements that support teaching and school leadership excellence; working with his senior leadership team to address critical, systemic human capital issues; partnering with his school board to develop human capital policy; and working with elected officials to drive a related legislative agenda are all part of the superintendent's human capital responsibilities.[1]

As his experience illustrates, human capital issues permeate the organization, and the approach to addressing them must be systemic and systematic.

Some systems will decide to name a single person who champions the human capital agenda and oversees all related initiatives. This approach can be a powerful way to focus attention on the work, ensure efforts are coordinated and strategic, and signal its importance, particularly if the person reports directly to the superintendent. Yet caution is required to ensure that employees don't interpret the appointment to mean that human capital work is one person's responsibility and that they don't need to attend to it within their own job responsibilities and as members of the larger organization.

Regardless of whether or not there is a single champion of human capital, school systems can take steps to ensure that many people own this work. Systems signal what they expect based on what they inspect. Evaluating all principals on a set of human capital metrics communicates the importance of managing human capital and making it a priority. Measuring central office services based on how well principals and teachers perceive the services support them and their work makes clear the central office's responsibility to schools, principals, and teachers. Requiring teachers to conduct self-assessments on teacher performance standards, indicating their strengths and weaknesses, goals for growth, and strategies to realize them, helps them understand that they are responsible for and expected to manage their own performance and careers. Measures and incentives that recognize the performance of communities of adults rather than that of individuals create a culture of collective responsibility that builds peer support and pressure.

Focusing Efforts

Addressing human capital management can be daunting for a school system. Management has many dimensions, all requiring time to think, thoughtfully design, and implement a new way of doing business—all tasks that are hard to do in our current school systems. Some of these new approaches also require money and the reconsideration of staff time and effort. Some require political action and state legislative reform. And some may be best addressed at the school level. Yet certain teaching-quality issues must be or are most efficiently addressed at the system level. These are key levers that the system is uniquely positioned to pull to affect teaching quality and reshape teaching careers. The five key levers are: teacher performance standards, tenure, compensation, differentiated treatment of teachers based on performance, and professional development.

Teacher Performance Standards

Performance standards provide clear expectations for teacher practice, a focus for professional development, and a foundation for accountability, all of which are fundamental aspects of human capital management. Performance standards also affect other key teacher-quality levers, including tenure and compensation. Without standards, any discussion of teaching quality and how to improve it is impossible.

Performance standards can include a mix of qualitative and quantitative performance metrics that are weighted and reported in a variety of ways. But however they are designed, they need to bear some relationship to student performance standards. Too often, the two are disconnected in a way that confuses the public and makes human capital management difficult. For example, in some school systems where 55 percent of third graders read at grade level and 50 percent of high school students graduate ready for college, it is common for 97 percent of teachers to be rated satisfactory. This defies reason and casts doubt on the validity of the teacher performance standards.

One way to link teacher and student standards is to measure the value a teacher adds in terms of student learning. At the same time, establishing qualitative indicators of the observable teaching and student behaviors that lead to student learning provides a way to focus on effective teaching practices.

Systems may choose to develop their own standards, but high-quality standards already exist. Adopting or adapting standards from resources currently available may provide a valuable starting point.[2] What matters most is that as part of the adoption or creation of standards, people at every level of the system talk about what the system values and how it defines effective teaching. These conversations can change how everyone thinks about his or her work.

Teacher performance standards have the greatest impact on teachers' practice if they include multiple levels of performance, rather than the simple binary ratings of satisfactory and unsatisfactory. Multilevel ratings provide more fine-grained data to teachers and the system about performance and growth over time. An increasing number of school systems are developing red–yellow–green rating tools, providing principals a quick way to distinguish high fliers (green) from low performers (red). This approach recognizes high performers, gives middle-of-the-road teachers something to aspire to, and signals concern to low performers. By including performance levels that recognize true excellence (perhaps 10 percent to 20 percent of the teaching force) as well as unacceptably low performance, the standards set the stage for differentiating treatment of teachers based on performance.

Standards and performance metrics are only as good as their implementation. The process of teacher supervision and evaluation is critical. Historically, the execution and quality of teacher supervision and evaluation has been inconsistent at best. One district estimates that it has evaluations on file for approximately 50 percent of the teachers scheduled for review in a given year. This suggests that supervisors do not evaluate 50 percent of the teachers scheduled for evaluation each year. The quality of the evaluations that are done is inconsistent. Some of the poor quality is the result of supervisors not having the time or training required to do a comprehensive review. Supervisors often resort to a single observation, a checklist, and little or no discussion about the teachers' practice, much less a conversation that includes both praise and critical feedback to inform improvement.

Given the inconsistent quality of supervision and evaluation, the current approach and its heavy reliance on principals and their administrative staffs need to be reconsidered. By asking, *who can most effectively evaluate teachers?* and *what support do they need to do so?*, systems can figure out if the approach simply requires training and accountability or if others might do the job better or at least participate in the process. Engaging peers in teacher evaluation is something that some school systems have explored and that has been a mainstay in other sectors for decades. Peer review can be targeted to serve all teachers, new teachers, and/or struggling teachers, depending on the needs and interests of the district.

Explicitly creating new capacity to support principals in their work with low-performing teachers is one way to enhance the quality of implementing standards. In some districts, peer review programs are designed to give struggling teachers a cycle of intensive support, supervision, and evaluation. Another approach, pursued by the Boston Public Schools, is to hire and place experienced principals with strong records of teacher supervision and evaluation in the human resources department to coach, provide technical support, and partner with principals who are struggling to document and dismiss chronically low-performing teachers.

Whoever does the evaluation must be held accountable by supervisors, using a mix of process and outcome measures. Process measures include the consistency and quality of their assessments of teaching performance. Outcome measures include absolute student achievement, the rate of growth, and the correlation between an evaluator's rating of a teacher and her effectiveness in realizing student growth.

Tenure

The beginning of a teacher's career is when it is easy to ensure a high bar for teaching quality. With clear expectations and accountability measures, novice teachers can be acculturated to the profession in ways that will build capacity and have long-term benefits. Districts can identify and target high-potential employees early on. Similarly, they can identify people who are not well suited to teaching and counsel them to leave the system, without the constraints that accrue with tenure and additional time on the job.

When systems don't have clear standards and processes for tenure review, teachers earn tenure based simply on their time on the job, as state statutes dictate. But tenure is a costly decision: lifetime employment is estimated to cost $3 million.[3] Therefore, school systems should pay close attention to the tenure review process.

Systems need to address two issues regarding tenure. The first is the role of tenure in ensuring teaching quality and signaling the importance of entering the profession. The second is state policy and its possibly negative influence on teaching quality.

The standards for tenure and the process by which it is granted are tremendous untapped resources for influencing teaching quality in most school systems. Systems have authority over the process for reviewing teachers for tenure, but few set up rigorous processes that both signal the importance of entering the teaching profession and ensure quality. Teaching-performance standards provide a strong foundation on which to build rigorous tenure review. Part of the review should include measures of teachers' impact on student learning and their teaching against standards of effective practice. In addition, systems can solicit feedback from parents and colleagues and assess teachers' level of engagement in professional learning and improvement over time. Asking teachers to reflect on their teaching, both to celebrate growth and to identify areas for ongoing development and career aspirations, can simultaneously inform the tenure review process and build a culture that emphasizes reflective practice and continuous improvement.

Making tenure a high-bar, high-stakes decision requires both the creation of rigorous standards for tenure and oversight on the part of principals' supervisors to ensure that principals are applying the standards fairly and consistently. Given that this high-stakes decision has historically been largely ignored, systems must hold principals accountable for their decisions and track the effects of them. Data on the ongoing performance of teachers whom a principal has previously recommended for tenure should be part of a principal's own evaluation. Such data also signal the importance of tenure decisions and the care with which they should be considered.

Basing tenure decisions on performance rather than time served enables school systems to differentiate the pace of tenure reviews. Some teachers demonstrate their talent quickly, and it is easy to make a decision about their future in the system in two years. The lack of fit between a teacher and the profession is also often easy to assess in the first year or two. Yet, often some teachers have promise and simply need more time to demonstrate that their performance warrants tenure. They may not perform at a tenure-worthy level at the end of the second or third year of teaching but often do by the end of the fourth or fifth year.

The issue of tenure may require state policy changes and a political strategy on the part of school systems, as state statutes often dictate the time frame for tenure decisions. Pursuing this policy may be part of a longer-term strategy to improve teaching quality. School systems can have the greatest influence if they partner with like-minded districts and policy makers to drive legislative reform. Districts can make a strong case by developing a rigorous tenure review process and showing that it can improve the quality of teaching. And they can implement it immediately and begin to influence teaching quality while efforts at state policy reforms are underway.

Tenure review is not simply about assessing teaching quality, but is a chance to celebrate the teaching profession and people's entry into it. The recognition can be achieved in very concrete ways, both in the symbolism of conferring tenure and in combining it with important rewards and incentives. Aligning significant salary increases with tenure and making tenure the gateway to additional career opportunities are just a few ways to highlight its significance and value.

Compensation

Compensation isn't the most important consideration for teachers, but it does matter.[4] It also matters to people thinking about the profession, because compensation systems indicate what organizations value and how they treat employees. The current predominant approach to compensation in public education values time on the job and pursuit of continuing education. There is no differentiation of value based on teaching in high-needs grades and subject areas, willingness and ability to work successfully with the highest-needs students or in the lowest-performing schools, or overall effectiveness. For these reasons, districts face layers of opportunities and challenges in reconceptualizing teacher compensation to support teaching quality and human capital management.

Systems can revamp compensation to align better with student achievement and teacher effectiveness by:

- Abandoning the practice of using time spent in the system and continuing education credits as the criteria for salary increases.

- Aligning compensation to teacher performance measures, including student achievement and system priorities.

- Creating individual, group, and schoolwide compensation incentives based on performance to balance a commitment to individual and collective performance and create peer pressure.

- Revamping the pension system to shift the emphasis from heavily rewarding teachers at the end of their careers to front-loading compensation and benefits early in their careers.

These items all represent new ways of doing business. Some are more radical than others. But any of these options require that districts create political will and alliances and that unions accept new measures and procedures to align compensation with teacher effectiveness and factors that have the greatest potential effect on student achievement. Some require changes in state legislation. Others are inextricably linked to one another. Yet these fundamental changes provide systems the greatest potential to align the incentive system for teachers to system priorities.

The traditional salary scale, created in the 1920s, was designed to eliminate biases and inequities. But there is increasing evidence that "seat time" and continuing education are not necessarily associated with teacher practice and student learning.

Systems can reallocate dollars that are saved by eliminating salary increases based on years of service and course completion to create incentives for exceptional teacher performance. They can be awarded at the individual, group, and/or schoolwide levels. Some combination of the three may create the right incentives for continuous improvement at the classroom and school levels. Individual awards can include salary differentials for teachers in high-needs content or program areas, those who have proved their effectiveness and choose to work in high-needs schools, and/or those who demonstrate excellent performance based on student performance and observations. Group performance awards recognize and reward the collaborative aspects of the work and create an environment in which peer pressure may have a positive impact on teacher performance. Systems' priorities, their existing culture, and the culture they are trying to build inform the right combination of these different approaches in each community.

Redefining the total compensation package—not just salary, but also benefits, including pensions—is a more radical step. Taken as a total package, teacher compensation is a very valuable and powerful incentive for teachers, especially in the later years of their careers, to remain in the profession.[5] In an economic environment where public pensions and retirement benefits are under increased scrutiny, the practice of rewarding the most-veteran teachers with salary and pension accrual at the expense of newer teachers is worth reconsidering. Currently, teachers at the beginning of their careers accrue almost no value from their pension contributions. By about the fifteenth year, however, the accrued value becomes large enough to be perceptible, even if it is still ten to fifteen years until it can be realized without substantial penalties. This benefit structure leaves midcareer teachers in the unenviable position of feeling that they must stay in the system to maximize the accruing value of their pensions, regardless of their career interests, job satisfaction, or performance.

This structure is not in sync with changing work-force demographics and school systems' need to compete for talent. It rewards staying in a career over performing in a career. It is geared toward an environment in which people choose a career and commit to it for decades, something that is quickly becoming an anachronism. Leveling the pace at which teachers accrue retirement benefits and allowing them to retain benefits when they leave would both acknowledge that people change careers frequently and allow experienced teachers who are poor performers to take the retirement benefits they have accrued if their evaluations indicate they should leave the system.

The success of the Denver Public Schools in redefining teacher compensation through its Professional Compensation System for Teachers (ProComp) makes clear that these changes are possible. Through the 2004 ProComp agreement between the school district and the teachers' association (Colorado is a right-to-work state), Denver began to use student growth and market incentives as factors in compensation. In addition to rewarding teachers for their students' academic growth and for being part of a school community that made significant academic gains, ProComp provides incentives to teachers who choose to work in schools with high percentages of students in poverty and in hard-to-staff positions. The introduction of ProComp shifted the conversation in Denver, and nationally, about teacher compensation. Denver continued to be a leader on the compensation issue in 2008 when it made significant revisions to ProComp. Perhaps the most important change was to increase the earnings potential for early-career teachers by increasing the value and number of performance and market incentives. Denver could afford to do so, in part, only by reducing salary-building incentives for teachers later in their careers.

Differentiated Treatment of Teachers

While teachers are expected to differentiate their instruction to respond to students' different performance levels and needs, school systems generally do a poor job of differentiating their treatment of teachers using the same criteria. Differentiating among teachers is in direct opposition to the entrenched culture of schools, whereby all teachers are treated the same. This tendency, which The New Teacher Project refers to as the "widget effect," has a disastrous effect on teaching effectiveness and staff morale.[6] It makes it nearly impossible to tap the talents of highly effective teachers or address the deficiencies of low performers. Establishing teacher performance standards is the first step for addressing these problems. Yet it must be accompanied by a clear commitment and structures and systems to provide support and accountability to teachers at different performance levels.

The identification and nurturing of high-potential employees as a human capital strategy is the lifeblood of successful organizations in other sectors. It is how organizations develop new innovations, address succession, and retain talent. They use clear performance standards to identify high-potential employees, nurture their growth, and ensure "bench" strength. For example, Boeing has transformed a room at its corporate headquarters into a "bull pen"; pictures, accomplishments, résumés, and career aspirations of top managerial talent are posted on the walls. The CEO and senior leaders spend time in the bull pen reviewing the talent pool, considering the talent gaps and how to address them, developing strategies to further strengthen existing talent and deploy it to support the organization's goals, and planning for succession. This process is largely unfamiliar to K–12 education.

Building and nurturing a talent pool requires that principals or other leaders in the system be personally involved and develop a systemic strategy.

Principals and others who interact with teachers must identify the most talented teachers by using a mix of observational and student achievement data. They then work with them to define their career interests and think about how to nurture and use talents and interests to greatest effect to strengthen the quality of teaching, school functioning, and/or system-level work. School systems can support principals' efforts by providing special leadership development training, career opportunities, and salary incentives to honor and reward these teachers for their performance. At the same time, systems can help build these teachers' skills in preparation for assuming leadership. Teachers need specific skills to successfully expand their focus from their classroom to the school or system levels or from working with students to working with adults. Teachers face clear challenges as they make these transitions, and the system is well positioned to prepare them for this work to ensure their success and ongoing commitment.

The system can further support this work by giving principals tools to identify talent and design a system to track, nurture, and deploy that talent. The system first defines the performance benchmarks and characteristics of high-potential teachers. Then it sets the expectation that principals are responsible for identifying and developing teacher talent. It can most easily achieve this by providing images of the work, developing strategies for how to do it, and holding principals accountable for it through their own evaluation. Tracking the teachers identified as high potential, the leadership opportunities they pursue, and their impact on student learning over time provides the system invaluable data. With these data, the system can identify principals who are good talent managers and schools that are breeding grounds of talent. This information can identify which schools can be training sites for aspiring teachers or lab sites for new teachers. Similarly, principals who are strong talent managers can be enticed to work in schools where their skills and the flexibility provided by the system will accelerate school improvement.

A new initiative underway in the Charlotte-Mecklenburg Schools to strategically staff schools shows how systems can identify top talent and deploy it to address its greatest concerns. The system has recruited top-performing principals (defined by schoolwide student growth) to lead teams that go into chronically underperforming schools. The principals can recruit five high-performing teachers (defined by student growth rates in reading and math), an assistant principal, and a literacy or academic coordinator to be part of their team. The principals are given a 10 percent salary increase that is maintained for the duration of their tenure in the school. Teacher members of the turnaround team receive a $10,000 recruitment bonus in the first year and a $5,000 retention bonus for each of years two and three. Everyone on the team makes a three-year commitment to the school.

Recognizing the serious impediment that chronically low-performing teachers pose to student learning and school improvement, the Charlotte-Mecklenburg initiative also enables principals to address the challenge of low-performing teachers. It gives the principals of these strategically staffed schools the authority to remove five teachers from the low-performing school that they think create the greatest impediment to school improvement.[7] The initiative draws on what is known about the profound impact of ineffective teaching on students and their learning.[8]

The presence of chronically low-performing teachers is an artifact of a weak teacher-evaluation system and low expectations for teachers. The problem cuts three ways. First, a weak culture of performance management in districts has left many teachers with meaningless satisfactory ratings that don't support their growth and development and often don't capture their practice well. Second, because of the weak culture and low expectations, poor-performing teachers are often either not identified as such or not provided the support needed to improve. Finally, unions have negotiated complex processes for documenting poor performance and pursuing dismissal that entail extensive documentation and convoluted time lines and procedures. These make it nearly impossible for a principal to pursue dismissal, avoid all the possible loopholes, and simultaneously run a school. As a result, principals are more likely to ignore poor performance or manage by cutting deals to get weak teachers out of their schools. This approach doesn't address the performance issue; it simply moves it to another school.

By creating meaningful teacher-performance standards, supporting principals, and holding them accountable for using the standards, school systems can make teacher performance management meaningful. Weak teachers are identified through this process, whether by their supervisor or a process of peer review. They are then supported and given the opportunity to improve their practice. If they don't improve, a fair, clear, simple process for moving teachers from the system—that doesn't have the system incur thousands of dollars in legal fees and settlement payments—must be in place. Local unions can follow the lead of some of their forward-thinking union colleagues nationally who have partnered with systems to develop simple and fair support and accountability processes for poor-performing teachers. In so doing, they demonstrate their commitment to teaching quality and extricate themselves from the thankless task of defending chronically poor-performing teachers who shouldn't be teaching children.

Professional Development

Professional development is the main vehicle for supporting teaching quality. Yet few school systems have robust training and professional development systems that are designed in response to student performance data, reflect best professional development practices, and are proven to effect student learning. Responsibility for professional development is often diffusely spread across a variety of departments with little coherence or alignment of efforts, leaving no one in charge. Individual departments tend to set their own professional development agendas, leaving teachers confused by the array of offerings and unable to focus on what is important. While the era of one-shot workshops distanced from the classroom realities that teachers face is waning, system professional development usually does not consistently reflect best practices. Given that school systems spend between 2.1 percent and 5.5 percent of their total operation budget on professional development, systems have a substantial opportunity to redirect money toward their priorities and improved student learning.[9]

School systems can address these problems by moving professional development dollars and services closer to schools and classrooms, dismantling entrenched central office training structures in favor of nimble training strategies that respond to individual teacher and school needs, and tapping promising practices already in existence. These tasks, the responsibility of the chief academic officer, are a key way the teaching and learning departments are implicated in and held responsible for human capital management. The systems can focus resources on providing support to teachers in the context of their classrooms and encouraging teacher collaboration. They can charge principals, as the leaders of learning, to work with faculty to assess professional development needs and design an appropriate response.

Differentiation based on school capacity can take various forms. In schools with strong capacity, faculty and the principal can drive training and development. Conversely, schools with low levels of leadership and/or teaching capacity need more external guidance and support. Differentiating the flexibility that schools have with professional development dollars and strategies based on the pace of student achievement growth and other indicators of school functioning allows those that are well positioned to drive their professional development to have that opportunity, while also providing more direction to those schools that need help.

Classroom-based instructional coaching is an example of a professional development strategy aimed at moving support into schools and classrooms, building capacity, and creating consistency of instruction across classrooms and schools. The implementation of coaching can be differentiated so that teachers within a school that has capacity can provide the coaching internally, while coaches are provided to schools that don't have internal capacity. Developing a model of teacher collaboration that mixes common planning time, peer observations, study groups, and so on, organized according to priorities defined by student achievement data, provides a strong foundation to further build instructional quality and collegiality. Providing more structure for the content and delivery of professional development can support schools that have more basic needs and less internal capacity to address them.

Where to Start

As the exploration of levers makes clear, the human capital landscape is vast and the need is enormous. School systems must direct human capital in a way that is manageable, responsive, and ensures success. Each school system's approach will be different. The context of the system, its history, existing infrastructure, approach to school improvement, demographics, performance, community resources and partners, opportunities, and most importantly, its work force, all inform the approach. For example, a school system with a long history of a predominantly white teaching force working with students who have much more diverse ethnic and racial backgrounds will place a high priority on ensuring diversity and equity. On the other hand, a system in which the race and ethnicity of the teacher population reflects the student population but where the most-effective teachers are concentrated in the highest-performing schools will likely have different concerns.

A school system pursuing an improvement strategy that gives principals authority over all aspects of their schools' instructional improvement strategy and holds them accountable for results will need to give principals real authority over hiring and firing teachers. While a school system that is implementing a centrally mandated curriculum, instructional expectations, and assessments is likely to be more focused on aligning professional development, performance management, compensation, and rewards to those mandates. A school system in a city with ten universities involved in teacher preparation has very different opportunities (and challenges) than a system that has one primary teacher provider.

Most school systems will find it obvious where to begin. There are clear human capital problems to fix. A system that perennially finds itself hiring 30 percent of its new teachers during the final weeks of summer and the first weeks of school needs to start there. A system that completes its hiring by late June but has a 40 percent attrition rate for new teachers at the end of their first three years needs to better understand who is leaving and why and then redesign its recruitment, screening, and induction to respond to the identified needs.

Systems commonly try to solve these problems one at a time. This approach makes perfect sense from a problem-solving perspective. Yet often, systems address human capital problems in a vacuum without any thought about the larger context in which they exist or the relationship between one problem (and its solution) and another. As a result, problems keep cropping up. Once it has bolstered induction support and new-teacher working conditions, for example, the system realizes that it has heavily emphasized support with no plan to assess teacher effectiveness before granting tenure. A system can pursue its human capital endeavors in this piecemeal way to try to eventually build a robust management system. But such a slow approach is likely to leave significant cracks through which promising teachers will fall, lessening the impact of this work on students and their learning.

School systems need to imagine the outcome of their human capital work. The vision may be to compete for the most talented teachers nationally, because the system has dynamic career opportunities and performance incentives for effective teachers that keep them engaged and leverage their expertise for the benefit of students, schools, and the system overall. Or perhaps the vision focuses on multiple pathways into teaching, increased compensation for new teachers, and efforts to make new teachers effective quickly. Maybe it's all these things. The specifics of the vision are less important than having one. The vision helps the school system focus, providing the desired state from which to design the human capital system. Understanding the vision and assessing current conditions relative to it help make clear the building blocks of the vision. They indicate the critical steps required to reach the vision, the sequence in which to take those steps to build organizational capacity, and the pace of the journey.

Building the Foundation

A key component of the foundation for high-functioning human capital management already exists in every school system: the human resources (HR) department. A system's capacity to effectively and efficiently recruit, screen, and hire people, pay them on time, provide benefits, treat them with respect, regularly evaluate and report their performance, and deal with incompetence is the underpinning for managing human capital. These functions have always been the purview of the HR department.

In reality, though, school systems are not uniformly effective in performing these functions. The most common challenges they face are ensuring appropriate, high-quality applicants for positions; designing and managing the implementation of an efficient marketing, recruitment, screening, and hiring process; treating applicants professionally; competing effectively for talent; anticipating and addressing future staffing needs; implementing a performance management system that ensures employees get regular feedback aligned with support and accountability; processing personnel transactions efficiently and accurately; using technology to expedite and streamline processes; and having useful, actionable data about the work force and the effectiveness of the HR department.

Given these common challenges, what might a high-functioning HR operation look like? Imagine a system where:

- Recruitment, screening, and selection processes are assessed by the quality of applicants and teachers hired. The system has created its own brand in order to compete for talent. It has an online presence and attractive printed materials that tell a compelling story about teaching in the district, the students, and the opportunities and benefits. The system uses social networking and other marketing strategies to reach targeted audiences. Recruitment is strategic, initiated early in the fall, and based on projected needs for the coming school year. The district has well-developed strategies to recruit diverse, high-quality candidates in high-needs areas and may recruit almost 50 percent of its new teachers from strategic partnerships.

- The system completes initial screening centrally to give principals a prescreened pool of candidates who meet a quality threshold. It uses technology to streamline screening and selection processes. All in-person contact is courteous, supportive, and professional. Teacher applicants visit schools, meet potential colleagues, and teach as part of their screening; teachers have a say in hiring decisions. For those hired, the process of on-boarding is facilitated by technology; getting on the payroll and signing up for benefits is simple and efficient. After being hired, new teachers are introduced to supports specially designed for new teachers.

- Once teachers are hired, the HR department addresses all their ongoing needs related to salary and benefits, performance, and movement from one job to another. It has systematized processes such as tracking and reporting attendance and performance review schedules and ratings. Ensuring the implementation of performance management of teachers is a top priority. The HR department works in collaboration with the teaching and learning division and other key areas to define the mix of quantitative and qualitative measures and then develops a system for implementation. It tracks teacher performance results, looks for trends, and supports principals in addressing chronically underperforming teachers and targeting high-potential employees for career advancement opportunities.

- HR is a service provider to both the teaching and learning division and the principals. It helps both groups drive their agendas for school and systemic improvement through staffing, support, and performance management. Department staff work on cross-functional teams with teaching and learning staff focused on instructional improvement priorities and their HR implications; they regularly visit schools to understand the needs of principals and teachers and how HR can best address them. The department may drive the training and development of teachers, or it may support the teaching and learning division in leading this work.

- Data guide high-functioning HR operations. Multiyear projections of staffing needs based on student demographics, anticipated teacher retirements, and staffing patterns guide strategic decisions and daily operations. HR tracks information on every teacher, including his or her basic personnel information, time and mobility in the system, college and university affiliations, performance ratings, students' performance results, and any commendations or disciplinary action. This information informs individual personnel actions and is aggregated and analyzed in various ways to better understand the teaching workforce and guide strategic action at the school and district levels.

Achieving this vision would create a strong foundation for a high-functioning human capital management strategy. Some systems might want to start by creating such an HR department. Yet the interrelated nature of human resources and human capital often results in them being addressed simultaneously, creating synergy. When a school system pursues an innovative approach to recruiting and preparing new teachers, it sees, in the experience of those aspiring teachers, that its screening and hiring process is cumbersome, inefficient, and unwelcoming. Conversely, HR data that document a high rate of attrition among the teachers who are having the greatest effects on student learning can drive innovations targeted at nurturing high performers. Pursuing a human capital agenda is difficult if the HR operation is completely dysfunctional. The basic operations of hiring and deploying staff must function well before human capital management can gain traction.

Given the pivotal role that HR plays in human capital management, where the department appears on the organization chart is important. In some school systems, the HR department is buried, often reporting up through a labyrinth to the chief of staff or operations. Such organizations perceive HR as focused on hiring, firing, and benefits management. In systems that prioritize human capital and see HR as a critical partner, the head of the department is on the superintendent's senior leadership team and often reports directly to the superintendent.

The organizational placement of HR is critical for several reasons. HR departments in many school systems, particularly large, urban school systems, are often antiquated. They struggle to execute the basic functions of hiring staff and managing employee information. HR departments need a strong head with deep professional experience and expertise (as opposed to a veteran educator who has an interest and shows some talent managing staff) to automate the department's key functions, prioritize customer service, approach recruitment in an innovative and entrepreneurial way, and fundamentally change the department's culture. To recruit such talent (often from outside), the system needs to signal its commitment explicitly through the organizational chart and reporting lines. Furthermore, in a system where human capital is a priority, the HR department head should be at the same level as the chief financial officer and the chief academic officer, signaling that human resource and human capital issues are as central to the success of the school system as the teaching and learning agenda and the organization's fiscal health.

Additional Infrastructure Required

In addition to a strong foundation for the HR function and systemwide commitment to human capital management, there are two additional elements of a school system's infrastructure that can either support or profoundly impede human capital efforts: (1) the principals and their role as human capital managers, and (2) the accessibility of human resource and human capital data to quantify problems, drive improvements, and assess progress.

Much of the daily human capital management happens (or not) in schools, led by principals, where teachers spend their days. Schools are where they are supervised, evaluated, and supported to grow. In schools, they build relationships with fellow teachers who support their continuous improvement and give them a sense of colleagueship. Finally, schools are where they experience success in teaching students and build a sense of efficacy. The pivotal person who influences all of these experiences is the principal. So, *how can the system best support principals in managing human capital?*

Focusing principals' attention on human capital changes the nature of their role and has the potential, over the long term, to save them both time and turmoil. Over time, they will increase the quality of teaching, retention, the level of teacher professionalism, collaboration, and leadership within their schools. Yet in the short term, they will likely see it as one more thing to do. Systems' ability to free principals to focus on human capital and ensure they know how to lead this work will make it possible for them to do it. A high-functioning HR department that functions on a model of serving schools as their customers (as opposed to one heavily focused on mandates and compliance) helps. The ability to off-load the time-consuming and energy-sapping task of dealing with chronically low-performing teachers is a godsend. The leeway to create meaningful teacher-leadership roles within schools gives principals the flexibility to retain their top talent and address school-specific needs. Principals who learn how to think strategically about their staffing, hiring, and budgeting to realize school improvement goals transform their HR tasks into human capital strategies. Learning communities in which principals can share their human capital strategies and challenges and get support bring the work to life and provide the assistance that makes it feel manageable.

Meaningful human capital data can help principals assess the situation in their schools, prioritize actions for improvement, and measure progress. The value of human capital data extends beyond principals. Data inform

2

Using Data to Support Human Capital Development in School Districts

*Measures to Track the Effectiveness
of Teachers and Principals*

Laurence B. Stanton and Kavita Kapadia Matsko

The Hansen school district enrolls 75,000 students in 125 schools. Enrollment is stable, but the percentage of students receiving free and reduced-price lunches has increased from 30 percent to 60 percent during the past five years. At the same time, the percentage of students meeting state standards has decreased by one or two percentage points each year.

The Hansen School District employs about 4,500 teachers and hires between 400 and 500 teachers each year. Historically, nearly half of its new teachers come from Hansen State, a third-tier state university located in Hansen. The district also hires a small number of teachers each year from State University, a first-tier research university, and from St. Peter's University, a national Catholic university located in a nearby suburb. The district recently began working with the state on an alternative certification program targeting science and special education teachers.

Two years ago, the district hired a new superintendent, Annette Ward. Shortly after her appointment, she announced her major strategy for improving student achievement—she would focus on the quality of the district's teachers. At her initial speech to district administrators, she said, "Developing our teaching force needs to receive as much, if not more, of our attention than district facilities or finances." She began by identifying six priorities:

- *Identifying and filling teacher vacancies earlier so the district gets the best candidates possible and every student has a full-time teacher on the first day of school.*

- *Increasing the number of high-quality applicants for teaching positions, particularly in high-needs subjects and high-needs schools.*

- *Supporting new teachers with intensive induction support during their first two years in the classroom.*

- *Identifying and retaining the best new teachers and removing ineffective teachers.*

- *Building a post-tenure career ladder for the district's best teachers.*

- *Matching teacher needs with professional development offerings.*

Ward knew from the beginning that announcing a thoughtful teacher-quality initiative wasn't enough; she and her team would have to implement a set of distinct but related strategies over several years. She also knew that effective implementation would require a continuous flow of information on progress that would allow her to make adjustments, shift resources, and hold people accountable. During her first few months, she found that, although the district had lots of human resources data, her staff could not produce timely answers to basic questions about their progress, such as: Are we getting better applicants this year than last? Are we hiring them earlier? Which universities provide the best teachers? Are new teachers staying in their schools? In the district? Are the district's lowest-performing schools getting good teachers? Are we removing ineffective teachers?

Although Ward and her colleagues are still in the initial stages of their work to improve teaching effectiveness, their priorities are based on three important assumptions. First, Ward believes that effective teaching can be measured and nurtured. Second, she believes that effective teaching is different from competent teaching. Therefore the district needs to be concerned about more than removing bad teachers; it also needs to be identifying and developing excellent teachers. Finally, Ward believes that improving the quality of teaching is a necessary prerequisite to improving student achievement. Building a shared belief in these assumptions is the central element of Ward's improvement strategy for Hansen. Because Ward understands that reliable, timely, and relevant data will be the only evidence that her assumptions are right, she charged her academic, human resources, and information systems officers with building a system to provide her with the data she needs to advance her human capital priorities.

Ward's concern with student achievement is echoed in districts across the country, but her emphasis on improving teaching quality, while not unique, is unusual in its focus. Experience tells us that identifying the right priorities and strategies is a necessary but insufficient first step. Too often, districts are long on good intentions (e.g., "we need to recruit better teachers"), but short on execution and accountability (e.g., "the best teachers just don't come to our district"). The challenge is making a connection between big, ambitious strategies and data-driven execution. Hansen needs to clarify responsibility for implementing strategies and then measure performance against specific agreed-upon goals. This level of clarity will shift the conversation from well-meaning rhetoric to informed conversations about performance and accountability for results.

This chapter describes how school districts committed to improving the quality of teaching and school leadership can begin to collect and use data to support their improvement strategies. We begin with a brief discussion of performance metrics and then describe five principles for developing human capital metrics. Next, we describe teaching quality as a continuum that needs to be evaluated using multiple measures and multiple data points. Building on that assertion, we describe and provide examples of how districts can use data to develop aspiring teachers, novice teachers, second-stage teachers, and school leaders. Finally, we discuss data governance and communications, with special attention to the use of scorecards and dashboards as vehicles to promote improved teaching effectiveness.

What Are Performance Metrics?

A human capital improvement strategy is only as effective as the district's ability to measure its success. Performance metrics are tools for turning data into information that can be used to manage and evaluate strategies. For example, two commonly used metrics are the percentage of students meeting state standards and the percentage of teachers who are certified under the No Child Left Behind Act. Although there may be a relationship between changes on the two metrics and a human capital strategy, neither number would provide a district like Hansen with the information it needs to guide its human capital initiatives.

Performance metrics fall into three categories: input measures, output measures, and outcome measures. *Input measures* report on resource utilization.

For example, tracking total spending on professional development would be an input measure that could be useful for comparisons if tracked over several years.

Output measures capture activities. A report of the number of teachers who complete a professional development course may be a useful measure of satisfaction with the course, but it is not a measure of improved teacher knowledge or skills.

Outcome measures describe what was produced. A report on the change in student learning resulting from better-prepared teachers would be a valuable outcome measure. Outcome measures, particularly those related to student learning, should be based on multiple measures and data points.

Although an effective system needs to include a mix of input, output, and outcome measures, in the end, the impact on student outcomes is what matters most.

Principles to Guide Development of a Human Capital Metrics System

Based on our experience working with districts, we have identified five principles for district leaders to keep in mind as they build systems for using performance data to advance a human capital strategy. The scorecard and dashboard data management tools embody these principles, but regardless of the tool, these principles can be used to develop a metrics system.

1. Alignment with a Human Capital Strategy

The district's human capital strategies should determine what to measure as well as the data to collect, report, and act on. Performance metrics without a strategy or a strategy without performance metrics are both suboptimal. To optimize results, a district needs performance metrics aligned with a thoughtful human capital strategy. For example, the Hansen School District is committed to focusing resources and attention on its high-needs schools—defined as schools with over 80 percent low-income students. Therefore, all data reports should highlight the performance and resources committed to high-needs schools. This helps leaders sustain attention on the strategy of allocating resources to address the needs of these schools.

2. Focus on Student Outcomes

Human capital performance metrics should focus attention on the district's ultimate goal—improved student outcomes. Where it is not possible to link student outcomes directly to the strategy, the district can use proxies for student outcomes or measures of implementation progress. For example, while teacher satisfaction with a professional development course may be significant, the course is only valuable if it contributes to improved student outcomes. Even though it may be difficult to make a direct connection between a particular professional development course and improved student test scores, metrics can link professional development to teacher behaviors that the district believes will result in improved student outcomes.

3. Support for a Culture of Continuous Improvement

Human capital performance metrics should support a culture of continuous improvement. The metrics should be based on an agreed-upon definition of excellence and provide staff at each level of the district with information on how they are doing in advancing toward excellence and what they might do to support and incent excellence. This is a vastly different notion than defining teacher effectiveness in binary terms (i.e., satisfactory or not satisfactory) for the sole purpose of deciding whether to rehire a teacher. District leadership should facilitate cross-level conversations about the data that result in establishing best practices, shifting resources, or even modifying strategy. For example, if data show that the district's high-need schools are not hiring graduates of a newly approved, alternative certification program, then that finding should lead to conversations with program's director, the human resources office, the district's regional superintendents, and principals of high-needs schools to determine what's happening. Are the alternative certification graduates applying to high-needs schools? Are they well prepared? Or is there something about the district's application or interview process that results in too few hires? Using these data should result in conversations based on data, not anecdotes, and result in solutions aimed at the actual problem and not the perception of the problem.

4. Support for Accountability

A system of human capital performance metrics should encourage accountability for improving human capital at the school, regional, and central office levels of the district. Cascading performance metrics can shine a light on the contribution of each level to meeting district human capital goals. For example, advancing Hansen's early teacher hiring initiative will require actions by principals, regional superintendents, and the central human resources office. Evidence of the necessary activities at each level can be identified, collected, and reported, so that progress can be noted and problems identified and resolved at the appropriate level. With monthly reports on the number of candidates referred to each of her schools, the number of interviews conducted and offers made by each principal, and the number of teachers processed and hired, a regional superintendent can identify and resolve staffing problems before school begins. This cascading system will promote transparency as well as clarity of ownership, ultimately resulting in shared responsibility for school and district goals.

5. Quality, Not Perfection

When identifying performance metrics, districts would be wise to avoid making the perfect the enemy of the good. Much can be learned and improved based on imperfect or incomplete data measures. The things districts are trying to measure—teaching effectiveness, leadership, student learning—are all complex and not easily summarized in a single number or even a set of numbers. What's most important in developing performance metrics is begun by identifying what matters. Once that happens, the measures can change over time as better information is collected and reported. For example, although many districts may not be able to employ value-added measures to assess an individual teacher's contribution to student-achievement gains, every district can calculate student progress across performance quartiles. Such data are useful measures of how well teachers are improving student performance.

Defining Teaching Quality—a Critical First Step in Managing Human Capital

If the goal is to improve the quality of teaching to accelerate student learning, districts need to begin with a clear and shared definition of teaching practices that result in documented increases in student achievement.

Measures of teaching practice include two types of data: (1) observation-based evidence of whether a teacher is effectively managing the interaction between students and curriculum content; and (2) student outcome-based evidence—derived from student work, curriculum-based assessments, or standardized tests—that shows whether students in a teacher's classes are making appropriate annual gains in achievement. Districts at the optimal level are systematically collecting and using both types of evidence to assess teacher performance. Districts at the emerging level systematically use one or the other type of evidence, and districts at the foundational level aren't yet using either kind of evidence in a systematic way, but are collecting data that describe the district's teachers and school leaders.

Observation-Based Evidence

In order to use qualitative, observation-based evidence to define the quality of teaching, district leaders, union members, school principals, human resources staff, and teachers themselves must develop a shared understanding of effective teaching practice. Several districts have adopted Charlotte Danielson's Framework for Teaching, which includes a rubric that identifies four domains of practice and describes four levels of performance for each component—unsatisfactory, basic, proficient, and distinguished.[1] Other districts use Marzano, Pickering, and Pollock's work to guide their observations.[2] Still other districts and charter networks have developed their own standards of excellent teaching and systems for measuring practice against the standards. All these systems share a commitment to measuring individual teacher practice using a common ruler. The observers of this evidence may include principals, coaches, teachers, or full-time specialists trained to use the instrument so that there is consistency across schools and regions. Who conducts the observations and the particular tool is less important than the district's commitment to defining the elements of excellent teaching and then implementing a system to effectively and consistently measure teacher practice.

The adoption of a common definition of *effective teaching practices* has positive implications throughout a teacher's career. It will prompt district staff to screen potential new hires more carefully for the skills and knowledge identified in the definition. The definition will also allow principals to identify and support emerging teacher leaders, to assist teachers in the middle range of development by acknowledging their need for significant support, and remove teachers who are not serving students well. A shared definition of teaching effectiveness will also help principals and district staff to differentiate professional development opportunities to meet the varying needs of their teachers. Together, these efforts will increase the quality of teaching performance in the district.

Student Outcome-Based Evidence

Improved practice, however, is an insufficient end goal. Tracking student outcomes is also a critical part of managing district human capital.

While principals and district administrators have always made links between student performance and individual teachers on an anecdotal basis, technology has now made it possible to create those links in a formal, evidence-based manner. These techniques enable principals and district administrators to see that students in some classrooms have made substantial gains in achievement from year to year, while other classrooms have made more modest gains. These value-added methods take into account students' backgrounds and prior achievements, so that they do not reward teachers who happen to have a class of high achievers or punish teachers who might have a class that began farther behind.

Several states and districts have begun measuring individual teachers' value-added gains for their students on annual state tests. Several factors, however, limit the benefits of value-added data. For example, value-added data may only be available for students with two consecutive years of state test data and also only available for teachers of tested subjects. This means that as many as half the teachers in a district may never have value-added data. Some districts are developing proxy measures of student learning using data from district- or curriculum-based assessments or student work portfolios to understand the impact of their teachers' performance.

Together, teacher-observation and student-learning data provide rich evidence for districts to learn from and act on. Such a combination makes it possible to study how teacher practice affects student outcomes. We know of no district that is currently using a robust mix of observation and learning data to evaluate teaching performance, however. Many districts are at the emerging level, with either observation-based evidence of individual teacher practice or student growth data linked to individual teachers. Those districts can move forward with the work described next as they continue to build systems that use both types of data. But without both measures in place, districts need to be very cautious of drawing conclusions about teaching effectiveness from measures with weak or nonexistent connections to quality teaching.

Using Data on Teaching Quality

Once districts have data describing their teaching force, they need structured ways to examine the data, learn from them, and use them as the basis for making decisions. Districts at the optimal levels can use quality data to sort teachers into multiple categories (buckets) ranging from low performing to high performing. Examining a teaching force using a continuum or ranking performance can help inform decisions about retaining, developing, and removing teachers. It can also help a district target professional development resources or identify potential future leaders. Tracking performance by effectiveness quartiles may be a useful method for tracking progress. Districts at the foundational stage of data collection may be able to do some sorting of data. These initial uses of data will probably highlight the need for better, more reliable information.

Examining the Distribution of Quality Teachers

Once teachers are sorted based on performance, district leaders can assess how teachers are distributed across the district. Are the strongest teachers distributed equally across their higher- and lower-performing schools? Subject areas? Geographic regions? Grade levels? Over time, understanding the distribution of stronger and weaker teachers will make it possible to build targeted strategies such as providing additional compensation for strong teachers who move to high-needs schools.

Differentiating Responses to Individual Teachers

Data can enable district leaders to differentiate the nature and amount of support teachers receive. Leaders should encourage teachers in the top performance level to stay in the district and develop them to assume roles where they can hone their own skills and areas of expertise and increase their contribution to the system. They should offer teachers in the middle targeted assistance to address their identified weaknesses. This could come in the form of coaching, specialized professional development, additional attention from the principal or colleague, or an adjustment in class composition. Struggling teachers can receive assistance before key decision points, such as tenure.

Removing Poor Performers

District leaders should monitor teachers in the lowest performance level closely, and if they don't show immediate improvement, the district should have a plan for removing them. All too often, poor performers are moved from one position into another, from school to school. If the district's priority is improving student learning, then it must be prepared to act aggressively to ensure that only the teachers who are effective stay in the classroom.

Identifying Effective School Leadership

The quality of a principal can be defined and tracked in similar ways. Aggregated school performance gains and a rigorous, evidence-based examination of a principal's leadership practice are comparable to teacher value-added measures, and the observation-based evidence required for determining teaching quality. Based on those two types of evidence, principals can be sorted into performance levels. If district leaders evaluate principals using a rigorous leadership framework that includes evidence of both practice and student outcomes, progress toward the articulated goals will accelerate.

In addition to helping districts achieve their goal of improving the quality of teaching and improving student learning, these processes also suggest an important shift toward evaluation that is based on evidence rather than anecdotes and years of experience. This reinforces a system of transparency and clear expectations.

Measuring Performance at Stages of a Teaching Career

Although practice and student-performance data are important for all teachers, there are also specific metrics that can be used for teachers at each stage of their careers: aspiring teacher, novice teacher, second-stage teacher, and school leader. Most districts are in the early phases of development of such metrics, but there are more sophisticated metrics to use that focus attention on the varied human capital challenges districts face.

Aspiring Teachers

Identifying teaching talent is among the most significant challenges facing school districts. Districts spend substantial time and money recruiting and interviewing prospective teachers from colleges, universities, and alternative preparation programs. But data can be an important tool to help districts identify and then target aspiring teachers who are most likely to advance student achievement, as well as to inform and strengthen local teacher-preparation programs. (See the box "Examples of Measures to Recruit, Hire, and Retain Aspiring Teachers.")

Denver and Louisiana are at the leading edge of the work to identify teacher talent. In 2007, leaders of the Denver Public Schools (DPS), deans of the local schools of education, and the leaders of alternative teacher-preparation programs began meeting to talk about improving the process of preparing teachers. A year later, those discussions evolved into a multiphase plan to use student achievement data and teacher observation data to better understand what it means to be a well-prepared novice teacher and to determine how well the various preparation programs were enabling teachers to meet those standards. (Under an agreement with the

---

Examples of Measures to Recruit, Hire, and Retain Aspiring Teachers

Foundational (descriptive information)

For each preparation program (including alternative certification programs):

- Number and/or percentage of new teachers hired
- Distribution of new teachers to high-needs schools, high-needs subjects, and school type, i.e., elementary, middle, and high schools
- Number and/or percentage of one- to three-year teachers receiving intensive support from their preparation program
- School and district three-year retention

Emerging (based on either observation or student value-added evidence)

For each preparation program:

- Number and/or percentage of new teachers at each performance level based on observations

or

- Number and/or percentage of new teachers at each performance level based on student value-added data

Optimal (based on both observation and student value-added evidence)

For each preparation program:

- Number and/or percentage of teachers at each performance level based on observation and student value-added data
- Retention rates of one- to three-year teachers at each performance level
- Distribution of teachers, i.e., high-needs schools, high-needs subjects, elementary, middle, and high schools by performance level

---

Colorado Department of Education, DPS also operates its own preparation program and licenses teachers.)

The first step was to figure out where teachers received their preparation. Since the district did not have complete information in its files, it enlisted the help of the universities. The district provided the preparation programs with the names of all district teachers and asked them to link each teacher to his or her preparation program.

The second step will be to develop a framework for effective teaching based on the practice of experienced teachers with high value-added scores. The district will identify 100 teachers with seven to fifteen years of experience, with varying value-added student achievement outcomes, and observe them to identify the teaching practices that are linked to their outcomes. They will then build a teaching framework based on the practices of the top-performing Denver teachers. Once the framework is completed, the preparation programs intend to assess their students using the framework to better understand where their preparation is effective and where it is falling short. The district also hopes to use the framework to encourage the state department of education to shift from a focus on credentials and time in the classroom as a measure of teacher quality to a focus on the practices of effective teachers.[3]

Louisiana, meanwhile, was the first state in the nation to assess the effectiveness of its teacher preparation programs using student outcomes. The study included more than 285,000 students taught by more than 7,000 teachers in 1,300 schools over the 2004–2005 and 2005–2006 school years.[4] It used value-added data to determine teacher effectiveness and then analyzed which preparation programs were more likely to produce effective teachers. Subsequently, the state formed a special research team to determine why and how some teacher preparation programs are having a greater impact on student learning. This work is helping to inform hiring decisions in Louisiana school districts. It will also provide teacher preparation programs with data to improve their quality.

Although the two data systems are different—Denver's will include both observation and student outcome-based data, while Louisiana is only using value-added data—both initiatives are transforming the nature of the conversation between school district leaders and preparation programs about the quality of teacher preparation. Both are providing the transparency of results necessary for continuous improvement. They are also beginning to hold preparation programs responsible for their results. Within a few years, Denver and Louisiana will produce annual scorecards that report the results of each teacher preparation provider. This process, focused on quality, will have a major effect on district recruitment and hiring decisions. It should also affect the quality of the programs; those that appear successful can offer lessons to those that are less successful. Ideally, those programs producing strong teachers will receive greater support, and those producing low-quality teachers will either improve or close. See figure 2.1 for an example of the kind of information such report cards can provide.

Figure 2.1 Report of second- and third-year novice teaching quality and retention by provider

		All Teachers, All Subjects, All Schools			
	Second- and Third-Year Novice Teacher Retention Data Organized by Teaching Effectiveness (Levels 1–4)*	SY 2005–2006	SY 2006–2007	SY 2007–2008	SY 2008–2009
Provider A	Total Novice Teachers	35	37	41	34
	Year-to-year school retention	80%	72%	78%	70%
	Level 1 (Top performing)	5%	0%	2%	4%
	Level 2	70%	62%	55%	60%
	Level 3	15%	25%	30%	30%
	Level 4 (Lowest Performing)	10%	13%	13%	6%
Provider B	Total Novice Teachers	21	24	28	27
	Year-to-year school retention	88%	90%	92%	90%
	Level 1	22%	30%	28%	35%
	Level 2	62%	57%	62%	62%
	Level 3	14%	10%	10%	3%
	Level 4	2%	3%	0%	0%

*Levels based on district quality evidence, both observation and outcomes

The figure shows the performance of two teacher preparation providers on two dimensions—school retention and teaching performance level. The data prompt a number of questions that district leaders and the providers of new teachers can address:

- What explains the different outcomes of the two providers?
- Do success rates vary by subject matter or for teachers in high-needs schools?
- Can provider A learn from provider B and improve its program?
- Are the district human resources personnel and principals aware of and using these data in their hiring?

Over time, continued conversations about these data among the district, school leaders, and teacher preparation providers will improve the quality of the programs and the district's teaching force.

Novice Teachers

Until recently, most districts measured new-teacher success by retention alone. If a novice teacher came back for a second, third, and fourth year and gained tenure, the district deemed that teacher successful. Since efforts to retain teachers are not typically linked to teachers' performance, there is often no way to ensure that those who stay in the district are the best suited to help students learn. In recent years, though, formal induction programs intended to both retain new teachers *and* improve their teaching practice have become commonplace across the United States. Data on the early years of teaching can be supported to improve teaching effectiveness and student learning.

In 2006, Chicago Public Schools (CPS) identified regions of the school district with the highest teacher-turnover rates and decided to invest heavily in intensive supports for new hires in those regions. Novices working in these challenging areas received assistance every other week from a mentor trained by the New Teacher Center, an organization based in Santa Cruz, California. The teachers also attended monthly professional development programs focused not just on retention, but also on improving their teaching practices. Mentors kept collaborative logs of working sessions with the novice teachers and set specific instructional goals at the end of every session. The logs also reported on the specific Illinois teaching standards addressed in each visit. This type of tracking ensures a more rigorous, instructional approach to mentoring than beginning teachers typically receive.

CPS offered principals in the participating regions professional development designed to help them sustain and develop beginning teachers. In addition, it made efforts to align and deepen literacy practice in the schools.

One year later, vacancies in one of the regions dropped from more than 100 to less than 30. That result suggests that the differentiated level of support provided to teachers in the high-needs areas paid off in higher retention rates. As a next step, CPS can track the effectiveness of the teachers receiving intensive induction programming and compare their student outcomes to teachers receiving different levels of support.[5]

An optimal system would augment such data with real-time data that could track the supports for teachers over the course of the year, rather than annually. See figure 2.2 for an example of how these data might be regularly compiled and shared.

Figure 2.2   Monthly report on novice teacher support

First- and second-year teachers successfully participating in intensive new teacher induction* (# participating in intensive induction, total first- and second-year teachers, % of first- and second-year teachers participating)	*August 31*	*September 30*	*October 31*
All schools	116	117	100
	134	145	142
	87%	81%	70%
High needs schools (duplicates categories below)	27	24	20
	32	30	27
	84%	80%	74%
Elementary schools	60	54	52
	66	60	56
	91%	90%	93%
Middle schools	22	23	24
	22	23	26
	100%	100%	92%
High schools	34	40	24
	46	62	60
	74%	64%	40%

*Successful participation includes attending all scheduled sessions and meetings with mentors.

The data in figure 2.2 show that program participation has been consistently high for elementary and middle school novice teachers. In stark contrast, participation by novice high school teachers began at relatively low levels and continued to drop, possibly because a substantial proportion of the district's new high school teachers were not enrolled in the induction program until September, after school started. The decline in participation by teachers in high-needs schools can probably also be explained by the decline in high school participants.

This report could prompt conversations among the high school principals, the leaders of the district human resources department, and the induction program sponsors. Is enrollment in induction structured differently for middle school teachers than for elementary and high school teachers? If so, does that explain the difference in participation? If not, what does? Is there a correlation between those not participating in induction and their dates of hire? Is the low high-school participation related to the quality of the program?

Another example of the use of data to monitor the progress of novice teachers is the information system used by Teach For America (TFA). TFA, which has thousands of teachers working in districts all over the country, uses student assessment results to determine the support that TFA teachers need. Throughout the year, TFA staff members provide ongoing support to TFA teachers based on student data. They regularly track TFA teachers' progress toward leading their students to meet achievement goals and provide targeted support to help teachers succeed with their students. Although this system is still evolving and varies depending on assessments and goals, it has been an effective way to identify teachers who need help. TFA recently developed a way to aggregate all its data on teacher progress and student progress nationwide, so that it can identify large-scale trends and more efficiently deploy support and resources to its teachers.[6] (See the box "Examples of District Measures of Success with Novice Teachers.")

An optimal system would use data on teacher effectiveness in decisions about tenure. Using such data, principals can determine whether to award teachers tenure, whether the teachers need additional help and support, or whether they should leave the profession. District officials, for their part, can use the data to judge whether principals are effective in managing their human capital.

Experienced Teachers

Just as retention and quality measures are collected for beginning teachers, data collection should continue during teachers' careers post-tenure to help districts and schools identify top-performing teachers and determine how to best capitalize on their effectiveness. Districts can also use performance data as a basis for encouraging effective teachers to move to or stay in high-needs schools. The Montgomery County, Maryland, Public Schools have developed a system based on test scores to try to bring to bear the expertise of effective teachers in high-needs schools. (See page 56, "Examples of District Measures of Success with Experienced Teachers.")

In developing its system, Montgomery County zeroed in on fifth grade advanced mathematics as a critical course on the path to high school and college success for their African American and Hispanic students. Data in-

---

Examples of District Measures of Success with Novice Teachers

Foundational (descriptive information)

- Teacher attendance for first-, second-, and third-year teachers by school/type of school/high-needs schools

- Most common reasons for novice teachers leaving schools/district (from an exit survey)

- Novice teacher satisfaction with support by individual school/types of schools/high-needs schools (from a survey of novice teachers)

- Number and/or percentage of teachers eligible for tenure/receiving tenure

Emerging (based on either observation or student value-added evidence)

- Number and/or percentage of novice teachers at each performance level based on observations

or

- Number and/or percentage of novice teachers at each performance level based on student value-added data

Optimal (based on both observation and student value-added evidence)

- Number and/or percentage of novice teachers at each performance level based on observation and student value-added data

- Number and/or percentage of novice teachers at each performance level in high-needs schools

- Number and/or percentage of possible tenured novice teachers at each performance level who receive tenure

---

dicated that if students were successful in the fifth grade advanced mathematics course, they were on a trajectory to complete algebra in seventh or eighth grade, which led, in turn, to success in high school math. The chief academic officer decided that it would be useful to identify teachers who were having success with African American and Hispanic students in the course. She identified 107 teachers who had taught the course for the past two years. Of those, ten teachers also had classes with five or more African American students and five or more Hispanic students in both 2007 and

Examples of District Measures of Success with Experienced Teachers

Foundational (descriptive information)

- Number and/or percentage of experienced teachers removed for performance
- Most common reasons for experienced teachers leaving schools/district (from exit survey)
- Teacher attendance for experienced teachers by school/type of school/high-needs schools
- Teacher satisfaction with school and district professional development

Emerging (based on either observation or student value-added evidence)

- Number and/or percentage of experienced teachers at each performance level based on observations
- Number and/or percentage of experienced teachers at each performance level based on student value-added data

Optimal (based on both observation and student value-added evidence)

- Number and/or percentage of novice teachers at each teacher performance level (based on observation and student value-added data)
- Number and/or percentage of professional development offerings linked to teacher performance level
- Concentration of top performance level teachers in high-needs schools
- Number and/or percentage of highest performance level teachers in leadership roles, i.e., coaches, mentors, department chairs, grade-level team leaders

2008. Of those ten teachers, three consistently had 80 percent or more of their students meet the proficient standard on the state exam. The chief academic officer then talked with each of the teachers' principals, all of whom reported that they were doing a great job with their students in the course. The district then had the three teachers meet with all the other fifth grade advanced math teachers for a knowledge-sharing session, featured their work at a senior staff meeting focused on performance in fifth grade advanced math, and had them describe their teaching practices at a board meeting. The relatively simple use of data to identify the teachers and then learn from them in a critical course recognized excellent practice, encouraged its replication, and helped create a course-based learning community that went beyond the school building.[7]

Providing performance bonuses is another way to differentiate support for teachers and encourage top performers to remain in the district and in high-needs schools. One example of such a system is the Prince George's County (Maryland) Financial Incentive Rewards for Supervisors and Teachers (FIRST) program. FIRST provides performance-based bonuses to high-performing teachers in high-needs schools. Unlike most performance-pay programs, though, FIRST measures performance with a combination of student-gains data using state and local tests and performance-based evaluations that include multiple observations and self-reflection.[8] The evaluations assess four dimensions of teaching, based on Charlotte Danielson's framework: planning and preparation, classroom environment, instruction, and professional responsibilities.[9]

Quality data can also be used to monitor the concentration of effective, experienced teachers in a school. The New Teacher Project (TNTP), a nonprofit organization that recruits and places teachers in urban districts, advocates for a quality-teacher concentration index (number of high-quality teachers/total teachers in the school). Concentration is important because students need multiple years of quality instruction to make substantial gains. TNTP believes that the concentration of high-quality teachers in a district's lowest-performing schools should equal or exceed the concentration in the district's other schools.

TNTP asserts that the most important questions about a district's novice and experienced teaching pool can be summarized in three numbers: the annual retention rate for top-quartile teachers, the annual retention rate for bottom-quartile teachers, and the ratio between the two rates. If the retention rate for top-quartile teachers is consistently higher than that for bottom-quartile teachers—a ratio over 1.0—then the district is doing something right because stronger teachers are staying in district schools at a higher rate than weaker teachers. If, instead, the ratio is below 1.0, the district is less attractive to strong teachers than weak ones.[10]

Figure 2.1 shows a hypothetical district where teaching effectiveness has decreased over time. In 2005, the retention of top-quartile teachers

Figure 2.3   Annual report on novice teacher support

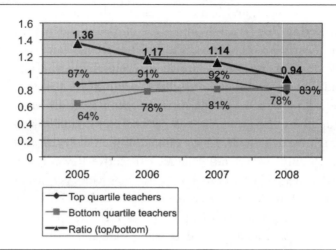

was considerably higher than retention of bottom-quartile teachers. But the ratio dropped below 1.0 between 2007 and 2008. Using these data, district leaders can ask themselves a number of questions: Why are our strongest teachers leaving the district? Is this pattern consistent across schools? Across elementary, middle, and high schools? Are there schools that are retaining more of their quality teachers than the rest of the district? What can we learn from those schools? How can we remove more of our lowest-performing teachers?

Performance data can also identify teachers who might qualify for leadership positions, i.e., coaches, mentors, department chairs. Using these data, district leadership can decide to establish new selection criteria for leadership roles or at least require those who consistently promote teachers with lower quality ratings to explain their decisions.

The data can also be used to provide professional development support to retain high-quality teachers. A high attrition rate of high-quality teachers beyond the early years may be an indication that teachers are not given enough incentives or opportunities to further their learning. Providing different kinds of professional development options for the most effective teachers can help districts invest in their future by developing their own leaders.

School Principals

Districts can also use evidence of effective practice and student outcomes to track and manage the development of principals. Several districts use a set of competencies for principals that generally focus on such criteria as community relations, staff management, and curriculum and instructional leadership to define an effective principal. The district or regional superintendent and new principal mentors usually gather evidence of success on the competencies through observations; surveys of parents, teachers, and students; and reports on key performance measures like retention of top teachers or student attendance. These data on principal practice and impact—combined with school-level, student value-added data—provide a district with information to make evidence-based decisions about school leadership.

As these data are collected over time, districts can sort or rank principals based on the evidence and then consider a range of interventions and supports. These could include providing incentives to high-performing principals to move to high-needs schools; differentiating the levels of support, supervision, or authority for principals based on documented strengths and weaknesses; and identifying areas for continued learning. For example, some principals may need practice in collecting reliable observation evidence about their teachers; others may need support in creating positive school cultures; and others might need strategies for effectively building relationships with parents. (See the box "Examples of District Measures of Success with Principals.")

We have not yet come across examples of districts that are systematically combining evidence of principal practice and student gains to inform districtwide school leadership strategy and support. Given the central role of principals in improving student achievement, we expect that during the next several years, many districts will begin collecting and using both types of data to support school leadership.

Data Clarity and Governance

As discussed, the quality of human capital is determined using two types of data—observation-based evidence of teacher or principal practice and student-outcome data derived from student work, curriculum-based assessments, or standardized tests. In most districts, these data are the responsibility of two different groups within the administration. The human resources (HR) office is usually responsible for data related to individual staff members; and the academic office, for student performance data. HR data systems are usually transactional in nature and capture and produce reports on topics like teacher applications, hires, and exits. They may

---

Examples of District Measures of Success with Principals

Foundational (descriptive information)

- Number of new principals (first, second, and third year as a principal)
- Number and/or percentage of new principals by source, e.g., outside the district, assistant principal, New Leaders, etc.
- Average principal tenure by school type/high-needs schools
- Principal satisfaction with district support for their development (from a survey of principals)

Emerging (based on either observation or student value-added evidence)

- Number and/or percentage of principals at each performance level based on observation-based evidence
- Number and/or percentage of principals at each performance level based on student value-added evidence

Optimal (based on both observation and student value-added evidence)

- Amount of principal professional development and support differentiated by principal performance level
- Number and/or percentage of principals in high-needs schools by performance level
- Annual retention rates of principals by performance level

---

also include subsystems that collect information on professional development, mentoring, and even evaluations. Student information systems collect and report on student enrollment, student supports, course taking, grades, and scores on standardized test scores.

While the technology office usually manages both systems and the research department analyzes data from both systems, the two data systems generally don't communicate or share information. Decisions regarding reporting and data access are generally made by their owner departments. A collaborative approach to data governance will help advance human capital strategies. Central office departments need to work together to clarify and then communicate the reasons for collecting data.

A good example of the miscommunication that can occur within district offices was Chicago's effort to measure teacher attendance. In 2006, the Chicago Public Schools identified teacher attendance as an important measure for its annual school scorecards. Since the payroll system required every teacher to swipe his or her identification card each day, the scorecard planners assumed that it would be easy to generate a teacher attendance rate for every school. The planners were mistaken. While the payroll system accurately reported whether a teacher was in a CPS building on a given day, it did not report whether the teacher was in his or her classroom teaching students. The initial prototype reports raised basic questions that were discussed with HR and instructional staff, principals, and representatives of the teachers' union. The questions included: Should sick and personal days be counted as absences? Should teachers who are attending professional development courses be reported as present? Should teachers who are assisting other teachers in the building but away from their classrooms be counted as present?

Eventually, the district agreed to define teacher attendance for scorecard reporting from the student's perspective—if the teacher is not present in her classroom, she is absent, regardless of whether she can qualify to be paid for that day. That agreement ensured that the scorecard met the district's human capital strategy needs.

Once a metric is defined for a particular purpose, an effective data-governance system requires identifying a specific person who is responsible for the quality of the data represented by the metric. For example, the chief academic officer may be responsible for defining high-needs schools, while the HR officer may have responsibility for defining strong teacher applicants. Clear definitions and ownership of data metrics allow people to focus on the significance of the data rather than arguing about its accuracy.

A collaborative approach to data governance will help advance human capital strategies. Failure to recognize the value of the different perspectives that the HR and academic departments bring can cause delay, confusion, and conflict.

Using Data as Catalysts for Action

Once the data have been collected and responsibility for their accuracy is clear, district leaders need to determine how its use will accelerate progress on its human capital strategies. Consistent with the aforementioned principles, the processes need to balance a commitment to continuous improvement with accountability for progress. This often requires substantial engagement by the superintendent. For example, if the number of applicants for special education teaching positions in a particular region is behind schedule, the superintendent might ask the regional superintendent and HR for an explanation of why the numbers are low and what's being done to fix the problem. The superintendent can then determine whether staff performance or the hiring process is preventing the district from meeting its goals.

Some districts use reports about particular performance measures as agenda items for senior staff meetings. A monthly data report with disappointing data can be used in a department or senior leadership team meeting as a prompt for a cross-functional problem-solving discussion. Why are the numbers bad? Who's responsible? What are we doing to turn it around? If the numbers are positive, can they be used as a prompt for a discussion to identify what's being done right? Who's responsible? How can we encourage more of such good work? In either case, districts can use the data to encourage leaders to address what's important.

Scorecards

When coupled with specific goals, coherent strategies, and accurate data collection, scorecards and dashboards can be effective tools for communicating human capital strategies and progress across levels of a school district. There are two parts of a balanced scorecard—a strategy map that describes its major elements and a limited number of metrics that are put together in a report describing the progress of the strategy.[11] Scorecards are often public documents reporting on annual district, school, or project progress, while dashboards are usually internal management tools. Scorecards are an effective tool for communicating strategy because they make the elements of success concrete.

Access to sophisticated and expensive technology, though helpful, is not a prerequisite to producing useful reports. Scorecards, because they are annual reports on a limited number of metrics, are less dependent on sophisticated data systems. A district at the initial level of data collection and analysis can populate a scorecard by manually counting several of the metrics.

None of the district or school scorecards that we reviewed link teacher quality with student performance. To the extent that they include any human capital metrics, they are limited to foundational-level data that describe the district teaching force:

- Teacher attendance
- Teachers retained from previous year
- Teachers and administrators who have earned National Board for Professional Teaching Standards certification
- Percentage of highly qualified teachers (under the No Child Left Behind Act)
- Teachers with graduate degrees

A scorecard for a district at the optimal level (using both observation and student outcome evidence to define quality) might report on the following human capital measures:

- Number and/or percentage of the novice teachers eligible for tenure at each performance level and those actually receiving tenure
- Ratio between retention rates of top- and bottom-quartile teachers
- Percentage of top-quality quartile teachers in high-needs schools
- Percentage of top-quartile teachers in leadership roles, i.e., coach, mentor, department chair, grade-level team leader

Human capital metrics on school scorecards can be problematic. Given the relatively small number of teachers at a school, it may not be possible to report on the number of teachers by performance level on a public, school-level scorecard without violating an individual teacher's privacy. Such information may be more appropriate for a dashboard that is not available to the public.

Dashboards

While scorecards generally report annually on key metrics, dashboard data are refreshed on a daily, weekly, or monthly basis. They provide internal school and district staff with real-time reports on the same or similar indicators to inform day-to-day management of improvement strategies. Dashboards can provide district-, regional-, and school-level views of the data. They are often set up to draw from a data warehouse that integrates HR, instruction, financial, and student support data.

Because the data in dashboards are refreshed regularly, they are more dependent than scorecards on good technology-based systems. Most dashboards are built on technology platforms that make it possible to query the underlying data system with the click of a mouse. For example, a regional superintendent could open her dashboard and view the number of new teachers hired to date in the schools in her region. From there, she might double-click on the number of new teachers to see how many of their new hires were graduates of a particular university. Then she could select a university and see a report describing the number and demographic characteristics of the new hires from that school.

Dashboards can also have multiple views—teacher, principal, regional superintendent, central office—so that people at various levels of the organization with different responsibilities for strategy implementation can see metrics that reflect their specific role. For example, in a district initiating a new-teacher induction program, the district dashboard view would report on mentors hired and trained, the regional dashboard view would report on the number of schools with the required numbers of mentors hired and trained, and the school dashboard view would report on whether every new teacher had been processed and assigned to a mentor.

Dashboards can serve as warning systems to help principals and district administrators address potential problems before they become serious. For example, an automated dashboard that reports on teacher attendance might provide a regional superintendent with a report on the number of teachers in each of her schools with lower than 90 percent attendance. Any school with more than two teachers below 90 percent would trigger a red flag on the regional superintendent's dashboard. The superintendent can then follow up with the principal to determine what's being done to address the attendance problems.

A dashboard can also provide operational data that are critical to execution of district human capital priorities. For example, in a district that is emphasizing the importance of tenure decisions and trying to ensure that all teachers who are up for tenure are evaluated in a timely and appropriate manner, the dashboard could report to principals, regional superintendents, and district HR directors on the status of evaluations for teachers up for tenure. Principals who are behind in completing evaluations could be encouraged to catch up, while those who are on schedule can be commended for being on track.

The system's capacity to provide this kind of robust functionality relies on the availability of the data in automated district systems, the integration of the data from various systems or subsystems into a data warehouse, and software to support the query functionality. While an integrated data warehouse with business intelligence tool software might be the ultimate vision for many large districts, it is not an absolute prerequisite for improving strategy support. Manually produced, paper dashboard reports can also help to focus attention and conversations on critical elements of district human capital strategy.

During the year, when an automated dashboard platform was being designed and constructed in Chicago, then CEO Arne Duncan distributed a set of paper dashboard charts at monthly senior staff meetings that reported on critical elements of the district human capital strategy at both the district and regional levels. The monthly reports included teacher vacancies, principal recruitment and hiring, and teacher attendance. The charts often sparked conversations at the meetings and were later the topic of conversations between the regional superintendents and their principals. They were produced on a personal computer consolidating manual and electronic reports generated each month. Since then, the district has built a data warehouse, and the same data are now refreshed daily or weekly on an automated dashboard. But then and now, the data, not the technology, provided the substance for the strategy-focused conversations.

One caution for districts that are able to combine data from different systems: more data are not necessarily more useful data. Once a data warehouse that combines information from the student, human resources, and financial systems is in place, it is possible to create hundreds or even thousands of human capital metrics. At this point, focus becomes even more important. District leaders have to resist the temptation to share all the data with everyone and instead continue to maintain focus on a small number of metrics that best describe the progress of the district's human capital strategy.

Although the use of scorecards and dashboards to track a district's human capital is still in its infancy, they are increasingly used as tools for data reporting. While they generally do not focus exclusively on human capital, most include some human capital metrics. We expect that, as the capacity to integrate data from multiple systems improves over the next several years, many more districts will build scorecard and dashboard systems that highlight human capital development in a more robust way.

Conclusion

This chapter is intended as a starting point for districts interested in using data to track the development of teachers and principals. We believe any effort to measure teachers' and principals' effectiveness needs to begin with a shared, districtwide understanding of quality teaching and school leadership. Measures of quality teaching and leadership should include both observed evidence of practice and student gains, but we recognize that few, if any, districts have reached this optimal level. Given the importance of the work and the many other demands on the attention of district leaders, we have four suggestions for district and school leaders setting off on this journey.

1. Start now with the data you have.

There is much to be learned from the foundational data described in this chapter, and every district has some of it. Sharing data that begin to describe the district's teaching and leadership capacity will encourage the right conversations and whet the appetite of school and district leaders to collect and analyze additional information.

2. Use human capital data to tell your student achievement story.

The superintendent needs to own the district's human capital strategy and use the data to tell the story of its strategy. Every time he or she gives a speech, visits a school, or convenes a senior leadership meeting, the superintendent should cite data that focus attention on the importance of teacher and principal quality to improved student achievement. That means discussing support for novice teachers at the Chamber of Commerce, talking about teachers who are up for tenure with principals, and identifying future school leaders with senior district staff. The superintendent needs to use the data to reinforce the idea that the quality of district teachers and principals is the major driver of improved student performance.

3. Keep it simple.

Our experience is that no one can keep more than seven things in his or her head at one time, so it's counterproductive to ask staff to pay attention to fifteen or twenty different human capital metrics. Districts should decide the five to seven metrics that are most important for the next year and focus on those. The following year, they can review the list and make adjustments. But for every metric that's added, they should subtract one so that there are always only five to seven things that they are asking people to track for the human capital strategy. Obviously, the district is collecting data in lots of other areas, but the five to seven priorities are what people can be held accountable for.

4. Celebrate good data and honor the people responsible for them.

When people see that district leadership is paying attention to the data, they will increase their efforts to move the numbers, and moving the human capital numbers will improve student achievement. So when a school or a department substantially moves an important number, district leaders should recognize the progress and reset the bar at the next level up.

The use of data to improve the quality of teachers and principals is taking root in school districts across the country. Although the work is still in its infancy in most districts, it offers new, hopeful possibilities for improving support for teachers, principals, district administrators, and, ultimately, the children in our schools.

3

The Principal as Human Capital Manager

Lessons from the Private Sector

Tony Milanowski and Steven Kimball

Although top-level leaders have always been seen as key contributors to the success of organizations, private-sector organizations and management thinkers have recently recognized that middle managers are the critical links between strategy and execution.[1] Further, research on performance in private-sector organizations has begun to show that the effectiveness of the manager who directly supervises front-line workers is an important influence on productivity, service quality, and other aspects of organizational performance.[2] For education, this research suggests that the effectiveness of principals in managing the recruitment and advancement of teachers will contribute to improvements in student learning.

One of the key ways these managers influence performance is through the attraction, development, and retention of employee talent—human capital management. Private-sector organizations such as General Electric, Microsoft, IBM, Target, Starbucks, and Sysco Foods see the management of human capital as central to their strategies for improving organizational performance. At the same time, these companies have decentralized responsibility for managing human capital to middle managers, who must build up their management capacity (see the box "What Is Human Capital?"). The most celebrated example is General Electric, where former CEO Jack Welch pushed the management vision through the company by both developing the capacities and removing those middle managers who could not or would not develop and apply them.[3]

What Is Human Capital?

Human capital is a term that economists invented to refer to the productive skills and technical knowledge of workers. It includes individuals' knowledge, skills, and abilities and the values and motivation they have to apply their skills to the organization's goals. Economists and businesspeople call these individual characteristics *human capital* in order to emphasize the importance of employee skills and abilities and the need for organizations to invest in their people, just as they do in physical capital, in order to succeed. As we move into a knowledge economy, human capital has become far more important than physical capital (machinery and equipment) in producing value.

In public education, human capital is likely to be even more important to organizational performance. Education is a human-capital-intensive enterprise, with around 80 percent of most school district budgets spent on staff salaries and benefits. Most of the key processes of learning are guided and influenced by the staff that interacts with children daily. In particular, teachers are a key source of value in public education. After more than a decade studying value-added measures of teacher effectiveness, most researchers believe that the quality of a student's teachers is the most important influence a school can have. In turn, it is also clear that school administrators—especially principals—play a key role in attracting, retaining, and developing quality teachers.

In most districts, principals help to recruit, hire, orient, and socialize new staff; evaluate performance and provide feedback; and make suggestions for performance improvement. Principals are commonly involved in helping teachers plan for professional development. In some districts, decisions on professional development programming have also been decentralized to the school level. Researchers have increasingly recognized the principal's influence on retaining people, something that teachers have long recognized. They are one of the most important factors in attracting and keeping high-performing teachers. Principals also have a more subtle but no less important influence on human capital through their effect on school culture. By intention or by default, principals help create a culture that either encourages staff to develop and apply their human capital or discourages them from doing so. In appendix A, the section, "Principals as Human Capital Managers and Leaders of Learning," lists some of the research that substantiates principals' effects on teacher attraction, retention, and school culture.

As the principal's role in human capital management becomes more clearly recognized, school districts need to learn how to build principals' management capacity. Public education can learn about how to build management capacity from those private-sector companies that have invested in human capital as a cornerstone of their performance improvement strategy. This chapter describes the most important human capital management roles of private-sector middle managers, explains how some leading companies develop the management capacity of middle managers, and concludes with some suggestions for how school districts might make human capital management a bigger part of the principal's role without adding yet more demands onto their vast responsibilities.

Like private-sector middle managers, principals are increasingly held accountable for performance, and many school districts are giving them a bigger role in human capital management functions, such as hiring and professional development. Also, in the past decade, principals have increasingly become instructional leaders. Looked at closely, the role of instructional leader overlaps that of the human capital manager in many ways. When principals evaluate teaching performance, recognize good instruction with positive feedback, and coach teachers on using assessment data or managing the classroom, they are acting as both human capital managers and instructional leaders. Yet many public-sector managers feel that private-sector experience just does not apply to their situations. Private-sector managers don't live in a political fishbowl, have more objective ways to measure performance, don't have a work force with lifetime job tenure, and are less likely to have to deal with unions.

Although public education does have some major differences from the private sector, the basics of human capital management are the same for both private-sector middle managers and principals. Schools—just like law firms, hospitals, manufacturers, and information technology companies—have to recruit, retain, develop, and motivate the people who make the organization perform. And while private-sector managers often have more flexibility than principals, they rarely have the free hand that many imagine. For example, while unionization has declined substantially, and labor contracts no longer constrain managers as much as they did thirty years ago, the explosion of employment law has limited managers' flexibility in almost all human resource (HR) areas. Legislation, court decisions, and state or federal guidelines now regulate hiring, performance evaluation, compensation, and benefits. Moreover, even private-sector organizations without unions have strong expectations for how middle managers treat employees so that unionization is not encouraged.

Of course, not all private-sector organizations provide useful models. The school district work force is largely fixed by state and district tenure rules, union contracts, and the difficulty of finding large numbers of replacement workers in the local area. Organizations that treat workers as expendable are not good models. The best models are organizations that treat their work force as an asset to be developed, retained, and involved in productivity improvement efforts. We call these high human capital investment organizations or high-involvement organizations.

Human Capital Management in High-Involvement Organizations

The best private companies see human capital management as a three-way partnership between the organizations' top leaders, the HR management department, and the middle managers who deliver much of the management that employees experience on a daily basis. The role of top management is to craft a vision for human capital management, continually communicate its importance, provide resources the other partners need, and hold both the HR department and the middle managers accountable for their roles. Middle managers and the HR department are then responsible for developing and implementing human capital management systems and practices that attract, develop, and retain employees who have the competencies needed to carry out the organization's strategies and attain its goals. As in most school districts, the HR management department is responsible for setting policies and providing services. The difference tends to be that in the best companies, the HR department is expected to actively assist middle managers, rather than regulate them or process paperwork, and to provide them with tools and training to help them carry out their human capital management roles.

Middle managers' roles in this partnership vary with the size and degree of decentralization of the organization. In general, in the private sector, the trend has been toward greater decentralization, with more human capital management decisions placed in the hands of middle managers, and HR department staff responsible for advising them and for managing systems where centralization allows economies of scale (e.g., screening applicants, administering pay). Where the HR department is well developed, it also provides important tools middle managers can use. For example, the HR departments at Kimberly-Clark and TRW developed electronic, multidimensional, performance evaluation tools that increased the involvement of professional staff in their evaluations, allowed managers to run the process more efficiently, and helped employees set goals directly related to business objectives.[4] At Microsoft, the HR department worked with managers to develop a career model they can use to answer employee questions about career paths and the competencies needed to move up, as well as to assess employee skills and suggest developmental activities likely to improve performance.[5] (See the box "Effective Human Capital Management Practice in Private-Sector Organizations." Also, see appendix B for a list of resources for learning about human capital management practices in these private-sector organizations.)

Middle Manager Roles

Although middle managers' responsibilities involve the classic HR functions of recruitment, hiring, performance evaluation, and training, their managing of human capital also includes everyday interactions with employees on their development and job performance. These interactions include giving informal feedback and coaching, recognizing good work, expressing support and encouragement, and helping employees solve problems. As mentioned earlier, middle managers are also important in the development and maintenance of organizational culture. The most forward-thinking private-sector organizations want to promote a culture that supports human capital development and employee engagement. This culture includes a shared conception of good performance, shared values about developing people, and sharing of expertise among employees.

Middle Manager Roles in Talent Acquisition

The talent acquisition partnership between middle managers and the HR department typically revolves around the manager as the customer for HR services such as recruitment advertising, application processing, and candidate prescreening. As active partners, middle managers provide the HR department with a specification of the job requirements and the competencies

Effective Human Capital Management Practice in Private-Sector Organizations

In the private-sector environment, a well-developed HR department does more than simply issue regulations and process paperwork. It has mastered HR transactional basics, with well-organized and efficient processes for major services it provides to all organizational units, such as recruitment advertising, application processing, and payroll. It also provides valued services to managers, including user-friendly tools to help them carry out their human capital management responsibilities, consultation on specific problems (e.g., employee discipline, union grievances), and assistance in developing solutions for particular challenges (e.g., a recruitment plan for a specialized job). It provides efficient services to employees, typically using electronic systems to do things like explain the application of policies, allow employees to update personal information, and provide benefits counseling. In addition, it measures the efficiency and effectiveness of HR processes, including its own internal operations, using metrics such as:

- Average time to fill open positions
- Turnover by recruiting source and employee quality level
- Percentage of employee development plans completed
- Percentage of professional development courses offered that focus on key employee competencies
- Employee and supervisor perceptions of utility of professional development activities in developing key competencies
- Competitiveness of minimum, maximum, and average salaries in the labor market
- Value of benefits compared to labor market competitors

Increasingly, top HR departments also identify the competencies—knowledge, skills, and abilities—that employees need to carry out the organization's strategy for success and develop practices specifically designed to acquire, develop, and retain employees with these competencies. In some cases, HR departments outsource routine functions such as benefits counseling and application processing in order to concentrate on this strategic role.

they want in a new hire, features of the job that can serve as selling points, and potential sources of applicants. They also provide feedback on the quality of the candidates that result from the recruitment effort. Middle managers also often participate in job fairs and campus recruitment visits. Middle manager participation in these activities is particularly important because research has shown that potential job applicants consider them far more credible as representatives of the organization than the HR staff. Many of the best applicants want to get a sense of the organization's direction and the quality of its managers. Savvy middle managers also go beyond the partnership to develop their own sources of applicants, especially for highly specialized jobs or those with shortages of applicants. They use current employees as sources of information about where to find promising job candidates, and they encourage employees to refer people with promise. They develop networks within and outside the organization to keep informed about people with the potential they might need.

While the HR department will often help middle managers develop and apply selection tools, such as tests or structured interviews, to help winnow the applicant pool, middle managers almost always have a decisive voice in who is hired, based on a job interview. Research has shown that the interview can vary considerably in its effectiveness in identifying which employees are likely to be good performers if hired.[6] One way private-sector companies try to make the interview more effective is to have the HR department and middle managers work together to develop competency models that can be used to guide the information that managers collect in interviews. At the Texas Children's Hospital, for example, managers use nine separate interview processes, based on nine job-family competency models. These models identify the key skills needed in each job family and the key actions employees must be able to perform to contribute to organizational success. Managers are then trained in a systematic, behavior-based interview process keyed to the competency model for each job.[7]

Another way companies have tried to improve the interview process is to involve members of the work group that the new hire will be joining. While the middle manager usually has the final say, adding coworkers provides more ears and eyes to pick up information the candidate provides, which lessens the effect of one person's (possibly biased) viewpoint. Companies such as Amazon.com, Whole Foods, and IBM use peer interviews to get a more complete view of potential hires and to give current employees a stake in the success of the new hire they helped select.[8]

Beyond interviewing candidates, middle managers also help the applicant make the right decision by providing realistic information about job requirements, working conditions, performance expectations, and organizational culture. This information helps applicants assess their fit with the job and the organization. It can reduce turnover of disappointed new hires later on. Middle managers also help close the deal when a job offer is made by answering questions about initial work assignments, conveying a sense of the organization's purpose, and expressing enthusiasm for the new hire. Middle managers can ensure the desired job candidate accepts the job offer by communicating the organizational mission, vision and culture, and describing the employee value proposition—the set of characteristics that make a company a more attractive employer than others. They help a talented person understand why he or she would want to join and stay with the organization. Elements of the value proposition might include training or mentoring opportunities, the team's quality, or career advancement opportunities, as well as pay and benefits.

After the hiring, the middle manager's next responsibility is to help the new employee move smoothly into the organization. While many organizations have formal, companywide orientation programs that cover the basics (ranging from benefits and work rules to company history and culture), it is typically up to middle managers to complete the process. Organizations realize that while socialization happens through various interactions the new employee has with managers and coworkers, actively managing the process is likely to have a more positive impact on new-hire retention and development. Middle managers contribute to socialization by introducing new employees to their specific jobs and work units, communicating performance expectations, and providing training, and through more subtle influences such as giving emotional support, identifying peer role models and mentors, and providing opportunities to work with and learn from high-performing coworkers. Because coworkers are important influences on socialization, matching the new hire with the right coworker mentor is a key contribution that middle managers can make. They can also continue to be actively involved with the new hire throughout the probationary period. A developmental plan with sequenced performance milestones for each new hire both eases the learning curve and provides information on the employee's potential as a long-term human capital investment.

Middle Managers and Talent Development

Many leading private-sector organizations have integrated their thinking about middle managers' roles in developing employee human capital under the heading of "performance management," which includes all activities that support maximizing the performance of employees with regard to organizational goals. These functions include performance appraisal, training and development, a planned cycle of assessment and improvement, frequent feedback, coaching, and collaboration with employees.

The first step in the performance management process is planning and goal setting. Typically, middle managers work to translate the organization's objectives and strategies into an individual employee's performance goals. Human-capital-intensive organizations have found that they should aim for a mix of specific, objectively measurable outcomes, goals for behaviors, and goals for learning and development. One current approach emphasizes individual employee goals that contribute to team or unit goals, which are in turn linked to those of the wider organization. In this way, strategic goals cascade from one level to the next in order to align effort. Middle managers build commitment by communicating the rationale for goals—how achieving the employee's goals makes a difference—and soliciting employee input on the supports needed to achieve them.[9]

The next step is to assess progress toward the goals. This does not mean simply reviewing performance once each year. One critical difference between performance *management* and performance *evaluation* is that managers make frequent, informal assessments of progress and provide feedback before the annual evaluation meeting. After making these assessments, managers provide coaching and suggest how to improve performance, and they listen to employees' concerns about roadblocks and challenges.

When formally assessing performance, in most organizations, middle managers use a performance appraisal system designed in cooperation with the HR management department. However, companies have found that the evaluation instrument is not the biggest issue; it is how they use the instrument that matters, including feedback and coaching and the fairness of the process. Therefore, middle managers are increasingly expected to use performance appraisal to help employees improve as well as to provide input for decisions on retention, pay increases, and promotions. As in public education, employees in private firms are naturally concerned about subjectivity and bias in performance evaluations. Companies are concerned as well. One way to develop consistency, used by Capital One and Intel, is a cross-calibration meeting during which managers discuss their ratings and the reasons behind them with their peers. The meeting helps develop a common understanding of good performance, promotes a more consistent use of the rating scale, controls rating inflation, and discourages idiosyncratic rating decisions.[10]

Though many organizations have a centralized training and development department, middle managers typically have an important role in identifying employees' training needs, working with them to develop training plans, providing feedback on how training is applied on the job, and coaching in the application of new skills. Middle managers also link employees with mentors and give assignments so employees can develop their skills. In organizations that emphasize human capital development, middle managers perform these functions as part of an annual performance management cycle and longer-term efforts to develop employees for future assignments. They may even encourage employees to rotate outside their units to gain needed experience.

Middle managers also contribute to talent development by helping to build a culture that respects expertise, encourages its development, and promotes knowledge sharing. They emphasize the importance of developing and sharing expertise during new-hire socialization; provide opportunities for teamwork around common problems that require developing and sharing knowledge; recognize, respect, and celebrate the development and sharing of expertise; and encourage informal communities of practice by providing time and technology for employees to interact. They also set an example by being open to and seeking new knowledge.

Middle Managers and Talent Retention

Many private-sector organizations think about retention in terms of a total-rewards framework that includes not only pay and benefits, but also recognition, learning and development, work environment, and work/life balance. These organizations recognize that while pay and benefits are important influences on retention, highly talented individuals require more than high compensation to keep them engaged. A considerable amount of research has shown that managers have an important role in talent retention. Their influences on retention include recognition of employee contributions, attention to working conditions, and a culture of engagement.

Middle managers in the private sector typically use pay raises (which usually adhere to policies and budgets set at higher levels of the organization) as one recognition tool. But the recognition they can provide to employees during day-to-day interactions is likely to be just as important in retention. Everyday recognition ranges from simple statements of thank you and good job to access to training opportunities or plum assignments. The key is to provide recognition consciously, based on an understanding of what particular individuals value. Another increasingly popular recognition is to celebrate successes, especially of the team or group.

Workplace conditions are an important influence on retention. In K–12 education, the working environment is gaining increased recognition as a factor in retaining employees.[11] To improve retention, organizations expect private-sector middle managers to address work environment issues proactively, identifying problem areas before they have a chance to fester. They encourage managers to recognize that many working condition issues are also productivity issues, because situations that make work difficult or unpleasant often take time and attention away from productive activities. Attention to basic working conditions issues is commonly part of quality and productivity improvement initiatives. For example, in GE's Work-Out process, employees can raise concerns about work conditions, and managers are expected to address them.[12] Companies concerned with retaining talent also recognize that the middle managers' conduct is an important aspect of the conditions in the workplace that employees experience. By acting with fairness, treating employees with respect, maintaining lines of communication, providing constructive feedback, and taking employees' goals and needs into account, managers become a positive feature of the work environment. Therefore, companies concerned with talent retention include positive treatment of employees in their management training programs and hold managers accountable by using tools like employee surveys and 360-degree feedback.

Middle managers also help retain employees by developing a culture of engagement. Concern with engagement has replaced job satisfaction as a focus for retention efforts because engaged employees expend their best effort on the job and remain connected to the organization in the face of challenges. Middle managers influence engagement in many ways, most of which are common sense: communication that keeps employees in the loop, recognizing good work, providing clear expectations and constructive feedback, showing how the work contributes to organizational goals, and involving employees in decisions that directly affect them. Managers accept and act on feedback *from* employees, understand what is important to them, and find out how to retain them. High performers, the employees that organizations most want to keep, are likely to be especially responsive to recognition and challenging work, and react negatively to job assignments that do not utilize their talents. Providing opportunities to work on challenging projects that develop skills and redesigning jobs to eliminate busywork and bureaucracy are ways in which middle managers have tried to improve the engagement of high performers.

Given the importance of engagement, companies as varied in as Abbott Laboratories, American Express, Washington Mutual Insurance, Sysco Foods, and Yum Brands (the parent of Pizza Hut, Taco Bell, and KFC) all survey employees regularly to track attitudes related to engagement.[13] They provide survey results to middle managers, who are expected to act on them.

Putting the Roles Together

Some middle managers in almost any private organization carry out some of the human capital management roles highlighted here. What the best companies do is to combine strong organizationwide *expectations* that middle managers be effective human capital managers with *training* in managing people, and with *tools* such as electronic recruitment and screening systems, talent inventories, and performance management systems. These organizations hold middle managers accountable for meeting human capital management expectations as part of their own performance evaluations and base bonuses and promotions in part on their record of effective management. For example, at Sears, 25 percent of middle managers' pay bonuses are based on measures related to employee engagement and human capital management, including employee surveys.[14] Performance reviews for higher-level managers at GE and McDonald's include an assessment of how they develop their middle managers.[15]

How Districts Can Help Principals Become Human Capital Managers

Some principals in some school districts are also carrying out the roles that middle managers perform in private firms, and do it successfully. School districts have also begun to develop some of the tools needed to support their principals. For example, they use more sophisticated teacher-induction programs that provide specific models for developing expertise and mentors to support principals' socialization efforts. Several leading-edge districts—including Clark County (Las Vegas), Nevada; and Fairfax County, Virginia—have developed strong recruitment programs that involve principals and provide them with a timely stream of candidates for teaching jobs. It is not yet common, however, for district leaders to hold principals accountable for human capital management the way companies that place a premium on human capital hold middle managers accountable. Putting these elements together—expectations, accountability, training, and tools—is the step that leading-edge districts need to take to increase the effectiveness of the human capital management efforts of their principals and other district leaders.

School districts can help principals become better human capital managers in a number of concrete ways. Many examples from private companies are directly transferable to school district practices. Next, we summarize seven important steps we think districts should take.

1. Communicate clear expectations about the importance of human capital management.

For a policy or practice to take hold in any organization, top leaders need to signal their support and demonstrate long-term commitment. Principals get their cues about district expectations not just from policy adoptions and budget allocations, but also from top leaders' patterns of actions and behaviors. District leaders need to clearly communicate the importance of the principal's role as human capital manager and take advantage of opportunities such as districtwide events, newsletters, and Web sites to reinforce the message and recognize effective practices. Further, they can dedicate resources to train principals and other district leaders in effective human capital management functions like recruitment, selection, induction, development, and performance management.

The Chicago Public Schools (CPS) has placed human capital management at the top of its educational improvement strategy. The district has had a Human Capital Initiative as one of three core strategies since 2001. The strategy has helped focus the district on developing systems for teacher and principal recruitment, induction, early development, retention, and talent management. Although the CPS initiative encompasses more than the principals' human capital management function, it demonstrates how a district can develop and sustain a strong focus on the importance of human capital to drive the organization's effectiveness.

To emphasize their importance, human capital management outcomes need to be measured at the school level. Districts should use a combination of staff surveys, exit surveys, turnover rates, professional development program participation, reviews of performance feedback that principals provide to staff, and observations of principal-staff interactions to develop a picture of how well schools are managing human capital.

Districts can show principals that their time devoted to human capital management is a valuable investment. For example, by identifying teaching openings early and initiating the recruitment processes sooner, principals can gain access to the top teaching talent entering the job market and avoid playing catch-up at the start of the school year. Similarly, they can show that investments in training and induction, mentoring, and performance management of probationary teachers result in a stronger staff, requiring less remediation later and avoiding the time-consuming process of removing a marginal, tenured teacher. With school-level human capital metrics, a district can illustrate that more effective school-level human capital management can lead to lower turnover, less absenteeism, more teacher growth, and, ultimately, higher student achievement. This helps convince principals that their investment of time in human capital management up-front will result in less time devoted to remediating problems later on. It allows principals to spend more time helping average performers become high performers, which is both more rewarding for principals and a necessity for teaching all children at high standards.

2. Develop a "principals' best-practices model" for human capital.

The next step is to establish a model of best practices, illustrated with clear behavioral descriptions. The model should include the main dimensions of human capital management—recruitment, selection, induction, mentoring, and performance management—and the less tangible but highly important aspects of school culture and working conditions. These last two are important ways that principals can affect the instructional program and student achievement outcomes as well as teacher retention.[16] Examples can be hypothetical vignettes, practices of strong principal human capital management within the district, and research-based case studies. Principals can use the model to assess themselves on how well their current practice meets district expectations. The model can guide training and development programs and be used as a basis for performance evaluation conversations as discussed in step five.

3. Select and train principals on human capital management competencies.

Because principals play such a central role in acquiring, developing, and retaining effective teachers, districts should consider human capital management skills when recruiting and selecting new principals. Selection committees can look for examples of leadership activities that the candidates demonstrated as teachers for indications of potential (e.g., how a teacher helped another develop). The committee can develop selection criteria from the district's human capital management competency model. It can also ask a candidate to respond to a vignette showing how these skills would be applied and participate in a mock teacher evaluation/feedback session. During the selection process, the district can reinforce the expectations for human capital management as a key part of the principal's responsibilities. Some likely competencies that hiring teams might consider are:

- Ability to analyze school goals and translate them into what staff need to know and be able to do
- Knowledge of what good teaching is and how to assess and talk about it
- Understanding of the principles of effective recruitment and selection
- Ability to provide specific, honest, and useful feedback about job performance
- Understanding how to coach and motivate people to improve performance
- Ability to understand and respond to the different developmental needs and interests of teachers based on their performance and stage of career
- Ability to learn about and understand individual staff member's interests, concerns, and values
- Ability to share leadership and decision making
- Ability to assess and act to improve school working conditions
- Knowledge of the basic principles of employment law and labor relations
- Ability to analyze data and metrics and use them to drive improvement

An important question is whether districts can rely on traditional university-based principal-preparation programs to build these competencies. Linda Darling-Hammond and her colleagues recently described exemplary university programs.[17] Common to these programs is a sharp focus on instructional leadership and supporting teacher development, what we have called performance management, via training in conducting classroom observations, including walkthroughs, feedback and coaching, and collaborative learning opportunities for teachers. But broader coverage of human capital management may be needed. In particular, programs must add hands-on activities for identifying the teacher competencies needed to formulate specific strategies for improving student learning, ways to recruit teachers likely to have these competencies, and ways to select candidates who best fit the school's needs. A well-designed preparation program that focuses on human capital development and management also introduces principals to the idea of an employee value proposition and the role of the principal in engaging teachers in the work of the school. Other topics might include:

- The shifting demographics of new entrants to teaching, and how to serve those interested in traditional careers, those unlikely to spend their entire careers in teaching, and the increasing number of career changers

- The needs of new teachers and how to build induction supports at the school level

- Professional development as a strategy, combining teacher-directed growth that promotes engagement with building the competencies needed to support school improvement plans

- The importance of the tenure decision and a thoughtful, thorough process for assessing teachers for tenure

Districts can take an active role in influencing preservice principals' training programs to emphasize human capital management. They need to communicate their requirements to colleges and universities. They can also develop their own in-house programs geared toward district needs. Several districts have developed, in partnership with area universities, alternative training programs that result in state-approved credentialing. Adding coverage of human capital management competencies to such programs is relatively easy. Both of these options allow districts to substantially increase the probability that the pool of potential principals has the human capital management competencies we advocate. Another option is to contract with external organizations such as New Leaders for New Schools to help recruit, select, and train principals who can demonstrate these competencies.

4. Evaluate and reward principals for effectiveness as human capital managers.

Performance management systems for principals should focus on human capital management. A district performance evaluation system for principals should include human capital management competencies, based on the best-practices model discussed earlier. In addition to other important leadership competencies, principals' performance goals should include developing human capital management competencies and goals for attracting, retaining, and developing people. Examples of teacher-selection instruments, induction, professional development programs, and teacher evaluations with related instructional feedback can be collected to assess competencies. In addition, the district can incorporate school climate surveys and staff turnover analyses. The analyses might assess how many teachers are leaving schools and who is leaving and why. To effectively monitor and provide feedback to principals, their supervisors likely need training in these areas.

Districts might consider performance pay systems for principals that include developing human capital management competencies and meeting school goals. Also, they need to respond to developmental requirements identified during the performance management cycle. Those principals who need training should have access to high-quality programs and then be monitored on how well they translate their learning into practice. All principals should be periodically retrained. (See the box "Measures of Principals as Human Capital Managers.")

5. Review district policies and practices at the high-leverage points for human capital management in schools.

Principals are key players at three high-leverage points for building an effective faculty: teacher hiring, the tenure decision, and professional development. Districts need to make sure their policies support sound principal decision making at these points.

To apply leverage when selecting the best teachers from the candidate pool, principals need flexibility and support. For example, recent studies

---

Measures of Principals as Human Capital Managers

To measure how well a principal is fulfilling the role of human capital manager, districts might want to consider developing a variety of indicators. These could include both implementation of processes and specific human capital quality indicators. Some examples are:

Process Indicators

- Percent of teachers hired after school year begins
- Percent of teachers evaluated as required by district policy
- Percent of teachers with completed professional development plans
- Average number of times per year teachers are observed in their classrooms

Outcome Indicators

- Teacher turnover, including turnover by performance level, experience level, and teaching specialty
- Teacher absenteeism
- Staff responses to school climate surveys

Quality Indicators

- Quality of performance evaluation feedback that principal provides to teachers

---

have highlighted the difficulties that district policies and contract provisions relating to voluntary transfers, excess requirements, and late-hiring practices pose for principals seeking to staff their schools on time and with the best teachers.[18] Districts should critically examine current requirements and labor contract provisions that may limit principals' flexibility in hiring teachers who would best fit the school's instructional needs. While some contract changes may be needed, working within current restraints to create more flexibility may be possible. For example, some districts may offer incentives, such as a bonus or conversion of sick leave, to teachers considering retirement if they make their intention known early in the year. Principals then would be able to announce openings and work to fill them before the end of the school year.

Districts should examine the tenure process as a point of greatest leverage for managing teachers, because most districts can make a sound decision if they invest the time in doing so, and because a poor decision is

- Alignment between area(s) identified in evaluations for improvement and teachers' professional development plans
- Number of teachers from school promoted to teacher leader jobs or assistant principals promoted to principal
- Percent of teachers to whom principal awarded tenure who have performance problems in the next five years

Creating these indicators requires that districts improve their data systems. In many districts, human resource information systems need to be upgraded to allow easier tracking of teachers across years and to include elements such as the results of evaluations and when they were completed.

Once these measures are in place, those who supervise principals need to use them as part of their efforts to manage *principal* human capital. Supervisors of principals need to set goals for improving school human capital indicators, provide feedback to principals on their performance, and coach them or identify opportunities to improve management skills. Supervisors themselves must learn more about effective human capital management, and the district must communicate, from the top down, that it is a priority. In addition, supervisors of principals and the HR department need to work more closely together to ensure that principals have the needed skills and advise them on handling human capital management problems.

very expensive to remedy. The period before a teacher is tenured should be treated as the final stage in the hiring process. During this time, the principal has an opportunity to see many valid examples of a teacher's performance. Districts should focus evaluation resources here, ensuring that probationary teachers' performance is assessed completely and often. Districts that grant tenure automatically, unless the principal objects, should consider requiring positive evidence of good performance as ground for an explicit and considered decision.

District budgeting, staff allocation, and professional development policies may limit principals' effectiveness in developing teachers. For example, current thinking on professional development suggests that a mix of job-embedded, team-based learning and outside courses may be most effective. Principals may need more flexibility in their professional development budgets; in the time allotted for school, versus district, professional development priorities; and in the time for teachers to work together on planning and implementing school-based professional development. Principals may also need flexibility in budgeting and allocating positions to create and fund teacher-leader roles—such as professional development coordinator, grade or subject team leader, or instructional coach—that provide job-embedded professional development and allow good teachers to take on the challenging assignments that keep them engaged.

6. Free up principals' time and energy for effective human capital management.

Traditionally, with training and increasing expectations added to their jobs, many principals aren't able to spend much time on human resource management issues, much less on a human capital management strategy for their school. Principals are expected to be the school's foremost instructional leader, accountability expert, facility manager, community relations specialist, and disciplinarian. When principals do focus on human resources, they may spend 80 percent of this time dealing with administrative procedures or with the lowest performers. Emphasizing to principals the importance of human capital management is not enough. Holding them accountable without enabling them to carry out the role is unfair and ineffective. Districts must also take concrete steps to support principals in this role. Here are a few possibilities:

Provide administrative support. A growing number of school districts have provided principals with school-based administrative managers to deal with finances, facilities, and routine HR functions.[19] This option can help principals free up time to focus on key human capital management and instructional leadership responsibilities.

Develop and fund teacher leaders to assist with school instructional leadership. Content area coaches, lead mentors, and curriculum coordinators are just a few of the formal teacher leadership roles that districts can support through budget allocations. Successful principals also cultivate informal teacher leadership within their schools and collaborate with teacher leaders on multiple tasks. Distributed leadership across tasks and people can create the expectation for teachers to participate beyond their classes in roles and initiatives important for school success. A culture of high involvement and collaboration can be a key outcome that also has carryover benefits for job satisfaction and teacher retention.

Offload responsibility for marginal performers. In the same way that administrative managers can free up principals' time for higher-value activities, central office specialists can manage the remediation and potential termination of nonperformers.

Review and streamline district administrative policies that take principals' time and effort. Administrative policies designed to hold principals accountable can also tie them up. For example, one urban district requires principals to audit weekly payrolls, expecting them to spend every Friday afternoon on clerical work. Another district emphasizes financial management to such a degree that principals believe this is their number one priority. Districts need to examine and streamline these policies and delegate the administrative work to allow time for instructional and human capital leadership.

7. Ensure that the HR department is an effective partner.

Along with examining current administrative policies and labor contracts, districts should also examine the effectiveness of their HR departments in meeting school leaders' needs. Too often, district HR departments are seen as paper-shuffling operations rather than key partners in the districts' educational improvement strategy.[20] When district HR offices live up to the low expectations held for them or embrace the role of regulator, they present barriers to effective human capital management at the school level.

Some districts have actively worked to restructure the district HR department to provide flexibility to principals to carry out their human capital management roles. They have replaced HR staff that lack capacity and then reorganized and retrained staff with a service orientation.[21] Some districts have appointed specific HR staff to certain schools so those principals have a point person for inquiries and assistance. HR can be a critical partner in the success of schools in meeting hiring and training needs. To that end, HR can develop performance indicators for effectiveness that include principals' satisfaction as one measure. Other performance metrics can measure progress in the HR function and identify areas needing focus. These include benchmarks for staffing schools, turnaround times for principals' requests for assistance, and measures of overall staff satisfaction with district HR transactions.[22] These measures can then drive further efficiencies in HR operations and provide the basis for performance management of district HR staff.

Finally, many districts have updated antiquated staffing, payroll, and benefits information systems with integrated HR information systems. These changes require considerable training of HR staff and systems users, but ultimately put many functions that required paper forms and processing by different units under one roof and directly accessible by school-level staff. The next step, one that some districts have undertaken, is to link HR information systems with teacher-specific outcomes, such as value-added achievement data. The combined systems create the potential for strategic planning and evaluation of the effectiveness of school improvement initiatives, professional development programs, or even individual teaching practices.

These seven steps and the innovations from the private-sector practice yield insights into how leaders of our human capital-intensive educational systems can strengthen the role of principals as human capital managers. These seven steps will not generate quick solutions but will help districts begin to address gaps or roadblocks to effective human capital management in schools.

The research clearly tells us that there is nothing more important for children's academic success than their teachers. Yet human capital management in public education is at a nascent stage of development. The sector can learn from other knowledge and service sectors that understand that people are their primary competitive advantage and that managers' most important work is to support and manage people. There are promising early examples of this work in school districts that build principals' potential and provide them necessary support. Public education needs to expand this early work and reframe the role of principal to make the cultivation and management of talent a top priority.

Principals as Leaders of Learning

A Redefinition of Skills and Responsibilities

Sandra J. Stein and Rachel E. Curtis

Principals are both managers of human capital and leaders of learning. Managing human capital—as explained in the previous chapter—is the hiring, professional development, and evaluation a principal needs to perform to improve the quality of the teaching work force. Leading learning means leading student learning by creating, through the process of human capital development, the conditions for a community of adults to continually build the knowledge and skills that most effectively generate student learning. It is an ongoing process of building structures and opportunities for teachers to collaborate, to improve practice, and to create a culture of continuous learning and improvement. The goal is not just to ensure that all individual teachers in the school are effective; it is to create a school environment where learning—for children and adults—is fostered, developed, and celebrated.

Just as the managerial role of principals in developing and deploying talent requires new skills and a different type of accountability structure, so too do the learning-leadership functions. This chapter focuses on principals as leaders of learning, how this work contributes to human capital development, and the implications for principals' preparation, the principalship itself, and district-level support and accountability systems.

New Definition of the Role of Principals

The idea of the principal as the instructional leader has had a powerful effect in shifting the focus of principals to ensuring high-quality teaching rather than managing schools. Yet the impact of this focus on teaching has been mixed, when judged by student learning results. The concept of leading learning grows out of the work of principals as instructional leaders and uses evidence of student learning as the anchor of all student and adult learning activities. Agnostic about instructional approach, the leading of learning orients the management of human capital around the very simple question of whether students are learning what we expect them to learn.

The research on principals as instructional leaders has long focused on organizing a school and its faculty for learning and "collective problem-solving structured by a common set of expectations about what constitutes a good result."[1] Yet, in practice, the emphasis has been on concepts of good teaching, which have been based as much or more on ideology than student learning results. That is, principals have tended to emphasize the kinds of instructional practices they favor or that particular curricular and instructional programs promote, regardless of whether they produce the desired results in student learning. Yet most teaching practices work for some of the students some of the time, and there is scant empirical research that connects instructional approaches to evidence of student learning. As such, for many educators, instructional leadership has come to mean the development of systems and strategies that support specific instructional approaches, with observation of teaching an exercise in determining fidelity to these approaches, whatever they may be. The focus has been on the means (teaching practice) more than the ends (student learning), and the principals' work framed as imparting expertise, observing for instructional allegiance, and providing professional development to bolster specific instructional approaches.

The work of principals as leaders of learning focuses on organizing and aligning human capital and all other resources in response to an understanding of: (a) concrete learning goals connected to clearly articulated content and performance standards, (b) reliable assessments of students' current mastery of the expected skills and content knowledge, and (c) responsive approaches to move students from wherever they start to content and skill mastery in ways that produce multiple forms of evidence of student learning. This approach requires school leaders to organize the school—through the use of time, people, and budgetary resources—to focus on inquiry, strategic instructional response, and adult learning, all in pursuit of student learning.

Although most communities expect schools to do far more than educate students to high standards, creating a dynamic learning organization that continually assesses its own effectiveness in concrete and measurable ways is emerging as the core of local, state, and national accountability efforts. In order for schools to thrive within this construct, the shift from a focus on teaching practice to evidence of student learning must be explicit, with school leaders the key engineer of organizational effectiveness.[2] This approach to school-based leadership cuts to the core of human capital management, reflecting the critical role principals play as lead learners and facilitators of others' learning and the prioritization of adult learning on behalf of student learning.[3]

This evolving definition of the principalship requires different knowledge and skills from those required in prior constructions of the principal as manager (managing the day-to-day functions of the organization) and the more recent interpretation of the principal as instructional leader (setting the instructional vision, observing teaching practice against a set of instructional expectations tied to specific teaching practices). The school management skills required to ensure a safe, orderly environment in which transportation, purchasing, and materials-distribution systems currently function evolve into a strategic, systems-thinking orientation that organizes all personnel and operational functions in support of student learning.[4] The ability to observe and comment on teaching and support a teacher to improve evolves to focus first on assessing and analyzing student learning, understanding what that analysis tells us about the necessary instructional response, and leveraging the collective expertise of the teaching force to improve every teacher's practice.

Implications for Human Capital

This redefinition of the principal's role and the work of schools puts human capital at the center. The orientation toward facilitating adult learning to address and respond to diverse student learning needs is, in effect, human capital management. When principals lead learning, they define the work of all adults in schools as driving student learning. Everyone analyzes multiple forms of student performance data to understand what they reveal about student learning and needs, and then to figure out which teaching strategies and interventions will accelerate that learning. The work of adults is then focused on the most promising actions, and the resources of the school are organized to facilitate this work. This conceptualization of school leadership has implications for many aspects of the human capital management of teachers, including induction and ongoing development, performance management, leadership opportunities, working conditions, school culture, and leadership stance.

Redefining the work of principals as leaders of learning also reframes the work of teachers, in ways that are compatible with teachers' job satisfaction. For example, once teachers feel confident in their practice, their interest is the pursuit of interesting challenges, opportunities for collaboration, and differentiated roles.[5] Orienting a faculty toward learning requires distributing leadership roles; this work needs leaders to manage teachers' talents by creating organizational conditions for experimentation, peer observation, collaboration, and collective inquiry.[6] It also requires devolution of the decision-making authority traditionally held by principals to teachers so that they can act on their learning on behalf of their students. The emerging cycle of inquiry—parsing student data, figuring out what they mean, crafting instructional responses, implementing those responses, and tracking the results—presents opportunities and challenges that require teachers to build their knowledge and skills together. Human capital management involves tapping those teachers already skilled at this work to lead these efforts and together determine the most effective ways for those new to the work to develop these skills.

With a focus on teachers building their individual and collective knowledge, professional development is iterative; it grows in complexity and sophistication in response to teachers' increased capacity. Principals, meanwhile, need to think in systemic and strategic ways about how they align all resources to student learning. Principals need skills in configuring teaching assignments and loads to ensure that the most effective teachers work with the most struggling learners. In addition, they need to provide every teacher with several opportunities during the week to collaborate effectively with colleagues to assess students' performance and progress and teachers' instructional responses.

Managing human capital by leading learning requires an orientation toward public learning that engages the principal in collaboration, exploration, experimentation, and teacher empowerment. In building a culture defined by high expectations, transparency, and public learning, principals model inquiry based on clear purpose and genuine curiosity. This leadership stance is a fundamental shift from the prevailing culture in many schools, where principals exercise authority by virtue of their position and teachers remain isolated from one another. Instead, principals align themselves with teachers in the pursuit of solutions in the areas where they are not yet generating student success. That alignment can take the form of formal or informal professional learning opportunities, of securing additional curricular resources, or of a schedule change that allows time for working with colleagues. The principals' ability to maintain their and the schools' focus on the core purpose—improving student learning—will determine the success of all human capital management efforts.

Realizing the potential of leading learning has significant implications for the preparation, support, and evaluation of principals. These three systems must all align. Accomplishing this alignment requires us to ask and answer three essential questions:

1. What are the most important knowledge and skills that principals need to facilitate the work of adults so that all students learn at high levels and all adults are engaged in continuous learning on behalf of measurable school improvement?

2. How can the most important knowledge and skills be taught in a way that is based in the real, day-to-day work of the principalship, provides aspiring principals the opportunity to practice the work of principals, and is responsive to local context?

3. How must the responsibilities of principals change, and how can school systems support and hold principals accountable so they can focus the work of schools in managing adults on behalf of students' learning and performance?

This chapter addresses each of these essential questions, focusing on how to ensure that leading learning is the cornerstone of principals' management of the talent and resources of their staffs. We suggest how principal preparation, effective support, and accountability for principals and the role of the larger school system might be redesigned to support principals to lead learning effectively in their specific contexts.

Five Minutes in the Principalship and What It Demands

You've run out of a seventh grade English Language Arts classroom in which the teacher has spent the last fifteen minutes discussing her reactions to Mildred Taylor's Roll of Thunder, Hear My Cry. *The teacher, in her third year on the job, was near tears as she used the text to describe the "brutality of racism" and the "evils of some people." Her students' test scores for the past two years have been quite low, and you are concerned about her contribution to her students' readiness for high school, as well as to your school's overall performance indicators.*

The students, seated in rows, rolled their eyes, played with their gum, applied makeup, talked to each other, or doodled in their notebooks. You left abruptly after receiving an urgent message from your secretary saying that a parent whom the school had been trying unsuccessfully to contact after her son got into a fight last week was in the office. The message that caused your PDA's urgent signal to buzz read, "Jared's mom here. Jared missing."

As you walk down the hallway, a security agent says, "Michael's gone loco again today, but he's on lockdown in 219," which you take to mean that one of your sixth grade students did not take his medication and is being detained in an office on the second floor so that he is not a danger to himself or anyone else. You nod, picking up your pace as she continues, "And that lock on the cart where the computers were stolen is still not fixed. I checked it this morning." You turn the corner to see a group of girls in the hallway. "Hello, ladies. Where are you supposed to be?" you say sternly. The girls disperse as two separate groups without talking to each other. You think you noticed hostile sneers pass between them.

Before you can think about the tension you perceived, a veteran math teacher approaches you with a three-ring binder. "Can you look at this and give us a sense if it's what you want?" she asks. "We met to plan the next unit, but we're all coming from such different places, and I don't think it makes sense yet. And between you, me, and the wall, I'm the only one who's done the item analysis of the last periodic assessment. Don't say I said this, but I'm not sure the others even know how to do it." Before you can answer, she places the binder in your hands, turns around, and addresses a slow-walking girl from the group you had broken up earlier, "Pick up the pace, Julia. You're burning daylight." As you finally arrive to your office, you find a young woman with a tear-streaked face. "Are you the principal?" she asks, and before you have a chance to answer she continues, "Someone here let his father take him. I'm gonna call the cops."

As this vignette makes clear, organizing every aspect of schooling, and especially the adult talent, for student learning and progress can be extremely challenging in the face of the day-to-day demands on school leaders. These demands provide constant and stubborn distractions from this core purpose. Just five minutes of the principalship require sophisticated and swift analytical skills and the ability to prioritize, respond, and focus uncompromisingly on instructional improvement for student learning outcomes. If we examine the vignette, we find that several skills are necessary to effectively address the varying and competing priorities, and to get back to the core purpose of student learning. Without careful consideration of adult talent and the management thereof, this core purpose cannot be met.

Deciding to leave the classroom observation to speak to a parent whom the school has been trying to reach—and who potentially has an urgent issue affecting the welfare of her child—requires the skills of prioritization and decision making. School leaders constantly distinguish what's urgent from what can wait, as they determine, moment to moment, how they are going to spend their time. These decisions are not without consequences. How can the leader focus on student learning, which never diminishes as the primary focus of the principalship, if he or she is running out of classroom observations to handle unexpected crises? Simply navigating the walk down the hall requires constant analysis of what is urgent and important and how to create a culture and climate where the expectations for interactions are clear and coherent, where rituals and routines are observed, and where the top priority is facilitating student learning. [7] What does the security guard's comment suggest about the way members of the school community talk about children? Why are the girls in the hallway during instructional time? Why does a teacher feel comfortable handing the principal a curriculum binder in the middle of the hallway with a casual request for review? What do these isolated events mean for a broader human capital strategy?

Skillful school leadership requires identifying the leverage for learning and for building human capital in every conversation, interaction, and decision. In order to talk with the seventh grade English language arts teacher, the principal needs to know how to have difficult conversations that get at the purpose of every instructional choice a teacher makes, relative to the specific students he or she is teaching. The principal's ability to strategically engage the teacher in reflecting on a series of questions, which, depending on the teacher's learning style and capacity could include: How and why did the teacher choose this book? What did she want the students to learn? How do the learning objectives map to the state standards of what we expect seventh graders to know and be able to do and the specific skills of every student? How can the teacher tell whether the students have met the learning goals based on the work they are doing? What do multiple types of student data—such as formative and summative assessments, student work products, classroom conversations—suggest about what each student already knows or where he or she is getting stuck?[8]

Answering these questions is only a beginning. Principals also discern the appropriate entry point for a given teacher based on skill and experience, and whether to delegate intervention to someone else. Perhaps another teacher is the best person to work with the teacher in a peer-coaching arrangement, or perhaps this teacher needs to plan with other teachers in the same subject area or grade level. The goal of facilitating teacher learning on behalf of student learning might start with questions about students' results on available assessments, how much the teacher knows about individual student's learning styles, and which literacy skills and subskills the teacher is attempting to address. Deeper analyses might include what the assessments, coupled with the students' learning styles, suggest the instructional response ought to be and how the teacher has attempted to differentiate her approach to various students, given their learning styles and current mastery of content and skills. Principals determine which strategic questions will probe the type of thinking that leads to more effective teaching and learning for individual teachers and how to strategically call on the universe of teacher talent in order to create a dynamic learning environment in which all are invested in collective success.

In mature learning organizations, all teachers consider the types of questions that will improve their own practice and that of their colleagues, individually and collectively, and have a basis on which to determine the type of support they need. Principals who build teams of teacher leaders who engage in high-stakes decision making, who know how to learn as a team, and who take collective responsibility for student outcomes are less reliant on their own personal energy and commitment and can count on a group of professionals to move the learning agenda forward. Matching the most talented teachers to the students whom they could benefit the most calls for thoughtful planning and execution. Creating time, space, and coherent processes for mentoring relationships among teachers, for teacher collaboration on curricular and instructional issues, and for appropriate development opportunities for teachers across the performance spectrum demands mapping a school community's talents and determining how to maximize those talents through organizational design.[9]

Principals require analytical savvy and a capacity for systems thinking to lead human capital effectively. [10] In order to align resources to an instructional improvement agenda that responds to student learning needs, principals convert seemingly fragmented budget streams, collective bargaining agreements, and decision rules about the use of time, people, space, and money into coherent and fluid approaches to sustaining and enhancing learning. For example, not only do principals have to know which funding streams can allowably cover which expenses, but they also have to make "all dollars green," which means articulating a clear improvement strategy to support teacher and student learning, programming the restricted dollars in alignment with strategic priorities first, and maximizing the flexibility of unrestricted dollars to fill in any gaps in budgetary coherence toward the strategic agenda. [11]

Communicating with teachers, other staff members, students, and parents is yet another critical component of leading learning. Talking with teachers about a lesson gone bad or efforts at curricular collaboration, conversing with security personnel about a specific child in crisis or efforts to guard against additional stolen property, discussing with students their need to be in class, and listening to parents voice their concerns all require clear communication that is appropriate for the audience. Such communication involves purposeful speaking, listening, the ability to read nonverbal cues, clear and cogent writing, and the skill of swift synthesis and analysis of multiple forms of information in order to fashion a response.

The capacity to demonstrate competence in everything from lesson planning to budgeting to the rules and regulations for reporting missing children relies on the ability to break down complex ideas into digestible pieces and, similar to working with teachers on improving their practice, to understand the entry points for engaging and attending to varied school community members.

What emerges is a robust set of skills for strategic thinking that starts with analyzing observable information about student learning and focusing all efforts on student learning and on the adult learning required to accelerate student learning. The ability to be a public learner who processes information quickly and leads a team of people to respond strategically to any obstacle or opportunity are critical skills for effective school leaders. The more transparent the analytical processes for determining student and teacher learning needs and their strategic responses, the less anxiety the school community is likely to feel about its approach to improvement. In order to do this work effectively and sustainably, school leaders must have a level of personal integrity and self-management that demonstrates to the entire school community a commitment to continual growth, a clear mental focus, stamina, courage, and resilience in the face of opposition or disappointment. Preparing people for this job is no small feat.

Principals' Preparation

Let's imagine two ways of preparing people for the human capital leadership work described. In one, we require prospective principals to take a series of courses that lead toward licensure or certification. The course descriptions demonstrate how all classes are aligned to the Interstate School Leadership Licensure Consortium (ISLLC) standards and each course syllabus asks aspiring school leaders to read, discuss, and write about some subset of the issues that came out in the earlier vignette. There are courses on supervising instruction, engaging parents and community, school culture, budgeting, school law, administration, and organizational change. Aspiring school leaders read, discuss, and write papers about the importance of instructional leadership, the need to build a team and distribute leadership across adults with various roles in the school, schoolwide discipline procedures, strategies for parental engagement, and school finance and budgeting, with each topic assumed to contribute to student outcomes. Faculty lead classroom discussions and grade assignments, some of which are completed by individuals and some by groups. Most assignments call for reflections on assigned readings as they apply to some observed school-based practice. After amassing a certain number of courses, and typically completing a school-based internship in which participants take on administrative responsibilities in their schools during the workday, aspiring leaders are eligible for certification to lead schools.

Imagine now a different type of preparation, one in which participants are thrown into a scenario that is similar to the vignette described earlier, for extended periods of time, with explicit attention to leading learning through human capital management and organizational design. Authentic and unrelenting work demands arise in a simulated environment and/or an actual school under the guidance of program faculty and mentor principals. Program participants make real-time decisions and then reflect on the observed consequences of those decisions. Aspiring school leaders face a set of complex challenges and have access to vast resources from the research literature, trade publications, district documents, and video archives that might help them think through the complex and multifaceted challenges and develop strategic responses.

Participants are put in teams and given collective assignments, and in order to complete the program, they have to demonstrate an ability to learn publicly as group members, and to develop the skills of forming high-functioning, purpose-driven teams that maximize the talents of each individual and that build on those talents in areas requiring additional skills. Program participants practice difficult conversations with various members of the school community, either in role-play or in an actual school setting. Written assignments include the results of a thorough analysis of the school data, accompanied by a plan for action that connects next steps to the current student-level data, letters to the school community, observations of instruction, and e-mails to a supervisor; each written assignment carries the expectation of rigorous analysis, clear logic, and impeccable grammar.

Participants receive 360-degree feedback on their individual performance as leaders, including how they manage themselves, their colleagues, resources, and time. Aspiring school leaders practice communicating in public forums with various audiences and receive concrete and actionable feedback from audience members and observers. They experience the challenges of filling vacancies (reading applications, interviewing candidates, observing model lessons), determining teaching assignments, constructing teacher teams, leveraging staff talent, and creating the operational conditions for continuous professional learning. They also practice getting out of the way of good work when the tensions inherent in many authority relationships impinge on the work moving forward.

Recent research suggests that programs preparing school leaders should be structured around several features, including research-based content, curricular coherence, problem-based learning, field-based internships or coaching, cohort groups, and close collaboration between the preparatory programs and the districts that employ graduates.[12] In order for programs with these features to be most effective, they must also adhere to the following principles:

- *Alignment to principals' competencies.* Program relevance is defined by its alignment to the competencies on which principals are evaluated. The focus of this chapter is on the competency of human capital management, or leveraging adult talent on behalf of student learning. In schools, this management takes the form of leading learning, and while it is but one of many required competencies for school leaders, its absence from preparatory programs will likely undermine the improvement efforts of the program graduates.

- *Responsiveness to district initiatives.* In order to be responsive, preparatory programs need access to the same data systems, analytical tools, policies, and practices that are expected from school leaders on the job, enhancing them as necessary. An assignment that asks participants to analyze student performance data from district assessments using the analysis tools the system has to identify struggling learners and then develop strategies for intervention mirrors a district's expectation for principals. Adding a mechanism for tracking the effect of the interventions on student learning enhances the district's expectations. For human capital management purposes, preparatory programs should have access to the system's human resources systems and relevant, allowable data.

- *Rigorous simulations of real practice.* When program assignments mirror the work of the principalship, are explicitly connected to school improvement, infuse the analytic tools of systems thinking, and are mapped explicitly to the district's principal competencies, the learning has immediate applicability. In job-embedded or residency programs, the preparation is most effective when it takes place in schools that are in the process of organizational improvement led by a strong leader. For example, engaging aspiring principals in an actual school's budget and staffing development processes, including the negotiations with the central office and local union chapter, allows for authentic and sustainable learning.

- *Flexibility and responsiveness in the recruitment of candidates.* From a school system perspective, managing human capital means identifying emerging talent and planning for anticipated vacancies at various school types and grade-level configurations. Examples of how principal preparation programs can support this include linking recruitment with intentional succession planning in anticipation of principals' retirements or unrenewed contracts; creating a clear pathway to the principalship for teachers who are high performing and are interested in school leadership; and recruiting candidates to lead specific school turnarounds and/or new school development.

- *Accommodation of various adult learning styles.* Because adults learn differently, the most successful programs provide multiple opportunities to learn the same content. In order to meet every learner, participants need opportunities to read or speak about, observe, and practice the skills they need to acquire.

- *Ongoing support after graduation.* This support consists of coaching, peer support, and online communities and maintains a tight focus on student learning, while providing new principals the technical support for all the things they are doing for the first time and helping them build their capacity to think strategically. Supporting new principals in the budget-development process provides a concrete example. A two-hour training session might start with central office budget staff talking about the technical aspects of budget development and submission. Then three experienced principals who are masterful at aligning their budgets to student learning needs and have realized strong student achievement results talk about their work, including how they manage the bureaucracy to the benefit of their students' learning. After the session, the new principals' mentors follow up, meeting with each of their new principals to help them apply the learning from the training to their budget-development process. Simultaneously, an online dialogue about how to budget effectively is initiated, giving principals a place to ask questions as they come up and share strategies.

Rather than tweak existing programs to align to these principles, practitioners and professors can come together to map backward from the necessary school leadership skills and knowledge to the appropriate educational experiences that will develop those abilities. This process is challenging, but not impossible, and the investment in robust preparation avoids principals having to learn everything they need to lead while on the job. [13]

Implications for the Principalship, School System Support, and Accountability

Training school leaders following these principles prepares them to act strategically, with an overriding focus on student, teacher, and organizational learning. Experience tells us that the context, culture, and expectations principals face on the job affect their behavior profoundly, by either reinforcing or contradicting the way they have been trained to work as principals and the imperative focus on leading learning. For this reason, we must address the issue of the local district context in which these principals work, which implicitly and explicitly incentivizes specific principals' behaviors and sanctions others. Coherently defining the responsibilities of principals and the ways in which school systems should organize to support them, while holding them accountable for student learning, is essential so that principals can operate within a reasonably aligned set of expectations that are measured transparently.

There are several challenges to this alignment. While many districts clearly articulate that the principal's priority is student, teacher, and organizational learning, some still expect principals to take on other functions, such as managing the disparate obligations of food preparation and custodial services, at times without direct line authority. While most district leaders want their principals to focus their time observing classrooms and creating structures to support teacher learning and improvement, the procurement systems can still require considerable amounts of a principal's time to purchase necessary resources. As a result, although districts communicate that principals' primary role is to lead learning, a district's own practices often demand inordinate attention to address administrative minutiae. Instead of fully reconceptualizing the principalship to emphasize learning, many districts have superimposed new expectations on top of existing administrative obligations.

However, some districts are beginning to recognize that the multitude of demands is creating problems. As growing claims that the job is too large for one human being to manage gain attention,[14] some districts have attempted to redefine the role of the central office and the organization of the school system as a whole to support the emphasis on learning and to figure out how to reasonably hold all district employees accountable for learning outcomes.[15]

Even when there is consistent focus on student learning, though, the multiple and, at times contradictory, federal, state, and local accountability systems can exacerbate the problem of mixed messages. While states have by and large aligned their systems to the federal metrics embedded in the No Child Left Behind (NCLB) Act, which look at the proportion of students at the basic, proficient, and advanced levels of achievement, some districts have begun to analyze students' year-to-year progress in addition to absolute performance (New York City being a widely known example). In these contexts, it is possible for a school to make considerable progress, even in the context of low performance, and be considered highly successful in a local context while unsuccessful by the state's accountability system.

The various accountability systems motivate different approaches to school improvement. For example, in New York State, the focus on performance categories on the annual state assessments encourages schools to identify and invest in students on the cusp of grade-level performance metrics (for instance, if the state rewards schools for students scoring at levels three and above on a four-point scale, then schools are inclined to focus on students scoring in the "high twos" to bump them to the next performance level). However, New York City's progress reports reward year-to-year gains of the students in the school's and city's lowest-performing third of students, thereby creating incentives to focus on that group. Districts can help explain to principals the convergence and dissonance in the various accountability systems and to explicitly explain where to focus efforts when the systems do not align.

In addition to the accountability systems, a district's approach to its own human capital management through support and supervision influences principals' perception of their job responsibilities. Just as principals need to take a systems view of the principalship, so too does the district central office in order to leverage its own potential to advance organizational learning efforts. By exploring the actual versus imagined constraints in which school districts operate and looking systemically at the work required to lead learning in schools, central offices can reinvent themselves in support of the broad learning agenda.

The following recommendations suggest a place to start the conversation about the kind of systemic change at the levels of principal, school, central office departments, and school system organization and practice that would be required to orient all levels of the system toward learning.

- *Identify the work that could be eliminated at both the school and central office levels without adversely affecting students and their learning or the district's standing.* Every principal can rattle off a list of things he or she is asked to do that take up precious time and have nothing to do with the work of leading for learning. To give everyone in the system more opportunity to focus on the most important work of student, teacher, and organizational learning, these nonessential activities need to be identified and addressed. You could use the quick and dirty approach of bringing together small groups of thoughtful principals who reflect the continuum of experience and performance and ask the question, "What could you stop doing without any adverse effect on students, their learning, and the district's obligations?" Or you could use a more formalized process to analyze responsibilities, like the GE Work-Out.[16] Either method makes it possible to identify the work principals are required to do that serves no meaningful purpose and (1) could be eliminated, (2) could be done using technology, or (3) should be done by others. The issues that principals raise will have implications for the work of the central office, and before engaging in this process, the central office leadership must be ready and willing to make changes in how and whether specific aspects of the current principals' portfolio are addressed.

- *Create the expectation, build the capacity, and focus accountability at the central office on each department's or division's ability to make principals' work easier and save them time.* Because of the regulatory nature of public schooling, a culture of compliance can permeate many school district operations. Teachers expect students to comply, principals expect teachers to comply, the central office expects principals to comply, and the state and federal government expect the districts to comply. Yet a focus on compliance can stifle innovation, ownership, and empowerment. The district's challenge is to redefine the work of principals through clearly articulated expectations, timely support, and transparent, aligned accountability to focus on leading student, teacher, and organizational learning. To do so, the central office must organize itself from student learning up, rather than from the district leadership down.

Imagine if the performance of everyone in the organization were measured based on the ability to support the next level: teachers support students, principals support teachers, central office supports principals, and the state supports central office and schools toward agreed-on goals of improvement. This concept is simultaneously simple and radical. As part of this effort, district-level departments would conduct internal audits of the requests they make of principals to answer the questions: Why is the request important and how does it support learning? Which requests are generated by the district versus the state or federal government, and therefore what do we have the authority to change? If it is not within our purview to change something, how do we advocate for an alternative approach? How do we determine whether students, schools, or the district are left vulnerable in terms of either basic safety or legal challenge if we eliminate any historical practice? What information do we gather to analyze and assess our next steps? A district's coherent vision for maximizing student, teacher, and system learning serves as an important anchor for these analyses and a sound rationale for changing standard operating procedures. Districts can probably do far more at scale centrally than is common practice, particularly for state and federal reporting requirements; centrally coordinating the requests from various offices that require the same information would be an enormous step.

- *Identify the work principals currently do that could be delegated to others without any adverse effect.* One of the challenges principals face is that they are perceived as the "go to" person by their staff, parents, the community, and central office staff. This expectation, premised in the logic of hierarchy, often leads to a bottleneck and leaves principals in the position of reacting rather than leading proactively. This issue can sometimes be as much a matter of principals feeling more comfortable doing simple managerial tasks and appearing responsive to constituents as it is a lack of clear delegation skills or appropriate staff. The addition of a business manager as an allowable position or the creation of horizontal accountability structures could ease the demands on principals and still accomplish the necessary administrative work.

- *Consider organizing the roles of the other administrators and teachers in schools differently to allow principals to focus on instructional improvement (and maybe attain some additional benefits for the school or system).* Both the skill levels and the roles assumed by assistant principals, teacher leaders, and even secretaries can widely diverge across schools. In addition, the process for becoming an assistant principal is often inconsistent, with little clear articulation or assessment of the skills required for the position. Reconceptualizing some of these roles offers the opportunity to enhance these positions and bolster the work of organizational learning. There is tremendous potential to tap teacher leaders to facilitate collaboration among teachers, participate in the leadership team, and assume the administrative responsibilities associated with each. When thinking about other administrative tasks, it is worth looking at several districts engaged in the School Administration Manager (SAM) Project.[17] This initiative aims to more clearly define the operations work of schools and the knowledge and skills needed to do it strategically, and to recruit and train people with business management experience to assume these roles. Thinking creatively about staff's professional growth and career aspirations, resource use, and other meaningful incentives can make it possible for principals to build capacity and accelerate improvement.

- *Define the appropriate role of principals' supervisors who translate the district's expectations to principals and ensure the people in these roles can do that work.* Principals' supervisors must do for principals what we are asking principals to do for teachers: they must create the conditions for accelerated and sustained learning. Following the adage that we "inspect what we expect," principals' supervisors must explicitly focus on the work principals do to lead learning. If the supervisors spend their time checking to see if all the reports requested by the central office have been submitted but do not observe classrooms and ask the principal about individual and collective student and teacher performance results and how those data are informing instructional practice, they signal that the district values management of paperwork over leading learning.

For principals' supervisors to focus on the most important work of leading learning, they must: (1) understand what that work entails and what it looks like at a sophisticated level of implementation; (2) know how to coach and build a principal's skills in key areas by asking the types of questions that stimulate learning; (3) buffer principals from the distractions of the job that impede the work of accelerating student learning and advocate for them when necessary; and (4) know how to use the tools of supervision and evaluation to drive improvement.

Districts across the country struggle to find well-prepared people to assume the role of principals' supervisors. Often a strong principal is hired into the role based on the assumption that knowing how to lead a school serves as a qualification to supervise others leading the work. Yet one of the greatest challenges for principals who make this transition is their own leadership experience. They often inspect for what they believe to be effective, based largely on their own history. This view does not always allow for the variability of school contexts and the multiple means to the same end. Principals' supervisors need the opportunity to explore together the implications of different school and community contexts for leading learning and the most effective ways they can facilitate principals' growth and performance. Finally, once someone leaves the principalship to assume the role of principal supervisor, she or he must make every effort to stay current with all of the new initiatives, analytical tools, and processes and procedures introduced. In some districts, these changes can be rapid and unrelenting.

These recommendations ask us to rethink how the work in schools and the system is defined and addressed. They would allow principals to concentrate on sustained school improvement through human capital management efforts that focus on leading learning. When reviewed collectively, these recommendations make clear that principals work at the nexus of the school and the system. Any coherent response to the myriad responsibilities of school leaders and how they are prepared for their work must take a systems perspective. That view looks into the school, up the organization to the work of the central office, and across into any institutions involved in leadership preparation to identify opportunities to maximize adult talent on behalf of student learning needs.

PART II

Recruiting, Retaining, and Leveraging Talent

5

Attracting and Retaining Strong Teachers

A Model of High Support and High Accountability

Robert Schwartz, Mindy Hernandez, and Jane Ngo

Thanks to the research of Richard Ingersoll and others, the education policy community has increasingly recognized that the perennial warnings about looming teacher shortages are largely misplaced. This is not to argue that we don't need to increase the supply of teachers in certain fields—math, science, special education—or that many high-poverty urban and rural districts won't continue to struggle to attract teachers. Rather, what the research suggests is that the United States is losing teachers at a faster rate than it is producing them, especially in their beginning years. This problem is especially acute in urban districts, where roughly half of all starting teachers leave within five years.[1] In a profession in which beginners typically take at least two or three years to become reasonably accomplished in their practice, too often the neediest students are consigned to schools heavily staffed by novice teachers.

There are several possible explanations for the high attrition rate among beginning teachers. Some people leave in order to start a family. Others discover after a year or two that they are not suited to teaching and move on to another occupation. Some—especially those who sign on through Teach For America—enter teaching as an initial public-service commitment right after college before choosing their long-term career path. Some enter with the intention of making teaching a career but are frustrated by the working conditions in urban schools or by the flatness of the profession and limited opportunities for advancement. Finally, some of the attrition can be explained by the fact that many young people today simply think differently about careers than did earlier generations, when most people assumed they would choose one line of work and stay with it for life. High turnover is hardly unique to schools: social workers and nurses have similarly high turnover rates. In fact, the Bureau of Labor Statistics reports that the average employee today holds 10.8 jobs from ages eighteen to forty-two, with the majority of the jobs held before age twenty-seven.[2]

What are the costs of a human resource system that loses virtually half its professional work force within the first five years of employment? The financial costs alone of such high turnover are substantial. Not only do districts and schools lose the benefits of professional development and other resources they have invested in departing teachers, but there are significant costs in recruiting, hiring, training, and placing new teachers.[3] While the total costs—including costs to student learning and school cohesion—are difficult to quantify, even rough estimates are staggering. For example, Boston Public Schools spent an estimated $3.3 million to replace nearly 200 first-, second-, and third-year teachers from 2004 to 2005.[4] The Alliance for Excellent Education estimates that with the number of teachers either changing or leaving public schools, the national cost of attrition could be upwards of $4.9 billion per year.[5]

But the financial costs pale in significance when compared to the educational costs, largely because the schools suffering the highest turnover rates disproportionately serve the highest concentrations of low-income and minority students. Successful schools, especially in inner cities, require sufficient stability of staff to build a positive culture of high expectations and a set of collegial norms for good instructional practice. Such norms cannot be created overnight, nor can trusting relationships be built with students and families if faculty are coming and going through a revolving door. What's more, novice teachers—who tend to be less effective than experienced teachers—are disproportionately slotted to fill these vacancies.[6]

Significant as these teacher turnover costs are, if the attrition were planned—i.e., the result of a performance-based evaluation system designed to weed out the least effective teachers—one could at least argue that there might be some offsetting benefits. But this type of attrition is almost nonexistent. While in a handful of urban districts, especially those with Peer Assistance and Review (PAR) programs, there is a serious attempt to provide enough attention and support to struggling beginners to make an informed, evidence-based judgment at the point of tenure about a teacher's performance and potential, the tenure decision in most districts is largely *pro forma*. Tenure is the default position, denied only in exceptional circumstances or extreme cases. As long as teachers keep reasonable order in the classroom, do not refer too many students for disciplinary action, and maintain civil relationships with their colleagues and administrators, the likelihood of their being denied tenure based on performance (as distinct from budgetary or programmatic reasons) is virtually nil.

As a result, substantial evidence indicates that our current human resource practices and policies result in adverse selection: we lose far too many of our most promising teachers and retain too many mediocre ones.[7] Beginning teachers who score in the top quartile on college entrance exams are two times more likely to leave teaching after five years than teachers who score below the top quartile.[8] This trend will continue unless and until we are willing to fundamentally rethink and redesign the way urban districts recruit, assign, support, evaluate, and compensate teachers in their early years. This chapter details one possible strategy for reconceptualizing induction into the teaching profession that addresses this challenge.

Premises Underlying the New System

We propose a new strategy for attracting a stronger pool of entrants, ensuring that more of them are reliably able to increase student learning and substantially reducing the likelihood that those who are unable to do so are granted tenure. Three major premises underlay our design. The first is that, whatever their formal credentials or pathway into teaching, without major support, only a tiny fraction of new entrants into urban schools are likely to be effective in their first year. For instance, Public Agenda found that new teachers feel there is a significant gap between their course work and issues they must cope with in the classroom, such as diversity and students with special needs.[9] Further, alternatively certified teachers, who are more likely to work in high-needs schools, are much more likely than traditionally trained teachers to consider the support they receive from other teachers or mentors to be inadequate in the following areas: working with children with special needs (59 percent versus 31 percent), communicating with parents (52 percent versus 31 percent), creating strong lesson plans (41 percent versus 26 percent), and managing classroom disruption (45 percent versus 30 percent).[10] The ongoing debate between proponents of traditional university-based certification programs and advocates of alternative programs deflects attention from the evidence suggesting that from day one, virtually no program equips its graduates to be successful in urban classrooms.

The reason that so few beginning teachers are equipped to succeed is explained by our second premise, namely, that teaching is fundamentally a craft, best learned through an apprenticeship on the job under the close supervision of one or more master teachers. We do not devalue the importance of ensuring that all teachers are familiar with the scientific knowledge base of learning and child or adolescent development and that they know about the social organization of schools and the historical and political context within which they operate. Essential as this background knowledge is, the professional practice of teaching can only be acquired in classrooms, working alongside expert practitioners who can help guide their learning and development.

Our third premise is that without a clear framework for the evaluation of teaching and a commitment to collect and use evidence of teacher effectiveness at key checkpoints leading up to the tenure decision, little will change. In a recent report entitled, "The Widget Effect," The New Teacher Project documented how little attention districts pay to instructional effectiveness in important decisions they make about teachers, including tenure. Among the twelve districts in four states that were part of the study, none took teacher effectiveness into account in designing professional development plans; only one (Cincinnati), in hiring and placement decisions; and only one (Toledo), in the tenure decision.[11] Given a world in which student achievement data are routinely excluded from teacher evaluation instruments and virtually all teachers are rated satisfactory, it is not hard to understand why high achievers might opt out in search of fields that recognize and reward performance, and why the public might resist the call for across-the-board increases in teacher compensation.

Core Elements of New Design for Teachers' First Three Years

There are four core elements in the new system we envision for attracting and promoting to tenure a high-quality teaching work force:

1. A performance-based entry into teaching that would allow only those candidates who can demonstrate effectiveness to move directly into full-time assignments, while directing all others into a sheltered apprenticeship year.

2. An apprenticeship year during which most new teachers would have a reduced teaching load, close mentoring and support, and built-in time for continuous professional learning.

3. Gradually increased responsibilities in years two and three, with clear measurable performance standards, against which teachers would be regularly assessed and given feedback.

4. A high and inelastic bar for awarding tenure, at which point successful teachers would become eligible for significant increases in responsibility and pay.

Recruitment and Eligibility

As we've suggested, the arguments over traditional versus alternative routes into teaching are diversionary. This field needs the best talent it can attract, and until there is much better evidence than we have about the efficacy of one entry path into teaching over another, we ought to remain agnostic and encourage more choice and competition among providers. Our design assumes that teachers will come from both these routes. The few predictive measures from research on teacher effectiveness—e.g., verbal ability, academic major, ranking of college[12]—underscore the importance of focusing more attention on recruiting academically talented students and worrying less about the locale and sponsorship of the preparation program.

Districts should recruit and select teachers based largely on two factors: evidence of baseline academic competency (e.g., grades, writing skills, subject matter expertise); and dispositions and beliefs important for success in urban classrooms (e.g., commitment to students, belief in the academic potential of all students, resilience, tenacity).[13] Focusing on these two criteria will require districts to redesign both their recruitment and screening processes. Recruitment will need to focus more on the academic quality of candidates than the quantity of candidates recruited. Screening will require establishing a clear baseline of academic competency and developing and adapting the early tools currently in use to assess dispositions and beliefs.

Two-Tiered Entry Process

In the system we are proposing, most beginning teachers would be hired as apprentices, as described later. However, any new applicant would have the option of requesting employment as a full-time, full-fledged teacher. But earning such a position would depend on evidence of competency. Any teacher who had full-time experience in the classroom as part of preparation would submit a portfolio with sample lesson plans, evidence of student work, and a short reflective essay on teaching practice as part of his or her credentials. In addition, those selected for a final interview would teach a sample lesson. Such a screening and selection process may not yet be common in urban districts, but it is the norm in high-performing suburban districts.

As suggested in chapter 1, the precondition for the process is a common framework for observing and assessing teacher quality. One such framework, developed by Charlotte Danielson, identifies four domains of practice (planning and preparation, the classroom environment, instruction, and professional responsibilities) with four levels of performance for each domain: unsatisfactory, basic, proficient, and distinguished. Our view is that no teacher should be hired for full-time employment whose practice is deemed less than "basic" in such a framework, and "basic" should represent a significantly higher threshold than many districts now use for initial employment. In addition, the applicant's portfolio should also contain evidence of reasonable student learning gains.

Our presumption is that only a small fraction of the beginning teaching work force in any district would be able to meet this performance standard. The urban teacher residencies described in chapter 6 are an example of a program that would allow aspiring teachers to accumulate evidence of student learning gains. Candidates who had completed a graduate-level teacher education program, during which they would have had at least a semester-long internship and sufficient opportunity to assemble a teaching portfolio with accumulated evidence of student learning gains, might also be able to meet the standard. But we emphasize that decisions about granting full-time teaching positions must be based on demonstrated performance, not the credentials teachers might hold. The predictive power of certification or degrees is so weak that we believe urban districts should no longer rely solely on either in selecting teachers. For instance, a New York City study found large and persistent differences in teacher effectiveness among certified teachers, suggesting that classroom performance during the first two years—not certification—can better predict a teacher's future effectiveness.[14] The requirement must be observable evidence of effectiveness against a fixed standard, accompanied by evidence of demonstrated success in increasing student learning. If a candidate from an alternative program with no advanced degree and only six weeks of summer teaching experience can meet the standard, fine. We bet that fewer than 10 percent of beginning teacher hires in most districts will do so. Therefore, the apprenticeship year model outlined next would be the dominant mode of entry into teaching.

The Apprenticeship Year

In our proposed system, any teacher who does not meet the performance threshold described would be hired as an apprentice teacher for an initial year. The key characteristics of the apprenticeship year are:

- An 80 percent teaching load, under the close supervision of a trained mentor teacher, with the other 20 percent reserved for a structured induction and development program.

- Consistent evaluation and support, with a rigorous assessment at year's end to determine whether to renew the teacher's contract for a second year.

- The same salary as a regular first-year teacher, but for an eleven-month year.

The apprenticeship year would begin with a four-week summer program, principally focused on district expectations, instructional practices, curriculum, content-specific pedagogy, and classroom management. Depending on the apprentice's prior preparation and certification needs, there would also be units on such topics as child or adolescent development, reading across the curriculum, and teaching English language learners and students with special needs.

During the school year, apprentices would be linked together in cohort groups organized by grade level or subject matter, all working under the guidance of a mentor teacher. There would also be substantial opportunity for apprentices to observe expert teachers throughout the district and to reflect with them on their practice. Right from the beginning, apprentices would be integrated into their school's professional learning communities, initially as observers but eventually as active participants. In addition, more formal kinds of professional development activities tailored to their needs would take place in the 20 percent of time devoted to learning. This would range from nuts-and-bolts instruction in lesson planning, student assignments, and feedback on student work to more ambitious topics like formative assessments. The curriculum for the ongoing professional development seminar would largely draw on the problems and challenges the apprentices themselves identify from their everyday work in classrooms. Built-in time for planning and reflection under the supervision of a master teacher would allow for the immediate testing of new concepts and ideas in a relatively protected setting. This approach of action learning, the process of collaborative problem solving of everyday issues, is regarded across many industries as the most efficient way to develop critical talent.[15] This is a luxury that beginning teachers are almost never afforded.

The school district would run the apprenticeship year, which might be coordinated in partnership with a higher education partner or a teacher preparation and induction support provider. In addition to overseeing the program design and implementation, there are two essential conditions the district must create in order for the apprenticeship experience to work as envisioned.

First, apprentices must be placed in schools that are reasonably stable and well led, and that are willing to create a master schedule that allows space for the coaching and collaboration described. Using these criteria means that a subset of the system's schools would host apprentices and should be chosen with care. The initial selection process for apprentices should be school-based, with teachers as well as administrators engaged in the interviewing in order to ensure a good fit between the apprentice's strengths and the school's needs. These terms may not seem difficult to meet, but they represent a major shift in the assignment practices in many districts, where seniority and transfer provisions in collective bargaining agreements often result in beginning teachers being sent to the schools that are the hardest to staff.

Second, districts must be willing to invest in the careful selection, training and placement of mentor teachers. They should choose mentors based on their effectiveness in increasing student learning, their pedagogical content knowledge, and their ability to facilitate adult learning. To the degree possible, they should assign mentors to work with apprentices only where there is a match of disciplinary field and grade-level experience. Most of the interaction between mentor and apprentice should focus on improving instruction, helping the apprentice deepen his or her own practice in alignment with the district's overall improvement strategy. A critical responsibility of mentor teachers is to help their apprentices prepare for the end-of-year assessment, described next, that will determine whether or not the apprentice is invited to return for a second year.

Assessment at End of Year One

At the end of the first year, there would be a rigorous assessment of each candidate's performance. A panel of teachers and administrators from the candidate's own school would conduct the assessment. They would base the evaluation on three factors: evidence of student learning, drawn from district and state assessments (ideally including value-added measures); a summary of periodic observations of practice, using a common framework (e.g., Danielson's); and a teaching portfolio generated by the candidate, which would include samples of annotated student work, a reflective essay on the candidate's practice, and whatever supplemental material the candidate chooses to include.

The district would develop and employ a transparent rubric and weighting system and define three levels of performance:

- *Green*—the candidate is on track for tenure. There is reasonable evidence of student growth and in at least some domains of practice, the candidate's observable performance has moved from basic to proficient.

- *Yellow*—the evidence is more mixed, but there is some evidence of student learning and some demonstrable improvement in observed performance.

- *Red*—there is limited evidence of student learning, and several domains of practice are rated unsatisfactory.

Apprentices with a green rating would advance to full-time teaching status in year two, perhaps with a retroactive bonus compensating them for the extra month of work the previous summer. Apprentices with a red rating would not have their contract renewed. Those with a yellow rating would be renewed, but with an individual development plan specifying the areas in which they must improve in order to be on track for tenure by the end of the year. We think it would be a mistake for a district to set any arbitrary targets for the percentage of apprentices in each rating category. As districts collect data over time, they will become more accurate in predicting a teacher's growth trajectories and thus better able to determine the likelihood of a teacher being able to move from yellow to green by year three.

The Second Year

When those apprentices deemed on track for tenure move to full-time assignments on regular ten-month contracts, the mentoring relationship would continue, but with less frequency. These teachers would continue to participate in biweekly professional development seminars with other second-year teachers. Teachers receiving yellow ratings would receive additional summer training and close mentoring during the school year. At the end of the year, there would be a second performance review, with the same evaluation components and criteria. For teachers receiving a green rating in year one, the expectation is that most would earn a rating of proficient and that evidence of student learning would be increasingly robust. If problems emerged in the second year that were not apparent in year one, a yellow rating with a development plan for year three could be an option, but the expectation for virtually all teachers in this category would be continuing positive progress toward tenure.

Particular attention in the second end-of-year review would focus on those teachers who are rated yellow at the end of year one and who have individual improvement plans in year two. Those who successfully complete all elements of their plan and show continuing evidence of student growth would receive a green light to proceed to year three. Those showing partial completion of the plan, with at least some aspects of their teaching practice now being rated proficient, would also have their contract renewed, but would be given very clear signals about the progress they need to demonstrate in order to be seriously considered for tenure. Those teachers who have made little or no progress in completing their plan, and whose practice remains mostly at the basic level, would not be renewed for a third year.

The Tenure Bar

In the third year of our system, teachers would become full-fledged members of the faculty. Rather than continuing to participate in special seminars for apprentices, they would be full participants in their school's ongoing professional learning community activities. Their mentor teacher would be available to advise them on assembling their tenure portfolio, but the expectation would be that these teachers are now able to function on their own.

The third-year review process would be considerably more rigorous than the earlier reviews. The review panel, composed of teachers and administrators from across the district, not the candidate's own school, would be looking at two and a half years of student data. District leaders would establish in advance a districtwide standard for learning growth that all candidates for tenure would be expected to meet, as well as a threshold score on the district's teaching effectiveness instrument that would indicate that the candidate is proficient in nearly all key domains of practice. The third-year evaluation is designed to ensure that every teacher who receives tenure has the knowledge, skills, and attributes to educate all students to high levels and to continuously improve his or her practice.

Given the consequences of the tenure decision, it is important that the review process allow for some human judgment, not just a mechanistic examination of performance numbers. As part of their portfolio submission, teachers would explain or defend any portion of their record that is in question, including any shortfalls in student performance. The mentor teacher and principal would also submit letters assessing the overall performance of the teacher. Teachers whose application for tenure is rejected would have a right to appeal, as would a principal who believes that the school would be substantially weakened by the loss of the teacher. If the system works as designed, however, the performance record of most teachers who survive to the point of tenure would be sufficiently well documented so there are relatively few surprises or contested cases.

This proposal raises the practical question of what to do in the case of a candidate who is teaching in a particular area (e.g., physics) for which there may be no other qualified candidates who meet the tenure standard. The question is: *How should we treat the teachers who have demonstrated competence at the yellow level but have not reached the tenure bar, when it is quite possible that districts will be unable to replace them with teachers who will be able to match their level of performance?* Should districts have the option of hiring such teachers on term contracts rather than being forced to choose between awarding them tenure or terminating them? The process in other institutions suggests possible options for such teachers. Law firms, for example, sometimes deny a person partnership in the firm but make that person "of counsel." Some professional schools shift a junior professor from a tenure-track position to a lecturer position in order to avoid the "up or out" consequence of a tenure review. While these options may not be ideal, they may be necessary to ensure that the tenure bar is not lowered in response to a market shortage.

Giving Meaning to Tenure

In a perfect world, one might ask, "Why tenure?" Citing the arguments against it is easy. Tenure rewards the security-conscious, leading risk-averse teachers to stay regardless of their productivity or drive, and discourages those seeking innovation and change. It prevents schools and districts from responding to demographic or economic changes by retaining teachers based on performance rather than seniority. It limits the public's willingness to make teachers' compensation more competitive with other professions that do not guarantee what outsiders interpret as a promise of lifetime employment. Whatever the merits of the historical argument that teachers need tenure to be protected from political cronyism or the whims of tyrannical principals, one could argue that in today's world, civil service rules and collective bargaining agreements provide sufficient due-process protection to make tenure superfluous.

Even if one grants these arguments, however, the political costs of trying to abolish tenure seem to us to outweigh the potential benefits. To return to our original argument, the big problem with today's teaching force is not that people are staying too long. Rather, it is the unacceptably high attrition rate in the early years, and the widespread perception that too many of the best people leave early and that too many weak or mediocre teachers stay too long. Our strategy, therefore, is not to attack tenure, but rather to make it a much more meaningful certification of performance.

We are not fond of comparisons drawn from higher education, but in this case, the K–12 system could learn from higher education's example. While one might quarrel with the excessive focus on scholarly publications in the tenure decision, the tenure process in the university world is a rigorous one. Tenure is earned, not granted on the basis of time served. It is accompanied by a significant boost in salary, status, and governance responsibility in most institutions, and the awarding of tenure is typically an occasion for public celebration. We envision something similar in urban districts: a significant salary boost, immediate eligibility for teacher leadership positions within the school, a public ceremony, and celebration.

Establishing Existence Proofs

Before addressing some of the policy barriers and implementation challenges of our proposal, we should ask, "Just how radical is this proposal?" Virtually every key component is in place somewhere, especially if we look outside the United States to countries like Japan and Switzerland that make major investments in the induction process for beginning teachers.[16]

In the United States, half the states require all new teachers to participate in state-funded mentoring or induction programs, although these vary widely in quality and intensity. Thanks to the work of the New Teacher Center and others, we already have high-quality mentoring programs and at least some evidence that such programs can increase teacher retention and success.[17] Two states, North Carolina and South Carolina, provide a reduced teaching load for beginning teachers. Several urban districts, most notably, Toledo and Cincinnati, Ohio, have very substantial experience through their PAR programs using panels of teachers and administrators to make consequential judgments about the performance of beginning teachers.[18] Finally, a few urban districts, led by New York and Denver, are putting in place a more serious evidence-based process for awarding tenure.

What we don't yet have, however, is a large district that is approaching the entire process from initial recruitment and assignment through the tenure decision in a coherent, comprehensive, systemic fashion. We need one or more existence proofs that this kind of sustained investment in assigning, supporting, and evaluating beginning teachers will not only result in a substantially higher-quality teaching force, but also produce significantly improved outcomes for students.

Implementation Issues

For the most part, districts could implement the model we have outlined under the current regulatory framework in most states. The most important state variable affecting the employment of beginning teachers is certification. The fact that alternative programs are now widespread suggests that most districts have significant flexibility in initial hiring (even the "highly qualified teacher" provisions of the No Child Left Behind Act create a significant loophole for entrants through alternative programs). The more serious problem arises from state requirements for permanent certi-fication, which in some states include obtaining a master's degree within a certain time period and in virtually all states specifies required graduate-level education courses. These requirements are reinforced by the design of teacher-compensation systems in most districts, which reward teachers for credits accumulated beyond the bachelor's degree.

As we observed earlier, there is scant evidence that certification and ad-vanced degrees are correlated with teacher effectiveness. In our view, certi-fication should be linked to performance, not credentials. We hope that if districts agreed to raise the bar for tenure and put in place the kind of rig-orous evaluation process we propose, states might consider aligning their certification systems with tenure.

In the near term, one challenge for districts would be to design the content of the 20 percent nonteaching time of the apprenticeship year to enable this learning to count for certification purposes. A strategy would be for districts to form partnerships with urban universities, as described in chapter 6, in order to allow course credit for district-designed and -led professional development.

The larger challenges districts would face in moving toward the adop-tion of our system relate to the kind of infrastructure districts would need to build in order to make such a system work. They would need to de-velop or adopt a framework for observing and assessing teacher practice and train people to use it. They would have to identify and train a team of mentor teachers. They would need enough stable schools with competent principals to provide appropriate placements for their apprentice teach-ers. They would need sufficiently robust and reliable data systems to track teacher performance over time and assessment systems that would allow for some form of value-added analysis. Finally, they would need the kind of working relationship with their teacher organization that would allow for the creation of joint teacher–administrator panels to conduct the an-nual assessments of teacher performance. Not all these elements would need to be in place in order to get started, but districts would need to de-velop a realistic time line for building such an infrastructure.

Finally, there is the issue of cost. The most immediate new expense is associated with supporting the 20 percent learning time for apprentices, i.e., the need to hire five apprentices for every four slots. There are signifi-cant additional costs to free up and train mentors and to train and support review panels. One obvious place to look for funds to reallocate would be in the compensation system. If districts could recapture the funds they now spend to compensate teachers for lane changes"—i.e., for graduate credits and degrees—they could not only accumulate a significant amount of money to give newly tenured teachers a salary increase, but also offset some costs of the apprenticeship model. In one large urban district, the *annual* costs of lane-change increases was estimated to be $239 million, an amount more than sufficient to support a high-quality induction program such as the one we have outlined.

Any cost analysis of the proposed system has to account for the costs of maintaining the current system, especially the nonfinancial costs. Even if the new system achieved no reduction in teacher attrition, a sizable proportion of the attrition rate would be planned—that is, driven by performance rather than other variables. Thus, the overall level of teaching quality would be higher than now in most urban districts, a result that would almost certainly lead to improved student achievement.

Reforming how teachers are inducted into teaching in their first three years needs to be part of a larger strategy for reforming how schools are staffed and led, which is why this chapter should be read along with the chapter on the second stage of teaching (chapter 7) and the earlier chapters on the role of principals as human capital managers and leaders of learning (chapters 3 and 4). We now have a substantial body of evidence to support the proposition that the single most important strategy for improving the performance of our schools is to recruit, develop, and retain high-quality teachers and principals. Organizations like Teach For America, The New Teacher Project, and New Leaders for New Schools have definitively demonstrated that highly talented people can be attracted to the mission of improving educational outcomes for urban students, and school districts like Chicago's that have taken advantage of these and other new sources of talent have already seen the benefit.

We believe that talented young people would be attracted to the high-support and high-accountability model we are advocating, especially if they knew that achieving tenure would then give them access to the kinds of differentiated roles outlined in chapter 7. While it may be true that very few talented young people are going to choose teaching (or any other career) for life, we simply do not accept the inevitability that teaching will become an occupation that the most talented people pass through on their way to a real profession, while their less talented colleagues settle in for the duration. If we raise the bar for entry into university-based preparation programs, reduce barriers to entry through alternative routes, and create a rigorous but supportive performance-based path to tenure, we contend that we will likely screen out less ambitious and committed candidates and select those looking for a challenging profession with ample opportunities for growth. They may not stay for life, but they are much likelier to stay longer if they experience success, are supported in their continuous learning, and are recognized and rewarded for performance.

Creating and Sustaining
Urban Teacher Residencies

A New Way to Recruit, Prepare, and Retain
Effective Teachers in High-Needs Districts

Barnett Berry, Diana Montgomery, Rachel E. Curtis,
Mindy Hernandez, Judy Wurtzel, and Jon D. Snyder

By plan or default, many districts have portfolios of pathways into teaching. They are a response to the varied needs of school systems (e.g., meeting needs in math and science, placing energetic and committed teachers in start-up schools) and their efforts to recruit and retain a large, diverse work force. They are also a response to the reality that there is no one pathway into teaching that is likely to meet the needs of all districts or prospective teachers.

However, many districts have found that their existing pathways are inadequate. In many cases, they do not supply enough teachers in critical-needs areas, such as special education. And they do not ensure that all teachers are capable of providing high-quality instruction for the district's students.

The urban teacher residency (UTR) model represents a pathway that responds powerfully to the long-standing challenges of how to recruit, prepare, and retain bright and capable teachers for high-needs urban schools. Somewhat reflective of the medical residency model that pairs professional course work and embedded clinical experience, UTRs are founded on the belief that new teachers in urban schools should enter the classroom with a minimum of one year of guided clinical experience in an urban classroom in order to develop the knowledge and skills needed for effective teaching. Residents integrate their master's level course work with an intensive full-year classroom residency alongside experienced, prepared mentors before becoming teachers of record in their own classrooms. UTRs make five distinctive contributions to the portfolio of preparation pathways by providing:

1. Systems for preparing a critical mass of teachers who are highly capable, well-educated, and prepared to stay in the profession for more than just a few years

2. Models for teacher learning that help transform traditional, university-based, and alternative certification programs

3. Opportunities for universities and districts to capitalize on the expertise of their best teachers as teacher educators

4. Entry points for reconfiguring a district's human capital system to bring a coherent approach to recruiting, preparing, supporting, and retaining quality teachers

5. Leverage for school reform that systemically focuses on improving school conditions that promote high-quality teaching and high levels of student learning

Urban Teacher Residencies Up Close

UTRs can vary in how they are designed and implemented. However, they share a common set of principles that can serve to define the components of a high-quality residency program, inform the design of new residencies, and distinguish teacher residencies from other kinds of preparation programs. The principles are:

- Weave education theory and classroom practice tightly together
- Focus on resident learning alongside an experienced, trained mentor
- Group candidates in cohorts to cultivate a professional learning community and foster collaboration
- Build effective partnerships
- Serve school districts
- Support residents once they are hired as teachers of record
- Establish and support differentiated career goals for experienced teachers

This chapter looks at the two most established UTRs—in Boston and in Chicago. Although the two programs offer different applications of these principles, they both pair master's-level pedagogical training and education content with a rigorous full-year classroom practicum under the supervision of expert teachers who have been trained to mentor novices. UTRs provide teaching candidates with both the underlying theories of effective teaching and a yearlong, in-school residency in which they practice and hone what they are learning alongside an effective veteran teacher in an urban classroom.

Residencies attract and recruit high-capacity, committed college graduates and midcareer professionals who are interested in teaching in low-income schools. Generally, once a resident is selected, she or he is placed in a school under the guidance of a mentor who acts as the resident's confidant and guide. In Boston, residents are placed in host schools for a full year. (Host schools are Boston Public Schools that have been selected to receive a group of residents based on established selection criteria such as a supportive context and enough teachers who meet the requirements to serve as mentors.) In the Boston Teacher Residency (BTR), the resident works alongside the same mentor for a full academic year. In Chicago, residents switch schools or training academies midyear, which gives them a chance to study under a new mentor in a different grade level and school environment. Residents work in classrooms with mentors while they complete their course work in curriculum, teaching, and learning at partner universities. During this year, residents gradually take on increasingly more complex classroom responsibilities. The resident studies and works with her or his mentor as she or he writes lesson plans, conducts classroom management, grades papers, and assesses student progress. The mentor and resident meet one-on-one to discuss these elements of teaching; and with the mentor acting as a guide, the resident begins writing lesson plans, leading classroom discussions, and gradually taking on the full responsibilities of a classroom teacher. As a resident tackles each new aspect of teaching, the resident and mentor continually meet to discuss, review, and assess progress.

Residents receive a stipend, a master's degree, and credentials at the end of the year and pledge to spend at least three or four years teaching in the district where they served their residency. After the year of intense mentoring, residents become teachers of record in their own classrooms in an urban high-needs school and continue to receive mentoring in the form of induction support for at least the next three years.

Launching Urban Teacher Residencies

In 2003, Thomas Payzant, then superintendent of the Boston Public Schools, needed more math, science, and special education teachers, and more teachers of color, who could all implement complex instructional reforms. Unable to solely rely on local teacher-education programs and recognizing the limitations of his own bureaucracy, Payzant and other district leaders collaborated with the Boston Plan for Excellence (BPE) to develop a new approach to recruiting and preparing teachers with the skills and qualities needed for its high-needs schools. The new program was deliberately housed at the private, nonprofit BPE so, as one community leader told us, "It would not be subject to the district bureaucracy, which can suppress innovation, [nor to] the annual district budget cutting process."[1]

Initial financial support came from outside funders with the commitment that BPS would take on increasing fiscal responsibility for BTR until it ultimately became the majority funder by reallocating its professional development funds from a wide variety of local, state, and federal sources. Today, BPS provides approximately 60 percent of BTR's operating funds. It's important to note that BTR was created eight years into Payzant's tenure when a clear instructional strategy was in place—one on which the residency program could be built and organized.

Today, BTR has changed the traditional consumer-producer relationship between school systems and institutions of higher education by giving BPS an alternative source of new teachers and ensuring quality control. BTR has grown each year in terms of numbers of residents, and at full capacity, it will provide the BPS with 25 percent to 33 percent of its new teachers each year.

In Chicago, the Academy for Urban School Leadership (AUSL) was founded in 2001 by a group of philanthropists led by Mike Koldyke, a venture capitalist and founder of the Golden Apple Foundation who saw that local universities could not prepare enough qualified teachers for Chicago's 408,000 students. He also saw a need to recruit and prepare nontraditional, midcareer adults for teaching, while capitalizing on the expertise of veterans. AUSL partnered with National-Louis University (NLU), which reworked its master of arts in teaching degree so that residents could earn state certification while taking course work that would equip them to teach in urban schools.

In running the residency, AUSL quickly realized that without sound leadership and similarly skilled colleagues in the schools where it placed its graduates, they would have difficulty reaching their potential. To have control over these factors, AUSL gained autonomy from the Chicago Public Schools (CPS) by becoming a school management organization that runs low-performing Chicago schools. AUSL hires the principals and administrative teams and is able to ensure administrative commitment to and support of teacher development and school improvement. In 2006 and 2007, the first turnaround schools run entirely by AUSL opened in Chicago. These schools are staffed with a critical mass of AUSL graduates and experienced principals; AUSL aims to have a total of twenty turnaround schools up and running in Chicago by 2012. AUSL now functions as both a teacher preparation program and a school management organization; the district considers it a crucial part of its strategy to change the district's lowest-performing schools.

Defining Principles of Urban Teacher Residencies

One way to understand the Boston and Chicago residency programs is to look at them through the lens of the seven Urban Teacher Residency United's (UTRU) principles.

First, *UTRs tightly weave education theory and classroom practice together.* Residents practice what is taught in courses and continuously test, reflect on, and improve their skills. They demonstrate their proficiency not only through course grades, but also through performance-based assessments and projects that are informed by research and theory but grounded in actual classroom experiences. For example, a resident teacher in Chicago studies lesson plan development in her university classes and then works with her mentor to create a lesson plan for class. After the lesson plan is implemented, the mentor reviews it and possible improvements with the resident.

Residents and university professors often compare their course work with their classroom experience and report back the following week on how suggested strategies worked when implemented in their classroom settings. In Boston, course assignments include bringing in student work or videotaping classroom implementation of an instructional technique learned at the university. To support the tight integration of theory and practice, many of the professors are outstanding, experienced teachers in the district.

In Chicago, National-Louis University modified its traditional two-year teacher education program to integrate its course work with the year-long AUSL teacher residency. Some changes were structural and logistical in nature—for example, all residents attend classes on Fridays and some-times after their school day. Other changes were more substantive; for ex-ample, the university changed its format for lesson plans based on input of AUSL staff and mentors. There is also a university liaison who works with the residents' mentor to collaboratively assess the residents' work. In addi-tion, NLU has modified course content and sequencing to better meet the needs of residents preparing in and for an urban school context.

Second, *UTRs focus on learning alongside an experienced, trained mentor.* Residents work side by side with mentors in a full-year classroom appren-ticeship before taking on their own classrooms and becoming the teacher of record. In Boston, each resident is paired one on one with a mentor. Chicago pairs one (and sometimes two) residents with a mentor. Mentors go beyond a focus on the technical aspects of teaching to cultivate a dis-position of inquiry, concentrate attention on student thinking and under-standing, and foster disciplined talk about problems of practice. For BTR, the minimum requirement for consideration as a mentor is three years' teaching experience. Both programs look for mentors who are reflective, able to talk about their practice, collaborative, committed to their own continuous growth and improvement, and able to show demonstrated suc-cess as a teacher as indicated by students' standardized test results.

In Chicago, residents spend four days a week in their mentor's class-room, along with frequent coaching sessions after school. The fifth day is dedicated to their own course work and seminars. BTR mentors spend at least two hours per week with their residents working one on one with structured protocols to guide and focus their work together. Boston resi-dents also spend four days a week in their mentor's classroom and one day per week engaged in course work and seminars. In both programs, men-tors participate in summer professional development sessions and con-tinue to meet monthly for ongoing professional development during the school year.

Residents identified the power of a full-year mentoring program and noted consistently the valuable support they received from their mentors and program directors. Residents experience a full-year school life cycle, from setting up classrooms to closing. They learn firsthand how to build culture and community, organize long-term instructional goals, create formative assessments, and use data to reflect on their teaching practices. The depth of the relationships residents and mentors build over the year cements a strong bond of trust and respect.

The two programs provide support for mentors. BTR pays its mentors a $3,000 stipend; AUSL gives mentors a 20 percent annual salary supplement. And both provide professional development for mentors to ensure that they are skilled in taking on the task of mentorship. As one AUSL mentor put it:

> An important lesson AUSL has learned is the importance of professional development that is specifically focused on the knowledge and skills necessary to be an effective mentor. A teacher who takes on this dual mission must be willing to divide equal attention between their students and their resident. They also must be prepared to supervise and manage adults, which for many mentors can be a surprising aspect of this job. The quality of our UTR rests in many ways on the skills, capacities, and commitment of our mentor teachers.

Third, UTRs *organize teacher candidates in cohorts* to cultivate professional learning communities and foster collaboration among new and experienced teachers. Residents engage in a tightly prescribed sequence of course work and clinical experiences together. The cohorts meet regularly and form an intellectual community that connects practice with course work, as residents work together in the same school "carry[ing] the conversation from place to place."

The cohort model extends beyond the residency year as an effort is made to place residency graduates together. One AUSL administrator explained: "AUSL has set the standard in terms of recognizing the importance of linking the training of teachers and school redesign. You need to put a cluster of [residents] in one building. . . . There need to be enough new transformative teachers to create a transforming environment."

Fourth, *UTRs build effective partnerships* that bring together diverse organizations for the common goal of improving student achievement through high-quality teaching. UTR program staff believe that their partnerships are absolutely crucial to supporting teacher learning over time and to effecting long-lasting reform in urban schools. For a district, partnering with a program like BPE or AUSL is critical, because as nonprofits, these organizations are nimble. They can hire faculty and consultants in timely ways, execute contracts efficiently, adapt programming quickly, and mediate institutional turf. Both BTR and AUSL have entrepreneurial, can-do attitudes and market their respective programs in sophisticated ways. Both act like small start-ups, less encumbered by the constraints experienced by the large bureaucracies of universities and school districts.

Fifth, *UTRs serve school districts*. UTRs exist to address community and school district problems, while maintaining their independence from school systems so they are not beholden to district vagaries, internal politics, and bureaucratic dicta. Admissions goals and priorities for UTRs are consistent with the hiring objectives of the district, and the district commits to hiring graduates from the program. AUSL and BTR place a priority on recruiting in the areas of science and mathematics, and BTR residents graduate with dual licensure in special education. In the 2007–2008 cohort, almost 60 percent of BTR recruits and 32 percent of AUSL recruits were being prepared to teach in high-needs subjects. In addition, 55 percent of BTR recruits and 57 percent of AUSL recruits in the 2007–2008 cohorts were people of color. For administrators in Boston, BTR is the district's primary recruitment strategy for ensuring a diverse teaching force.

As one of the BTR partners explained, "Universities have to prepare teachers for more than one district—this is their reality; but in doing so, they do not prepare teachers adequately for Boston. How they are prepared has very little to do with what they need to teach." In contrast, residents learn the district's instructional initiatives and curriculum, while they come to understand the history and context of the community in which they will teach.

UTRs can also serve districts by informing them and pushing them to improve their practices. For example, BTR's work on new teacher screening and induction has spurred BPS to revamp the way it screens candidates and supports all of its novices. BTR's development of teacher competencies informed the district's development of its Dimensions of Effective Teaching.[2] BTR, district professional development, and teacher evaluations are all being aligned to these teaching competencies. In Chicago, meanwhile, CPS gave AUSL the opportunity to run its own turnaround schools after observing the success of AUSL's training academies and turnaround schools.

Sixth, *UTRs support residents once they are hired as teachers of record.* UTRs recognize that even well-prepared novices in high-needs schools demand long-term support and professional growth and offer increasingly sophisticated approaches to both. For example, in Chicago, after graduating from the residency program, individualized coaching and induction support continues through year two of teaching, and additional professional development support is provided for graduates in years three and four. An induction coach works with the new teacher once or twice a week. New teachers are assigned a grade partner and cluster leader. There is common preparation time with grade-level partners, and other preparation time is used for observations. Coaches are trained in using the cognitive coaching model. Because these teacher supports are all rooted in a common definition of quality teaching, they are beginning to pay dividends for the schools and the students served.

Seventh, *UTRs establish and support differentiated career roles for veteran teachers.* The UTRs have begun to create opportunities for excellent experienced teachers to take on roles as mentors, supervisors, and instructors, while continuing to hold positions as K–12 classroom teachers. With AUSL mentors earning a 20 percent salary supplement, these experts can be recognized and rewarded and can hold meaningful leadership opportunities without becoming administrators. Both BTR and AUSL are beginning to see their most successful residents become mentors. As one AUSL leader noted, "As AUSL has grown, we have recognized the enormous talent that exists within our mentor teachers. Three of our current mentor coaches are past mentor teachers. We have also tapped mentor teachers to create writing and math benchmark assessments and curriculum to be used across our network schools. AUSL is working to increase leadership opportunities for our mentor teachers while not taking them away from their important work of educating students and training resident teachers."

The Effectiveness of UTRS

While UTRs appear to be a promising innovation, the critical questions are whether UTRs are making a difference in schools and classrooms and, if so, whether those differences can be measured. Preliminary evidence suggests that this innovation holds promise for improving urban teacher and school quality. Only a few years in operation, UTRs do not yet have sufficient data to determine the impact of their graduates on student learning. However, both BTR and AUSL see this question as the one that defines their success and are investing in the data and analysis to answer it. And both programs can point to other measures of success.

Skills and Competencies

School administrators' assessments indicate that UTR graduates enter teaching with well-developed skills and competencies that enhance their effectiveness as teachers. When asked to compare the effectiveness of BTR graduates to other first-year teachers, principals rated 88 percent of BTR graduates as effective or more effective than their counterparts, with a majority rated as significantly more effective. Over 94 percent indicated their desire to hire additional BTR graduates. When a Chicago principal of a turnaround school was asked about the differences he sees in AUSL graduates and other beginning teachers, he described how AUSL graduates "take advantage of the mentor coaches in sophisticated ways that other teachers do not; they know how to ask for and receive constructive feedback." He also noted that the AUSL teachers tend to be more reflective about teaching and better versed on the best practices, and added: "Whenever you have a teacher like that, you'll see impact in student achievement."

In addition, clustering the residents in schools and supporting them so they stay in the same schools over time seems to foster school cultures of consultation, shared learning, and data-driven decision making—all essential practices for schools that want to improve teaching and learning.

Hard-to-Staff Areas and Diversity

Both AUSL and BTR have been successful in recruiting high-caliber candidates of color—57 percent of AUSL residents and 55 percent of BTR residents are minorities. All UTR teachers teach in high-needs schools. Boston has also been particularly successful in recruiting and preparing teachers for high-needs content areas. For example, 57 percent of BTR's middle and high school residents teach mathematics or science, and every resident receives a certification in special education along with certification in a content area.

Retention

UTRs, compared to both higher education and alternate preparation programs, retain their recruits for a longer period of time. After three years, 90 percent of BTR graduates and 95 percent of AUSL graduates are still teaching. Compared to Boston's overall retention rate of 53 percent at the end of three years, the current retention rates for the UTR programs are extremely high. Causes for the high-retention rates likely include the high-quality preparation program, ongoing support, the up-front commitment to teach in high-needs schools, and the financial penalties if those commitments are not honored.

Mentor Skill and Retention

The UTRs' investments in selecting, preparing, and supporting the mentors who work with residents have further developed the veteran teachers themselves. These new roles for experienced teachers have led to renewed enthusiasm and motivation and contributed to the retention of some teachers who might have otherwise left the classroom or district. Finally, the leadership skills that mentors develop position them to be part of a potential pipeline to leadership positions.

Impact on the Human Capital System

Although the UTRs are relatively young programs, there are examples in Chicago and Boston of ways that BTR and AUSL have begun to have an impact on their districts' human capital systems. BTR has spurred important changes in how BPS recruits and screens teachers. BTR and BPS staff members recruit side by side at career fairs and generally work in a coordinated way to direct potential teachers to appropriate preparation pathways based on individuals' strengths, interests, and needs. BTR and BPS have adopted one set of standards for teaching, and those standards are becoming an increasingly integral part of the professional development and teacher assessment systems throughout the district.

Chicago is a far more decentralized system than the smaller Boston district, yet the impacts of AUSL are clear. AUSL is a significant part of the CPS plan for improving low-performing schools, with increasing numbers of turnaround schools being placed under AUSL governance. The close link between AUSL and National-Louis University has resulted in changes in the university's preparation program. The most direct change is in the course of study designed specifically for AUSL residents. However, faculty report that the success of residents in the AUSL training academies and high-needs CPS schools has prompted new kinds of clinical placements in other NLU preparation programs as well.

In both districts, recognizing the importance of supporting new teachers in hard-to-staff urban schools has led to a differentiated program of induction and mentoring that directs the most intensive resources to teachers in the highest-needs schools. For example, Chicago recently became the home of a New Teacher Center (NTC) site. The NTC mentors are placed in the regions with the greatest need for improvement in student learning. Boston has also adopted an intensive model of induction support with well-prepared induction coaches. At both sites, coordination between the UTR and the districts ensures that mentoring services complement rather than duplicate each other. Similarly, both UTRs' emphasis on new roles for exemplary teachers is starting to influence thinking on teacher career ladders in the two districts.

Budget and Financial Structures

Policy makers and community leaders considering whether a UTR should become one of their district's pathways into teaching will want to know how much these programs cost and how they are funded. The two UTR programs highlighted in this study demonstrate how different design and implementation decisions, as well as different district contexts, have profound impacts on total program costs.

In Boston, for example, BTR relies on BPS-operated host schools to provide the training site. BTR pays half the salary for a teacher at each school to serve as a site director and stipends to the mentors. AUSL has a very different approach, in which the UTR has taken over operations of selected CPS schools, some of which serve as training academies, while others are designated turnaround schools where large proportions of teachers hired are AUSL graduates.[3] CPS contributes a portion of the funds required to operate these schools, but AUSL must raise additional funds to fully support their operation. Another key difference, largely due to the fact that Chicago hires from many alternative certification programs while Boston does not, is that Chicago pays residents a higher stipend.

BTR and AUSL each have four major budget areas: up-front recruiting costs; preparation costs, which include financial support to residents during their training year; induction costs; and the costs of running an effective program that includes coordination and communication across programs and participants. Both programs invest heavily in recruiting excellent candidates for their programs, in sharp contrast to traditional teacher-preparation programs that rarely have been funded by their university administrators and state higher education agencies to proactively recruit top-notch teacher candidates. Both BTR and AUSL invest heavily in training and preparation, including compensating faculty engaged in instruction, mentors and faculty who work with residents, and mentors who work with residents in their classrooms throughout the entire academic year.

UTR programs also provide significant financial support to residents. They pay stipends and health benefits to residents during their year of training, which helps attract a diverse pool of qualified candidates in high-needs areas. Since residents are not teachers of record and thus are not getting a teacher's salary and benefits, stipends and health benefits are necessary in order for UTRs to be competitive with other programs that target similar populations of candidates but enable them to earn a full teaching salary after only a brief preparation period. BTR and AUSL also offer other financial incentives to attract candidates and retain graduates. For example, in both programs, candidates are able to readily acquire loans to cover the cost of tuition to universities for the master's degree. There are also built-in financial incentives for graduates to fulfill their teaching commitment in the districts' high-needs schools. BTR forgives a portion of residents' tuition costs for each year of teaching. AUSL requires proportional repayment of the stipend for teachers who teach for less than the contracted four years. Induction is also a major area of investment, as both programs pay for a corps of induction coaches who support graduates in their beginning years as teachers.

Finally, while specifics vary, the programs share many common categories of administration costs, as a function of similar needs to support residents and coordinate among schools, partners, and program participants. Each UTR employs staff to maintain program operations and has directors on site at each school where residents are placed. Funds are required for positions that are dedicated primarily to planning and coordination, as well as embedded in the salaries of others who invest time to ensure partnerships function effectively.

A fiscal snapshot of BTR provides a window into how funding and costs play out in that program's budget. In 2007–2008, expenditures for the thirteen-month BTR program totaled approximately $3.4 million, with about 12 percent allocated to recruitment, 76 percent to preparation, and 12 percent to induction expenditures. These numbers are based on dividing program administration and coordination costs among the three key program areas. These expenditures result in a total average cost per resident of approximately $38,000.

The sources of funding for the UTR programs are currently a mix of private and public resources. In both programs, private-sector funds were the sole source for initiating the UTRs and continue to be one source for sustaining them. In Boston, private funds were invested in the start-up of BTR, with an up-front commitment by the district to fund an increasingly larger portion each year. BTR had transitioned to primarily public sources of funding by 2007–2008. Currently, a significant portion of funds are public resources, with the district covering about half the program costs and federal AmeriCorps and Transition to Teaching grants contributing a sizable portion of resources as well. AUSL continues to have a large portion of funds from philanthropy, which makes an important contribution toward supporting the rapid increase in the number of turnaround schools that the program will operate.

Long-term Financing of UTRS

Funders have thus far found the appeal and promise of the UTR model compelling. However, long-term sustainability of these and other UTRs will require stable sources of funds that support the work. Federal funding may be available for the start-up of new UTRs, particularly in the form of the Race to the Top and Innovations funds that the U.S. Department of Education is making available through stimulus funding. Yet long-term sustainability will undoubtedly rely, in significant measure, on rethinking the use of existing state and district funds or different uses of federal funds such as Title I or Title II of the Elementary and Secondary School Act.[4] Based on data and analysis from Education Resource Strategies (ERS), an organization with a strong track record of analyzing urban district spending for teacher support, five strategies to support sustained district and state funding of UTRs emerge.[5]

1. Cost savings from reduced teacher attrition are redirected to support UTRs

The much higher retention rates of BTR and AUSL graduates result in significant cost savings to the districts. For example, recent research conducted by the National Commission on Teaching and America's Future on the cost of teacher turnover shows that in the Chicago Public Schools, the cost of a teacher leaving the district can be as much as $13,650 per teacher—and over 37 percent of teachers leave in their first five years. The study estimates the annual cost of all teacher turnover in CPS is $64.5 million.

While these savings only accrue over time and may be difficult for policy makers to see in districts' budgets, the savings are nonetheless real and quantifiable and can be taken into account in the financial sustainability equation. With UTR retention rates nearly twice as high as those in typical urban districts, UTRs could pay for themselves quickly.

2. Strategic reallocation of district teacher professional development funds

In Chicago, the district spends about $250 million on professional development annually. However, expenditures on new and experienced teachers can vary widely. Although districts offer fewer one-shot workshops than they once did, districts continue to spread professional development spending across a multitude of departments and initiatives, often with neither an explicit strategy nor an ability to assess impact. For example, a single school may benefit from district resources invested in math coaches as well as teacher certification instructors and new teacher mentors. All of them may focus on helping a novice teach more effectively but do so in duplicative or even conflicting ways.

By aligning new teacher support to district priorities, curricula, and instructional materials, and focusing that support on clusters of new teachers strategically placed in schools, UTRs offer an example of strategic use of resources for new teacher support. As districts analyze the array of new teacher support strategies they have in place, they may find opportunities to eliminate repetition and direct resources toward the strategies with the most potential for impact.

In addition to investments in professional development, districts also commit millions of dollars to salary increases that teachers earn by pursuing graduate credits. Many districts pay twice—reimbursing tuition to teachers for the cost of their graduate credits and providing salary increases on attainment of graduate credits for the tenure of a teacher's career. For example, recently BPS spent $29 million in one year for additional course work and graduate credits and degrees. This amount grows substantially if one calculates the credit attainment as an ongoing cost over the course of a teacher's career. In many districts, teachers can earn salary increases for a wide array of courses, some of which have little direct relationship to the content or students they teach. Tightening these policies might increase the impact of the investments on teaching and learning. Offering alternative ways for teachers to increase their salaries, such as through the job-embedded mentoring that UTRs offer, would result in more strategic use of district funds.

3. Change in districts' practice of billing at teachers' average salaries

UTRs might be also able to find fiscal support and sustainability by changing the way districts bill for teachers' salaries. Most districts' school budgets reflect the cost of each teacher using the district average, not the actual salary of the teachers in the school. With this practice, the cost of highly experienced teachers at certain schools is, in effect, subsidized by the lower cost of schools that have a larger portion of young, less-expensive teachers. A modified funding and billing system could be adopted for more equitable funding. Funds could be distributed to schools based on a weighted student-funding system in which dollars follow students to schools. If schools are then billed based on actual teacher salaries, those with larger proportions of inexperienced teachers would have more resources to invest in UTRs. Recouped dollars could go toward resident stipends and tuition as well as mentor salaries or developing mentors, if too few qualified teachers are available for this role.

4. Strategic reallocation of district spending on alternative certification

UTRs could also benefit from a more strategic reallocation of a district's alternative certification expenditures. School districts spend significant dollars to help uncertified or alternatively certified teachers meet state requirements. For example, in one large city, the school district provided $3,850 in tuition reimbursements to first- and second-year Teach For America teachers. District support of alternative route teachers tends to be directed toward a small number of its total new teachers. And, while these teachers may bring value to the classroom compared to uncertified teachers they replace, they are likely to leave teaching at a higher rate than UTR graduates, despite the district's investment. In addition, their training is not always specific to the district's curricula or instructional strategies, as is the case with UTR models. While many districts may keep strong alternative certification programs in their preparation and induction portfolio, they could focus more of their resources on identifying which alternative certification candidates are more likely to stay and make deeper investments in their preparation.

5. Strategic reallocation of state funding for teacher preparation

The cost of teacher preparation is traditionally borne by individual teacher candidates (tuition payments to their preparing institutions), the federal government (grants and loans to students to pursue their college and graduate studies), and state governments (subsidies they pay to support public colleges and universities within their states). State governments subsidize public teacher preparation programs with hundreds of millions of dollars a year (90 percent of all teachers are prepared in public institutions). Many state-supported education schools produce teachers who are in relatively low demand—e.g., elementary, social studies, and physical education. However, universities will be reimbursed all the same, no matter whether they are producing the math, science, special education, and bilingual teachers that urban schools need. Researchers and reformers have long lamented the fact that university leaders use teacher education as a cash cow—preparing anyone who wants to get a degree with as little expense (and clinical training) possible and few skills and supports to teach in challenging public schools.

To further deepen the problem, of the approximately 200,000 licensed teachers graduating from university-based preparation programs annually, only about 70 percent of them actually end up teaching.[6] The return on this investment is compromised when 30 percent of the people that universities are preparing never enter the profession, and only a small proportion of the remaining 70 percent are prepared to teach in high-needs content areas and/or high-needs schools. Consequently, the higher education community invests in teacher education students and graduates who widen the supply-and-demand gap. The percentages of aspiring teachers who do not graduate may include candidates who were appropriately counseled out of becoming teachers; however, this also demonstrates a costly form of quality assurance that could have occurred earlier with more attention to proper screening of those accepted into the program. As we suggest in more detail later, directing state funding to teacher preparation to programs with a demonstrated ability to meet the needs of urban districts could provide additional support for UTRs and potentially strengthen other teacher preparation programs as well.

Moreover, states could consider restructuring certification requirements so that teachers can earn certification through participating in a UTR program, being a mentor to a resident, or other job-embedded work aligned with their districts' curricula. The money that districts and states currently spend on certification could be redirected toward UTRs.

Lessons Learned

The right implementation of a UTR program will vary based on the unique ecosystem of each district and community. But despite the two very different contexts in Boston and Chicago, there are some district and community preconditions that are important for any aspiring UTR. We propose six action steps districts and their partners should take to understand, analyze, and plan around the relevant conditions on the ground. It's worthwhile to note that no district, including BPS and CPS, has all the conditions detailed next in place. But the action steps can guide an analysis of a district's readiness to implement a successful program and direct attention toward important features for initiating and sustaining a successful UTR.

Assess the readiness of a school district, institution of higher education, and/or a nonprofit organization to undertake the work of developing a UTR.

First, *districts* must have a sustained, well-developed teaching and learning infrastructure in which good teaching and learning are clearly defined and consistently supported. Districts need well-aligned curricula, instructional materials, and pedagogical approaches, and the UTR must be part of the district's coherent framework and overall strategy for improving teaching quality. Diagnostic and summative assessments should be in place to inform instruction. In addition, districts should have a clear understanding of their particular teacher-talent needs (e.g., more special education or middle school math and science teachers) and be able to communicate these to the UTR and its partners.

Second, *higher education institutions* must develop an organizationwide commitment to investing in teacher education and rewarding faculty who teach in residency programs. The right kinds of pedagogical course work need to be designed, and faculty who teach the classes must have expertise and experience in teaching in high-needs schools. There must be institutional support of faculty who work with UTRs, most commonly by providing time to teach the courses and valuing their contributions in the university tenure decision-making process. The tenure incentives for most professors run counter to the needs of school–university partnerships. Many higher education faculty may be willing and able to support UTRs, but policy makers have not enacted the incentives and policy tools to encourage them to do so.

Third, *nonprofit organizations* must have the expertise to lead teacher education efforts and a staff with the necessary content knowledge to help build teaching and learning programs. These third-party organizations play an important role that may be critical for bringing together partners from disparate institutions. School districts and institutions of higher education, in particular, may have similar goals for producing well-prepared teachers, but also bring their own bureaucracies, histories, and relationships that must be at least recognized and possibly overcome for a successful UTR partnership. Nonprofits must have the capacity to serve as boundary spanners between school districts and universities, as well as between those entities and other parties. These organizations should have the capacity to raise funds to help launch and support the UTR, and its leaders need to understand the values, culture, and interests of each partner and know how to negotiate necessary changes that must occur.

Identify high-quality schools and classrooms in which to prepare residents.

As with any new teacher, the school conditions under which residents learn to teach influence their practice. Research has shown how certain working conditions—especially those factors related to trust and relationships among teachers and administrators—affect teachers' retention, which affects their effectiveness in the classroom.[7] For UTRs to be successful, districts must have a sufficient number of schools at all levels where the culture is collaborative and collegial for adults, encouraging and supportive of all students' learning and high performance, and constantly focused on learning and continuous improvement. This requires excellent school leaders and mentors.

First, school administrators must know how to transform organizational structures to promote collaboration and integrate teacher learning with student learning. They should provide opportunities for teachers to take on leadership roles and provide time during the day to support teacher collaboration. UTRs have found time for teacher collaboration by "buying more of it" but could also consider adopting innovative school schedules. (In Japan and other nations, teachers regularly have time for lesson study, and novices have reduced teaching loads.) UTRs demand a culture of excellence that drives constant learning and collaboration. Too few school leaders have the knowledge and skills required to create and sustain these conditions; therefore, principals themselves may need training and support in promoting this type of work environment.

Second, there must be the necessary number of excellent teachers who can act as strong mentors, and they should be working in high-needs areas. These criteria may sound basic at first, but the experiences of Boston and Chicago suggest that it is a challenge to meet them. Setting high expectations for the schools and classrooms that will serve as training sites is critical to ensuring program quality. AUSL has approached this challenge by taking over full operation of turnaround schools; BTR has a more district-embedded strategy of working with selected host schools that are BPS-operated.

Define clear standards for high-quality teaching and support teachers' progress toward meeting those standards.

A centerpiece of both BTR's and AUSL's programs is a set of standards and common expectations for what high-quality teaching looks like. Standards, drawn from emerging research on teacher effectiveness, should drive the curriculum design of any UTR and the recruitment, selection, support, and evaluation of residents, mentors, and school-based program staff. While the UTRs prepare teachers for the district curriculum, they also attend to the underlying theory of the selected content and instructional strategies. By integrating educational theory with practice in specific curricula, teachers develop a deeper understanding of how children think and learn and the rational for pedagogical approaches. This approach leads to sound knowledge of specific curricula, while also broadening teachers' knowledge of how the content and pedagogy intersect with the needs and developmental levels of their students. This level of understanding is critical for long-term success in the face of changing curricula and for adapting existing curricula to students' needs.

For teachers to be effective, there should be coherence in the standards that guide their preparation and the standards to which they will be held accountable when placed as teachers in their own classrooms. In some cases, the UTR will develop the standards as part of developing the residency program. In other cases, the district in which residents work will have standards that the UTR will either adopt or adapt. In still other instances, the UTR will partner with the district to develop standards collaboratively, with the intention that these will be the standards for preparation, recruitment, selection, induction, tenure, and teacher leadership decisions.

While there is no best way to do this, there are a few guiding principles that must drive whatever process the UTR pursues. Districts need to be clear about expectations for new teachers, recognizing that even a well-prepared teacher is not fully developed, while also establishing clear standards that novices need to meet by the end of year one and to be awarded tenure. An effective and sustainable UTR depends on having in place clear standards for high-quality teaching that are consistent with or identical to the district's standards for all teachers. The district and the UTR and its partners need to work closely to ensure this coherence.

Develop teacher leaders and expand teachers' career options.

UTRs, by design, introduce a variety of teacher leadership roles: mentoring residents, coordinating the work of school-based clusters of mentors and residents, and teaching UTR course work. Developing teacher leaders allows districts to spread teaching expertise and keep its best educators; however, doing this well poses significant challenges and opportunities.

For example, UTR sites need to have a group of effective teachers and a strong school leader that may require school districts to recruit and use teacher leaders differently. Historically, teachers have been selected and placed individually in schools, often defined by district-union internal transfer rules and hiring practices. UTRs require districts to cluster cohorts of new teachers and mentors and to focus recruitment and placement efforts on teams with key teacher leaders rather than on individuals.

In addition, there may be insufficient numbers of expert teachers who can mentor and prepare novices. If so, the district, university, and community partners must actively cultivate teacher leaders and devise new policies that can free up time and space for their best teachers to be mentors and teacher educators, while still allowing them to teach. Currently, both AUSL and BTR are beginning to use their highest-performing graduates as mentors, offering a career pathway for its graduates. However, districts have done little to capitalize on these efforts by designing more expansive leadership roles and aligning professional compensation with their teacher development systems.

Attention to the importance of teacher leadership is on the rise for some institutions of higher education. However, many institutions could do more to prepare teacher leaders, especially in their roles as data coaches, assessment experts, and teacher educators. Indeed, the mentors UTRs are beginning to recruit and prepare could serve new roles in transforming university-based teacher education.

Collect evidence to improve programs and build political will.

UTRs are beginning to assemble evidence on the effects of their programs on teacher retention and student achievement. These data will be critical for improving their efforts and attracting the support of policy makers, practitioners, and the public. UTRs must be able to quantify who they attract, how they are prepared, where they teach and under what conditions, and how effective they are in helping students learn—both as individuals and as small teacher teams. UTRs need to demonstrate more clearly the cost effectiveness of their programs in terms of both student learning and teacher retention. Each program has assembled an array of studies to assess their programs and tell their stories. However, there is no common database or overarching evaluative framework. In fact, despite the enormous contributions and efforts of program administrators, we could not assemble some of the data we sought, and much of what we did collect was unavailable in any comparable form. Organizations such as the National Council for Accreditation of Teacher Education (NCATE) and Urban Teacher Residency United (UTRU) or accountability requirements in federal legislation could promote attention to gathering data on the programs' impacts and effectiveness.

Determine how UTRs can play a broader role in strengthening a district's human capital system.

AUSL and BTR demonstrate two approaches to how UTRs can go beyond preparing teachers to have an impact on teaching quality and student achievement. In Chicago, AUSL has begun to manage turnaround schools and create the conditions where their residents can effectively learn and thrive. As one of many organizations that partners with this large and fairly decentralized district to manage turnaround schools, AUSL has deep involvement in and impact on this subset of schools but limited impact on districtwide strategy. In Boston, on the other hand, BTR partnered with the central office to inform and shape district policies and practices, identifying system barriers and bringing to scale some of BTR's most promising practices. The choice of how the UTR can best engage with and affect the district depends, of course, on district context and needs as well as the leadership and capacity within the UTR.

In Closing

The power and potential of UTRs lies in their commitment to: (1) address the real teacher supply and quality needs of school districts, (2) leverage the best K–12 educators as mentors and teacher educators in preparing the next generation of teachers, and (3) promote redesigned schools organized for students and teachers to learn. These commitments are simultaneously basic and revolutionary. They are neither proprietary to UTRs nor new. But UTRs represent a renewed approach that can alter the current debate over university-based teacher education and alternate certification as well as expand the vision for recruiting, preparing, and retaining quality teachers for urban schools.

UTRs may cost more in up-front investments than most university-based and alternate pathways to certification, but they have potential to offset those costs with the retention of novice teachers and their increased teaching effectiveness over time. They also have the potential to reframe teacher preparation and a career in teaching to include communities of continuous adult reflection and learning and dynamic, differentiated roles for effective teachers who aspire to leadership roles.

Keeping Second-Stage Teachers
on the Radar Screen

*An Agenda for Recognizing High-Flying
Teachers After Tenure*

Jane Hannaway and Brad Jupp

School administrators and researchers pay surprisingly little attention to what Susan Moore Johnson and colleagues call "second-stage teachers"— teachers who have obtained tenure, but who are still at relatively early stages of their careers.[1] Systems track the hiring, recruitment, and retention counts of entry teachers and the expected retirement rates of career teachers, probably because information on both these groups is essential to keeping schools adequately staffed. But once teachers pass the tenure hurdle, largely a procedural matter, systems pay little attention to teachers and their career development. Tenured teachers drop off the radar screen, becoming part of a largely undifferentiated mass, regardless of their talents, interests, or potential.[2] Yet they represent more than a third of the teaching force.

The contrast of this practice with human capital management in other types of organizations is striking. Most organizations use the relatively early career years of employees to identify and invest in up-and-coming leadership talent and to sort individuals into areas that develop specialized skills of value. Likely career trajectories become evident to employees, leading some to stay and others to leave. The consequence is a human capital management strategy geared to organizational objectives and focused squarely on the talents and skills of employees who contribute to those objectives. But in education, once tenured, teachers' careers are largely guided by an automatic pilot that charts a career course that differs little across teachers or over time and that is not based on the skills and talents of individual teachers.

The seeming disinterest in teacher career development is curious. Districts grant tenure using little information about teacher performance or potential; almost every teacher receives tenure. The high performance of tenured teachers is hardly assured. Once granted tenure, the teacher has a hold on her job for life. A district can break the hold, but only at high cost, involving extended due process that typically includes multiple classroom observations, lengthy periods of paid leave, and tough hearings that often resemble criminal trials. In economic terms, the school district commits to a large investment in the teacher at the point of tenure. The total accumulated salary and benefits of a teacher represent a big bet by the district, easily $3 million if the teacher works another thirty years and retires with full benefits.[3] Districts could get a much bigger return on that investment, both in financial terms and in terms of student learning, if they paid more attention to the cultivation, differentiation, and management of the tenured teacher work force.

The current career development model for teachers, to the extent there is one, is a one-size-fits-all model. Its features include: impersonal professional development that is, at best, program driven; the single salary schedule, a system of earning pigeonholes that prohibits recognition of a teacher's accomplishments; an inadequate evaluation system that rates everyone excellent; and a back-loaded set of compensation incentives that tends to keep many teachers on the job, even if their motivation for the work has waned. Perhaps most important, the career development model does not allow career-altering recognition, regardless of a teacher's skill or performance. The New Teacher Project report sees the education system treating teachers as interchangeable "widgets."[4]

This chapter attempts to put the second stage of the teaching career—from tenure to ten years—on the radar screen of administrators and reformers. We begin by reviewing what we know about who stays in teaching and who leaves at different career points. We then describe the behavior, attitudes, and perceptions of second-stage teachers. Finally, we propose a broad set of policy and practical actions so schools and districts can identify, develop, retain, and advance teaching talent in this critical segment of the work force, especially the highest performers. Our goal is to challenge school and district leaders to use readily available performance-management strategies in order to promote engaging, productive work experiences for second-stage teachers.

Teacher Attrition: Who Stays? Who Leaves?

First-Stage Teachers

Teacher attrition, at both the level of the school and the profession, has received considerable attention in recent years. Most of the focus has been on early career leavers; almost a quarter of teachers leave within the first three years, mostly in the first year.[5] The rates are higher in the most challenging schools.[6] Such findings have led many analysts to support policies aimed at teacher retention, and for good reason. (Chapter 5 outlines a proposal for redesigning the first stage of teaching to encourage well-qualified individuals to remain and ensure that those who do stay through tenure are effective.)

Second-Stage Teachers

Second-stage teachers appear to be restless and mobile and, thus, are probably a good target for career intervention. Departure rates show a U-shape relationship by age; rates are higher for younger and for older teachers. (Other professions are more likely to show a general downward slope.) A Florida analysis showed that, in the 2006–2007 school year, the highest departure rates were for teachers between ages twenty-five and thirty-four and those over age fifty-five. In the middle-age years (thirty-five to fifty-five years old), rates were low.[7] Part of the explanation for the U-shaped departure pattern for teachers is that younger teachers, not heavily invested in the pension system, explore other opportunities, For middle-age teachers, the structure of the pension system imposes large losses for early exit, and so they stay. Older teachers, over fifty-five years with enough time in service, can exit with good benefits, and do. Indeed, it often does not pay for them to continue working.[8]

Our own analysis of the Schools and Staffing Survey (SASS) and of The Teacher Follow-up Survey (TFS), conducted by the National Center for Education Statistics, shows a similar pattern.[9] Teacher turnover—the sum of teachers who move within the profession (whether from school to school or district to district) and teachers who leave—is highest in the first decade of employment. After ten years of service, job stability for teachers is high. In fact, 57 percent of all movement occurs in the first ten years of service, and only 43 percent occurs in the remaining three-plus decades of service. And the largest part of that later career movement can be accounted for by retirement. In short, the first decade of service is one of rapid movement—both leaving and moving—followed by a prolonged period of extraordinary job stability.

This same trend is evident in close-up research on local school systems. One study, commissioned by the Piton Foundation and the Donnell Kay Foundation, concluded that once a Denver teacher reached her twelfth year of service, the odds were one in 100 that she would leave the district. By comparison, the odds were one in three in her first three years of service and one in twelve in years four through twelve.[10]

We do not have information on the effectiveness of the second-stage teachers who leave teaching. But if we assume conservatively that the variation in effectiveness among second-stage teachers who leave is close to the variation in the teacher population as a whole, at least some reasonably significant number of the departing second-stage teachers are highly effective. The fraction may even be larger. Teachers with the strongest academic credentials are the most likely to leave teaching, presumably because they are most likely to have other options.[11] To the extent that highly effective teachers leave, the exit rates represent lost opportunities for schools and school districts to build a strong core of educational professionals.

Currently, the teachers who remain—perhaps disproportionately weaker teachers—tend to stay on until retirement, at least in part because of powerful incentives to remain in teaching, such as higher rates of pay under current salary systems, job security through tenure, and back-loaded pension systems. However, the pattern of long-term employment may be changing as younger workers become more accustomed to changing jobs frequently.

Why Teachers Leave

A survey of teachers who have left teaching suggests measures that might be taken to help retain teachers, in particular, strong teachers, longer into their careers.[12] Apart from pregnancy, child rearing, and retirement, the reason that teachers most often rated as important to their decision to leave was the pursuit of a different career. Although many teachers reported dissatisfaction with teaching, the attraction of different opportunities appears to be an important driver.

What is it about these different opportunities that departing teachers value? According to those who leave, it was not about salaries and benefits, at least not immediately. Ratings of salaries were about the same in teaching and in their new position, and ratings of benefits far favored teaching (47 percent, compared with 27 percent in the new position). Nor was it about the social value of the work. Some 42 percent of those leaving strongly felt that teaching provided opportunities to make a difference in the lives of others, compared with 26 percent in their new position.

Teachers who left saw their new position, however, as offering greater intellectual challenge (48 percent versus 30 percent) and greater chance for upward mobility (opportunities for promotion—58 percent versus 20 percent; recognition—53 percent versus 15 percent; professional prestige—47 percent versus 28 percent) as well as opportunities to exercise influence and control over workplace policies (53 percent versus 11 percent). In short, the reports of those who left imply that the current flat structure of the teaching profession restricted their professional potential in a number of ways.

These observations are supported by rich qualitative research by Susan Moore Johnson and colleagues on second-stage teachers.[13] Although the research involves small numbers of teachers that preclude generalization, it adds rich detail about teacher behavior, attitude, and perception between years four and ten of their careers.

The picture they paint shows teachers who perceive themselves as coming into their own and, having mastered the basics of a tough job, ready to take on leadership responsibility for improving practice. Teachers are committed to their jobs, but mobile, willing to move up or across their organization for new challenges, and also ready to move out if the job is frustrating. They are not opposed to state or federal mandates, but are animated by the prospect of new responsibilities in the school or recognition by school leaders. They love the work of teaching, but will actively seek advancement to other levels of responsibility. They consider differentiated roles and responsibilities as a natural part of the profession, and see this differentiation as one way to advance. They are also willing to work collaboratively with like-minded colleagues and strong instructional leaders. At the same time, they are easily discouraged by uncooperative colleagues, leaders who do not recognize their efforts, and clumsy systems that do not reward or recognize what they do on the job.[14]

Taken in its entirety, current research suggests an image of emerging professionals who want a sense of purpose and challenge in a job that they already see as infused with an important moral and policy purpose.[15] In turn, they expect to play an active role in their own career development, crave responsive leaders and systems, and want to advance their careers.

The expectations of second-stage teachers defy those set up by the current system. Schools and school districts, for the most part, are not structured to provide opportunities for advancement, recognition, and influence. They are fairly flat hierarchies with tightly bounded responsibilities. New challenges are slim. The job responsibilities of a brand-new classroom teacher, for example, are almost identical to the job responsibilities of a thirty-year veteran. To a large extent, teachers function relatively independently in their classrooms, and their work is seldom observed or recognized. With few exceptions, jobs outside the classroom are scarce. Jobs that combine part-time teaching with other career opportunities are even scarcer. This lack of opportunity, new challenges, and recognition appear to be a big part of the rub. Especially when coupled with poor school leadership or a school culture that lacks a sense of purpose or efficacy, these conditions may actually repel the most conscientious second-stage teachers from teaching and explain part of the attrition of teachers in these years, in spite of reports that suggest second-stage teachers would prefer to stay in the profession.[16]

The second stage of the teaching career does not have to be this way. There are ways for schools and districts to move beyond the current career model. Given the behaviors, attitudes, and perceptions of second-stage teachers, and confronted with the stubborn problem of improving the overall performance of our students, especially closing achievement gaps, it is possible and maybe even incumbent on schools and school systems to address this important segment of the teacher force more directly. The common practice of most schools and school systems is to let them fly under the radar, even though they want to be noticed, and to expect them to fly at that altitude, even though many want to fly higher.

New Avenues for Advancement: An Agenda for Policy and Practice

What follows is a broad agenda for using teacher-effectiveness information in order to create new avenues for advancing effective second-stage teachers. It assumes that in the second stage of their careers, there is still a relatively high rate of turnover, but that the longer teachers stay on the job, the less likely they are to leave. The agenda recognizes that during this stage of their careers, teachers remain committed to the broad policy proposition of improving student learning, but seek recognition and opportunity for advancement. It also recognizes that teachers' talents vary widely. Under this agenda, districts and schools would treat these circumstances as an opportunity, rather than passively allowing tenured teachers to continue with little or no direction or distinction. Principals and teacher leaders in schools and central office officials in school districts, as well as practicing teachers in classrooms, would make fair use of readily available performance information to structure new avenues for advancement of talented staff in exchange for greater professional responsibility, including improving student learning.

The agenda has two related objectives. First, it seeks to actively retain the most productive and skilled teachers in the school district, while at the same time supporting those who can become more effective through personalized professional development. Second, it prioritizes deploying the strongest staff in ways that promote the school district's ultimate objective—improving student performance. To do so, school and district leaders—not just principals, but teacher leaders and talent managers in central offices—must make differentiated judgments about staff performance, with the purpose of encouraging those with the highest potential to take on challenging assignments and make a substantial impact. To achieve this, our agenda sets out four strategic directions:

- Measure teacher effectiveness and use that information to make distinctions in the workplace
- Create incentives aligned with the measures of effectiveness
- Invest in leaders who can recognize and act to support effective second-stage teachers
- Invest in systems that recognize effective teaching as a reason for teachers to advance

As we pursue our second objective, we will give special attention to recently tenured teachers of great promise, or "high fliers," which we believe is important for two reasons. First, cultivating leadership early is a critical talent development strategy. Second, we believe that high fliers' example will create a sense of organizational updraft that will be relevant to everyone in the work force, showing that high performance is possible and proving that results matter throughout a teacher's career. They will be the pacesetters, signaling the productivity values of the system.

Most planks in this agenda would be useful when managing any or all of the segments of the teaching work force. We believe, however, that the second stage is a critical point of intervention, if only because the second stage is when teachers are highly motivated by twin drives—to improve and to advance.

1. Measure teacher effectiveness and use it to make distinctions in the workplace.

The first order of business is to define teacher effectiveness and give it the appropriate weight in both policy and practice. Teacher effectiveness should be defined primarily by a teacher's practical outputs: student learning outcomes captured by statistically rigorous measures of gains that are standards-based and criterion-referenced rather than relative, by other pragmatic indicators of learning of comparable rigor, and by a teacher's classroom performance observed by a principal or peer looking for evidence of student learning and classroom practices that have a positive impact on outcomes. Teacher effectiveness should, in other words, be assessed using a simple common-sense body of multiple measures.

More important than measuring effectiveness is acting on the information it generates. Not only should such information be used to support milestone career decisions like tenure, but it should also become a routine part of workplace decision making about classroom responsibilities, professional development, team assignments, and the like. Principals, instructional leaders, and teachers should be aware of their measured performance in the same way student athletes, their teammates, and their coaches quickly learn to attend to their stats. Above all, it should be part of the on-the-job discourse about performance, something transparent and shared for the purpose of continuous improvement, not concealed behind concerns that people might find out who on their team is better or worse.

Used transparently, performance information is a critical tool in the development of teaching talent and careers. As noted earlier, second-stage teachers expect this feedback. Teachers want to hear about how they are performing not only from principals, but also from coaches and peers. They believe their accomplishments should inform decisions for advancement within the ranks of the school's faculty. When they do not hear from school leaders and their accomplishments go unrecognized, they are likely to become less engaged with the job. As a result, their skills go undeveloped, or their attitudes harden into less-engaged workplace cynicism. Either way, the consequence is the same: talent is squandered for want of routine feedback. In addition, clear feedback on performance may encourage persistently weak teachers to move to other professions.

A number of school districts have implemented measures of teacher effectiveness by providing teacher "stoplight" reports. Every teacher in the system receives a rating of green, yellow, or red, representing highest-, middle-, and lowest-quintile performance, respectively. Districts share this easy-to-interpret rating with teachers and their principals annually, and there is an explicit expectation that principals will act on the information. The emphasis is on leveraging the talents of the highest performers, developing the middle performers, and supporting the improvement of the lowest performers. Principals are also expected to use this information to guide school improvement planning and teacher deployment to best support student learning. Looking at stoplight reports by school and disaggregating district results in a variety of ways helps the system track important issues of teaching quality and equity. Analyzing the distribution of low-performing teachers to ensure they aren't concentrated in the lowest-performing schools is one example of this. Identifying the high fliers and surveying them to better understand their career interests and inform how the district manages their talent and career advancement is another.

2. Create incentives aligned with the measures of effectiveness.

The national survey and qualitative work mentioned earlier clearly depict second-stage teachers as seeking simple performance recognition, opportunities for advancement in their schools, and opportunities to advance beyond classroom assignments into leadership roles. Teachers, like most individuals, are no doubt also motivated by compensation incentives.[17] A wide range of incentives should be part of the tool kit for second-stage teachers. They can help create the sense of updraft that these teachers need to deepen their engagement with the work and to stay committed to improving their performance.

Principals and teacher leaders should be empowered at the school level to make both programmatic and flexible use of incentives to recognize and reward second-stage teachers. Incentives can be monetary, but should also include recognition and opportunity to advance to positions of greater responsibility. The process should begin at the school level where the real work of education happens and where information about teacher performance is best. Teachers naturally look not only to principals but also to instructional leaders such as coaches or team leaders for signals that they are succeeding, as well as for opportunities to advance.

A mix of school-based and district-initiated incentives is likely to provide the greatest opportunity for high fliers, while addressing the varied needs of the system. At the school level, for example, exceptional performers could be assigned to formal leadership roles such as grade-level or department team leader, leadership team member, or mentor to aspiring and new teachers. These roles could be part of a career pathway within the school; a teacher could pursue them in addition to full-time teaching. Principals have the authority to organize them to best meet their needs and teachers' interests, allowing for part-time teaching and part-time leadership opportunities. These roles can be clearly distinguished and celebrated in schools as leadership opportunities for high fliers, with additional compensation, although that is not always necessary and may set a precedent. Inviting a single high flier or team of high fliers to design and implement a system of instructional and intervention supports for the students who are struggling the most is an example of how high fliers can be leveraged. This approach can be used for any persistent challenge the school faces. In this example, teachers would create the solution and assume a very substantive role in school improvement.

At the district level, performance pay is the most basic incentive that recognizes teaching talent. Beyond that, districts can develop incentives that recognize high fliers' talent and leverage across schools to address persistent systemic problems. For example, high fliers can be recruited as turnaround teachers. Under this approach, districts would provide training in teacher leadership and the elements of effective school turnarounds and then place groups of high-flying teachers in teams in low-performing schools to catalyze improvement and improve school culture. Teachers who take on this assignment would receive a substantial bonus or salary increase.

Districts can also create pathways to develop leaders for teaching and learning roles in the central office and for schools. They could invite high fliers to participate in a mix of training and internship opportunities intended to provide them the skills and experience required for these roles. This example is both a way to recognize and nurture talent and a strategy for succession planning for leadership in schools and the central office.

3. Invest in leaders who can recognize and act to support effective second-stage teachers.

Close management of second-stage teaching talent is unimaginable without leaders—not just principals, but also school instructional leaders and central office leaders—who place a premium on effective teaching. They must be capable of two critical and very distinct leadership functions. First, they must be able to use data from multiple measures of teacher performance to recognize effective teaching. This process is much more than just sorting teachers into two piles—effective and ineffective. It involves observing critical distinctions in teaching skill, as well as readiness and willingness to advance, and making refined judgments about relative strengths and weaknesses among faculty members. The differences would be based on where individuals stand in the arc of their personal career development and contingent on the context of the classroom in which they are working.

Second, leaders must be able to follow up quickly to affirm success and support development. Because the differences in performance will be highly individualized, the ability to respond must be at the personal level. Principals, coaches, and professional developers should be able to intervene quickly, affirmatively, and definitively in the course of working closely with recently tenured teachers. They must have a broad array of potential incentives, like those described earlier, as well as the leadership skill to use these incentives with precision—giving fair and meaningful career advancement advice to one teacher and supporting the classroom practice of another. Schools are dynamic workplaces. Second-stage teachers are at a place in their careers where this dynamism is in play. To be able to recognize subtle distinctions among younger members of the tenured teaching faculty without acting is at best an aesthetic gesture and at worst an act of futility that depresses a culture of effectiveness.

As chapters 3 and 4 make clear, districts must invest heavily in the development of the skills and knowledge of principals and instructional leaders if they are to create a culture in which second-stage teachers can experience personally relevant professional and career development experiences. To call on school leaders to address the needs of second-stage teachers is to come up against a smaller and more intense version of the paradox that Richard Elmore describes, "Current education leaders are no better equipped than the organizations they lead to meet the challenges posed by standards-based reform."[18] Currently, those leaders are not systematically recognizing and developing the talent in their schools. It is unfair to expect them to use sophisticated incentives—praise and critique, incremental advancement of an eager teacher or incremental delays while a motivated teacher develops the right skills, or small, localized bonuses or extra pay opportunities—when they have neither experience working in such a system of incentives nor experience administering it. In short, if districts are to develop the knowledge, skills, and talents of second-stage teachers, then it is imperative that districts invest in the knowledge and skills of their leaders.

To ensure that principals can manage both individual teacher performance and talent development, districts have to continually signal the importance of the work and support principals in developing the required skills and hold them accountable for using them. Creating stoplight reports, sharing them widely, and using them to differentiate support and opportunities is one way districts can signal the work's importance. Consistent messages about the importance of teacher evaluation and making the evaluation instrument and process meaningful signal it as a district priority and encourage principals to take it seriously. Rolling out instructional reforms with a clear strategy for using high fliers to ensure effective implementation and bolstering support for low performers indicates the value high fliers have to contribute to district work and the importance of differentiation.

Helping principals become aware of and adept at making strategic human capital decisions that differentiate treatment of teachers based on performance and school needs can result in improved student achievement, more opportunities for high fliers, and support that leads to improvement for lower-performing teachers. A simple example relates to how principals determine their staffing for the coming school year. Rather than simply asking teachers what or whom they want to teach and trying to accommodate them using anecdotal evidence about teacher performance and fit, principals could learn to make this a strategic exercise. They would review the stoplight data (and master schedule at the secondary level) to assess the extent to which teaching talent is leveraged to support struggling students; every department or grade level has a good representation of effective teachers; and, at the secondary level, teachers are teaching a consistent and manageable number of courses.

Principals can learn to solicit ideas from teachers about their assignments (if they don't already) or move beyond the simple question, What do you want to teach next year?, to ask questions that focus on teachers' talents, interests, and career aspirations, such as: What are your career aspirations five years from now, and what teaching assignment for next year would help you achieve them? Based on your students' achievement results, what should you be assigned to teach to provide the greatest benefit for students? What support do you need to improve your effectiveness, and what assignment would provide that? Why? Using the answers in combination with stoplight data turns a teacher assignment process that is often guided by adult interests into a strategic exercise focused on teaching expertise and responsiveness to students' needs.

Such an approach would eliminate situations that result in misuse of teacher talent and poor student results. For example, middle schools commonly find that six different teachers are teaching Algebra 1, some of whom are teaching out of their content areas. Or high schools find that they lose valuable resources when teachers who had been trained to teach struggling readers are assigned to other classes or transfer to other schools.

In addition to signaling the importance of human capital management and training principals in it, districts can use metrics of teacher effectiveness to create incentives for principals to support second-stage teachers. Tracking and reporting to principals the movement of second-stage teachers from red to yellow or from yellow to green is very similar to reporting to teachers the growth of their students. Principals become more aware of their responsibility for teacher performance. Setting goals with principals for an appropriate level of improvement and tracking the results provides a further incentive for them to address the needs of second-stage teachers. Tying this to principals' compensation is both an incentive and an investment in leaders who are true human capital managers.

4. Invest in systems that recognize effective teaching as a reason for teachers to advance.

Using measured effectiveness as a means to recognize and advance the specific career and professional development interests of second-stage teachers calls for a different approach to how school and school district business is done. It places a premium on attending to teacher effectiveness immediately after a teacher has been granted tenure. Since the current practice is to pay little, if any, attention to this segment of the faculty, doing so calls for the realignment of district systems, especially measurement systems, information systems, human resource systems, and professional and leadership development systems, none of which are currently focused on managing the talent of recently tenured teachers.

Measurement and information systems have to assume new burdens. Leaders and teachers alike would want to know more about their performance and that of their peers and of the teachers in their schools, now that the information matters. Under the current system, school districts do not expect to assess teacher effectiveness or track that information over time. Statistically rigorous measures of longitudinal learning, such as value-added measures, are easier to work with than before, but they are neither easy to set up nor perfect. The information subsystems that make them work, such as methods for associating students accurately with teachers, require concerted effort to design and implement. And though we may wish for multiple measures of student learning to balance the information provided by value-added measures, pragmatic measures of student learning—such as reading diagnostics, benchmark exams, end-of-course tests, or Advanced Placement tests—are less common and therefore less definitive. As with value-added measures, only more use will lead to better, wiser use. Too much caution therefore will only slow development in the field.

Human resource systems also need to be built or revamped. By and large, these systems are passive, especially after a teacher reaches tenure, and not geared to support school district leaders' active talent management. The systems make only the simplest distinctions among their teachers—counting years of service and hours of accrued graduate credit. They are designed after decades of policy, practice, and culture to not make distinctions based on individual teacher effectiveness. Thus, distinguishing among teachers based on effectiveness calls for new ways of keeping records, organizing and presenting information to school employees, and organizing teachers' jobs, so that teachers advance independently of one another, rather than in lockstep. These new measurement systems create a larger body of information that teachers, principals, and other leaders will have access to over the course of a career. Just as student information systems, including databases, reporting software, and user interfaces, have dramatically improved over the last decade, so too will human resources information systems have to evolve to meet new, higher expectations.

The management of teacher-evaluation information provides a good example of the kinds of changes required. Currently, evaluations of tenured teachers require almost no action by district human resource officials except in the highly unlikely circumstances that teachers are being lined up for dismissal. For the HR department, the teacher-evaluation process is largely an exercise in filing papers. Access is limited and confidential. Principals seldom drive to the central office to review evaluations when making hiring decisions, let alone use the information to inform tactical talent-management decisions. School and district leaders do not review teacher evaluations to differentiate professional development or ensure that individuals have appropriate curricular support.

Imagine the implications if teacher evaluations are used to make meaningful career decisions. Teachers would want their evaluations to be precise, at least in part because they would be reviewed in decisions to hire them into positions of advanced responsibility. Evaluators would need to be well trained in the process and able to write meaningful evaluations that were standards-based and calibrated to ensure consistency in ratings. The records would be important documents for leaders and teachers alike. They would need to be accessible online in a way that ensures teachers' privacy but also allows principals and others to refer to evaluations easily when making decisions. The information management system would allow for aggregating evaluation data across teachers and disaggregating performance on particular standards to assess progress and guide professional development.

Differentiated Treatment of High Fliers

Among second-stage teachers, high fliers have demonstrated the greatest capacity to accelerate student achievement and the greatest interest in new responsibilities, advancement, and recognition. Targeting these performers for retention and advancement and creating overall upward mobility in the teaching ranks have the potential to systematically drive improved student performance. By focusing on a relatively small number of high performers who significantly outperform average performers, districts recognize for advancement a group already making a difference. This avenue to retaining high performers does not exist in current practice. By focusing first on the high fliers, the district would send culture-altering signals. It would build a culture within the district in which performance and results have consequence for a career and set a high standard for teachers who have not earned tenure.

The identification of high fliers is easy once a system to measure teacher effectiveness is in place. By using a mix of value-added data, classroom observations, and measures of teacher collegiality, districts can apply consistent standards. Initially tying this distinction to tenure makes it more meaningful in a teacher's career, as it serves as both the entrance into the profession and the gateway to additional opportunities for the highest-performing teachers. Using these indicators, principals would have an important role to play in identification, recognizing their role as human capital managers.

Once high fliers are identified, their preparation and deployment set the stage for their success, job satisfaction, and impact. Early efforts at creating teacher leadership roles have taught us a lot about the skills that teachers assuming leadership need to make the transition from working with children to adults and from working at the classroom level to the school or system level.[19] Understanding adult development and learning and how to be influential at different levels of the system are critical skills high fliers need to accompany their content knowledge and teaching expertise.

By forming a "career development institute" (CDI), districts could recognize high fliers, teach them these skills, and create a new way of managing teacher talent that is not limited by any current policy constraints.[20] Participation in the CDI would be voluntary for those eligible, based on their performance; the district and principals would actively recruit teachers who are eligible. Participation would both be an honor and provide a new challenge. Initial involvement might last a year, as high fliers learn instructional leadership skills and apply them in new contexts: leadership within a group of teachers; leadership in driving school improvement at their school or others in their district; district professional or curriculum development and implementation assignments; work in district departments or on district initiatives where teacher talent and input are critical. The training could be differentiated so that high fliers could participate at an introductory level and then assume leadership roles, returning over time for more advanced training.

The CDI would recognize the broader impact that teachers can have in schools and the system while maintaining their classroom assignments. The focus would be on honoring the value of the classroom as the location of teachers' most significant impact and also signaling to the rest of the faculty the importance of outstanding classroom performance to the district. Participation would be the pathway to differentiated roles and pay based on the various roles and teachers' effectiveness in them. It would provide both the talent development needed to be successful in those roles and explicit training in career management to help teachers think about their work in teaching as a career that offers different opportunities, phases, and incentives.

Most assignments would either focus on enhancing teachers' impact in the classroom and on student learning or providing them with opportunities to pursue outside the school day or year. Teachers who complete a course in the CDI would be organized into a talent pool that would continue to serve a wide range of district jobs, including classroom assignments, but that could be a source of first consideration for turnaround assignments, teacher leadership assignments, and other jobs that require advanced knowledge and skills. While some assignments might take teachers out of their classrooms for temporary rotations of several years or for part of the school day, the emphasis would be on leveraging teachers' talents while they continue to teach children.

Schools and school districts would do well by developing a range of differentiated responsibilities for these accomplished second-stage teachers. School leadership teams would define some of the jobs at the school level in order to ensure immediate relevance to the needs of students in the school's community. Other jobs would be district-controlled and program-based, intended to drive improved student performance at a broader scale. All assignments would have financial incentives. The work opportunities would include jobs that are becoming more familiar to teachers, like mentoring and instructional coaching, and would also introduce new ways of leveraging teaching expertise that could drive new innovations. The roles we envision include:

- *Differentiated teaching assignments.* This approach could focus on assigning high fliers to either smaller than usual classes of the most struggling students to accelerate their learning or to larger classes of students learning at or above grade level. The goal is to maximize the impact of high fliers on student achievement, to use district resources efficiently, and to ensure equity.

- *Eleven-month contracts.* Adding another month to the contract of high fliers would allow them to work intensively over the summer in an area of district need that taps their specific talents. Curriculum development, benchmark assessment development, and taking a leadership role in summer training and development of teachers are all examples of projects for the additional month.

- *Summer fellowships in central office.* This approach would bridge the divide between schools and the central office. It both leverages the expertise of teachers to guide district initiatives and cultivates future central office leaders. With meaningful stretch assignments in departments, along with seminars that provide access to district leaders and build understanding of the district improvement strategy, high fliers could learn about the district's role in school improvement and student achievement and gain concrete skills.

- *Turnaround specialists.* This opportunity would cluster a group of high fliers in the most struggling schools to catalyze improvement. The teachers assume leadership roles with other teachers related to key elements of the turnaround plan (e.g., the use of student data to drive instruction, intensive literacy development) and work to improve the culture in the school to support improvement.

These examples offer a starting point for thinking about how to simultaneously recognize high fliers' talent and leverage it to drive improvement. Creating opportunities for high fliers to come together and think about their work and their impact will surely generate many more ideas. Making this reflection and conversation part of the CDI would likely further motivate participants, guide the system in deploying them, and generate innovations.

As districts consider the CDI idea and differentiated roles, they should probably start small with a limited number of initiatives likely to have transformative impact. The small scale would not require immediate perfection of systemwide solutions for information management or professional development, and would allow the district to deploy high fliers at a reasonable pace for opportunities that it could carefully manage to ensure the capacity and culture required for success. At its most fully functional, this approach to differentiating would be broadened to serve high-flying school and district leaders, model talent management at every level of the system, and build organizational capacity and succession planning.

Coda: An Agenda That's Doable

If anything, this agenda of policies and practices is moderate. The primary impulse in constructing it is to call for schoolwide and districtwide application of sound performance and talent management practices that currently occur randomly in our schools. The current policy climate discourages but does not entirely prevent leaders from using performance information to develop the careers of teachers after they are tenured. Great principals are always looking to combine talent and opportunity, and many second-stage teachers actively seek pathways for advancement that offer new challenges commensurate with their accomplishment.[21] And by focusing on a specific programmatic intervention—the creation of the CDI for high fliers—the agenda provides a concrete example of how a school district could consciously optimize its talent management efforts to create durable and lasting improvement in overall student performance. The premise of the CDI is simple: by focusing on top performers, a school district can preserve a population of potential gap-closing teachers immediately. Even if the framework poses some large-scale systems problems, such as rethinking access to and use of teacher performance information, they are the right problems for school districts to solve. Moreover, the CDI does not involve changes in collective bargaining agreements or state laws and policies. It is a doable agenda and points to relatively easy places to start, not only for improving career opportunities for teachers, but also for driving improvement in student achievement.

Once this simple agenda is established, it is easy to imagine building on it. Clearly, the work of managing the performance and talent of the teaching work force can be more extensive; just as we tend to the career development interests of second-stage teachers, we can also tend to those needs in other segments of the teaching work force. One virtue of the proposed agenda is that is treats teachers as if they were individuals, not replaceable parts. That individuality is evident in their performance and is articulated across their career through professional development, advancement to new roles and responsibilities, honest feedback from leaders and peers, support for learning new or difficult skills, and so on. These same principles of individualization could extend throughout the teaching work force, for instance, by creating new opportunity for teachers in other segments of their careers as well. In any case, the motivation would be the same: we can improve student performance by making the job of teaching more engaging for effective teachers.

$$\left(\overset{\curvearrowright}{8}\right)$$

Weaving the Pieces Together

A Framework for Managing Human Capital in Schools

Rachel E. Curtis

Building a human capital management system in education is about transforming how we do business to ensure that all students learn at high levels and graduate college- and career-ready. Transformation happens when we put together promising and related ideas and initiatives that are focused on the same outcome in a coherent, systemic, and systematic way that drives action and gets results. The previous chapters have outlined the components of a system. The first section is about making human capital management a priority, with chapter 1 highlighting high-leverage actions that districts can pursue to strengthen teacher human capital. The second section is about recruiting, retaining, and leveraging talented teachers.

Building a human capital management system for teachers that has the potential to transform student achievement requires school systems to simultaneously create and integrate infrastructure and innovations. To bring these two pieces together, this chapter combines the ideas from the previous chapters into a framework for a comprehensive system, illustrating the full spectrum of elements and how they fit together.

Intentionally building a human capital system is difficult in school systems where the prevailing culture is one of putting out fires. We can observe this reactive tendency when we scurry to fill teaching vacancies as the first day of school looms, or when we ignore chronically low-performing teachers because dealing with them is too difficult or, alternatively, pursue them tenaciously without addressing the underlying issues that led to their performance.

The preceding chapters have introduced various ideas about human capital. Some ask us to think in new ways about long-standing practices (teacher preparation, tenure), while others introduce elements that have not yet been part of the discussion about districts, school leaders, and their partners driving the quality of teaching. To help us synthesize these ideas and move from a reactive to an intentional and proactive stance, we need to show that by connecting the pieces, we can transform teaching careers, teaching quality, and student achievement.

The framework for managing teacher human capital integrates and synthesizes the big ideas outlined in previous chapters. After providing a brief explanation of the framework and its development process, this chapter examines each element of the framework, juxtaposing current conditions and best practices. It considers the interrelationship of the elements and how to integrate them to create a robust human capital management system for teachers. Finally, it reiterates the most important guiding ideas.

A Framework for Human Capital Management

We first introduced the initial draft of this framework in the summer of 2007 at a workshop on human capital management in urban education facilitated by the Aspen Institute's Education and Society Program. While developing the framework, we created a visual model that illustrates the elements of human capital management to orient people to a process that was largely unfamiliar in the education sector. The framework has since been shared widely and has undergone extensive refinement, informed by feedback from superintendents, human resources managers, and other practitioners in school systems; policy experts; higher education faculty and staff; leaders of nonprofit organizations that work in this arena in partnership with school districts; and experts in human capital management. The framework is an effort to simultaneously capture both the complexity and simplicity of the human capital enterprise in education. It reflects knowledge gleaned from the most promising work in education and other sectors that have well-developed human capital systems, policy trends, the research base on human resources, human capital management, and effective teaching (see appendix A for a resource guide to the research base that undergirds the framework).

We designed the framework to provide a common way of thinking about human capital management and guide our actions. It addresses the phases of a teacher's career, the critical benchmarks, and levers for support and accountability and signals the interrelationships of each (see figure 8.1 for a graphic representation of the framework).

Figure 8.1   Framework for human capital management in K–12

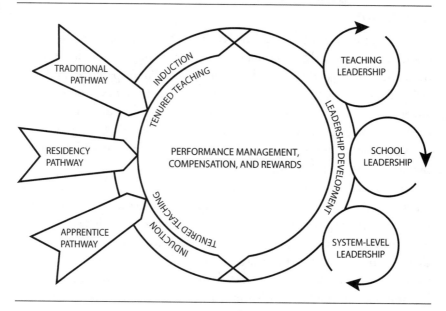

The goals of the framework reflect the ideas introduced throughout the book: increase the talent level of people entering the profession; accelerate the growth and development of all teachers, with a particular focus on high performers; and align training, development, compensation, and rewards with performance. The framework offers ways of thinking about how a wider pathway into teaching might look and how districts can think more strategically about teacher leadership. Three major elements of the framework—pathways into teaching; induction and tenure; and leadership opportunities—represent the progression of teachers through their careers. The performance management, compensation, and rewards element anchors the framework because it relates to every teacher from the point of hire on. The integration of these four elements has the potential to affect every teacher's growth, development, and effectiveness.

Looking more closely at each of the four elements of the framework allows us to juxtapose current conditions with a vision for the possibilities in order to illuminate the opportunities for improvement. Placing the ideas and innovations introduced in the previous chapters in the context of the framework helps us to begin to build a bridge from current conditions to the vision.

Pathways into Teaching

What's Broken?

As noted in chapters 5 and 6, the teacher-preparation monopoly run by higher education is dysfunctional. The programs tend to be far removed from the daily experiences and realities of classroom practice, and they lack accountability for the effectiveness of the teachers they produce. They are often expensive; have low entry standards, which are often not aligned to the characteristics of successful teachers; and have a history of being unresponsive to the market, producing teachers for grades and subjects that are in the least demand.

There are a series of perverse incentives built into the structure of traditional programs. Teacher education is a significant revenue generator for many universities, so programs have incentives to accept whoever applies, rather than to be selective. As a result, the programs often cater to a student population that performs less well than average on standard measures of talent,[1] and as many as half of those who graduate with a degree in education never teach.[2] In addition, higher education has little incentive to track or be held responsible for the effectiveness of its graduates. In most cases, the relationship between students studying to be teachers and the university that prepares them ends at graduating, before they ever begin teaching. When strung together, all these facts create a strange reality where the actual impact of the programs on students and their learning is relatively low. The lack of data about graduates' performance gives programs little information to drive improvement. Furthermore, the lack of accountability for graduates' performance in the classroom creates few incentives for the programs to do anything different.

It is not clear that the traditional, linear progression from preparation that culminates in state teaching certification, to district screening and hiring, and then to induction is the most efficient way to ensure every child has an effective teacher. Because preparation programs are not highly selective, districts weed through a high volume of applicants who have completed programs in search of the most qualified ones or mistakenly interpret program completion as a sign of quality. The expansion of teacher-induction programs in recent years is an acknowledgment by districts that new teachers need extensive support to be successful and that districts are responsible for providing it. While it is important for districts to support new teachers, it is striking and discouraging to see how much support many new teachers from traditional preparation programs need.

In the past decade, the primary alternative to traditional higher education preparation has been fast-track alternative certification programs. The design of these programs reflects an indictment of and shift from traditional programs. They offer little advanced preparation before aspiring teachers assume full responsibility for students and their learning. Prospective teachers learn for six to eight weeks in the summer, entering schools in the fall as the teacher of record. The follow-up support these teachers receive once they are in the classroom is often quite limited.

At least in part because their preparation fails to orient teachers to the realities of the classroom and schools, new teachers' attrition rate nears 50 percent in high-poverty districts at the end of three years.[3] Given research that shows teachers don't realize their potential as teachers for three to five years, this rate creates a revolving door for new teachers who never have the chance to hone their practice to the point where they provide excellent education to students.[4] Recent research gives the most damning assessment of current approaches to teacher preparation by illustrating that there is no discernable difference in the effectiveness of teachers in supporting student learning based on the type of preparation teachers have received.[5] This assessment has led to proposals to eliminate teacher credentials as a means of ensuring quality and instead measure teachers' effect on student learning as a more effective method.

Yet, despite the well-documented problems with traditional preparation programs, the answer is not simply to scrap preparation altogether and allow anyone to teach and measure their success after. That would create too many opportunities for teachers to do real damage to children's learning before their performance was measured. Rather, the answer is to reconceptualize teacher preparation so that it positively affects a teacher's effectiveness in facilitating student learning. The reconsideration of teacher preparation addresses these fundamental aspects:

- The environment and conditions in which prospective teachers best learn to teach
- The role of theory, research, and practice in teacher preparation
- The role of expert teachers and schools in training aspiring teachers
- The design of preparation that provides meaningful leadership roles and career pathways for expert teachers
- The boundary between preparation and induction and its permeability

- The criteria for screening applicants to preparation programs and the role of districts in this process
- The cost of teacher preparation and who pays for it
- Alignment of the supply and demand of trained teachers
- Indicators of teacher effectiveness and their use
- Graduate effectiveness data for assessing and driving preparation program improvement

How Can We Fix It?

The pathways in the framework—traditional, residency, and apprentice—address many of these aspects (see figure 8.2).

There are multiple pathways into teaching and guiding principles that inform each. The fundamental principles of pathways include:

1. *Responsiveness.* Preparation is aligned with the needs and interests of schools and school systems. The focus of preparation—whether run by the district, a higher education institution, or a partnership that includes community-based organizations—is defined by the demographics and staffing needs of the district. If community de-

Figure 8.2   Pathways into teaching

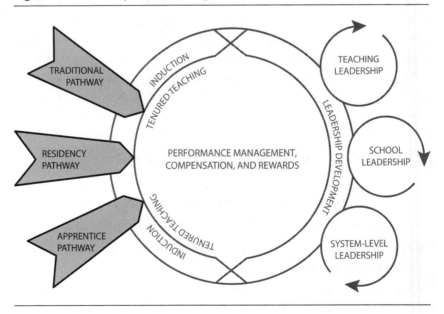

mographics project an increase in the number of Spanish-speaking children, for example, preparation responds by training prospective teachers with strategies to teach English language learners and preparing a significant number of bilingual and ELL teachers.

2. *Reality-based.* Preparation is closely tied to the real work of student learning, teaching practice, and schools, with expert teachers playing a significant role in preparation. Preparation occurs in classrooms under the tutelage of effective teachers. Prospective teachers participate in the adult community of learning by taking part in grade-level/subject area teacher meetings and school-based training and development. They are also intentionally introduced to the larger schoolwide issues and structures that require teacher leadership, such as student data management teams, instructional leadership teams, school site councils, and so on.

3. *High standards.* Standards for entering teaching are high, performance benchmarks are established along the way, and those whose performance does not measure up are counseled out of the system. Aspiring teachers might need more time and support to meet standards, so programs are structured to provide differentiated supports based on performance and need.

4. *Professional culture.* Preparation is structured to build and support a collaborative professional culture in teaching. Aspiring teachers are taught the habits of continuous improvement by reflecting on their practice through formal inquiry processes and more frequent, less formal reflections. They work collaboratively with their colleagues as well as teachers and staff in the school to provide the best possible instruction to students.

Each of the framework's three pathways—traditional, residency, and apprentice—reflects these principles. Across the pathways, there is selectivity at the front end to raise overall teaching quality. Most of the preparation takes place in the classroom, with the aspiring or novice teachers taking on more and more responsibility over time. Support is differentiated, and there are clear performance benchmarks, with poor performers winnowed out. The biggest differences among the pathways relate to when the aspiring teacher becomes the teacher of record and who runs the program. Districts need to think about the relative advantages of each pathway and how they could pursue all three pathways to meet their teacher staffing needs.

The traditional pathway is a vastly improved version of current higher education programs. The appeal of this pathway is that districts can choose the level of involvement they want to have in preparing teachers. The role can range from full partner in design and implementation to full delegation. This makes the traditional pathway appealing to districts with different levels of capacity. A district that has a clear vision of what it wants the traditional pathway to look like and staff who can teach or co-teach courses can be a full partner in program design and implementation. If the district's capacity is limited, it can find a higher education partner willing to refine its programs and defer most program design and execution tasks to the partner. The district doesn't need to build the internal capacity and infrastructure required to create and run a program.

The residency pathway, which is deeply explored in chapter 6, gives districts a voice in tailoring a program to its needs. With a mix of district, community-based organizations, and higher education institutions as partners, residencies can tap broad expertise and engage the district, without leaving the district totally responsible for program design and implementation. Residencies prepare teachers in response to district staffing projections to ensure that the teachers they prepare are those the system needs. They also prepare teachers for the district's students and the district curriculum, using the selected instructional materials and assessments in the training. As a result, residency-trained teachers generally transition smoothly after they graduate from the program and become teachers of record. The selectivity of residency programs gives districts a higher-quality and often more diverse pool than the traditional pathway. One of the greatest benefits of the residency pathway is that it requires districts to develop teacher leadership roles (e.g., mentors and site directors) and target particular schools to serve as training sites and placement sites for clusters of graduates. This helps districts develop schools with strong cultures of collaboration and adult learning and differentiated teaching roles that can serve as models. Because of the intense training, residency graduates can be clustered in schools with the goal of influencing culture and classroom practice and improving schools. The skills that graduates of residencies have in reflecting on their practice, engaging in action research, and pursuing continuous improvement prepare them to be powerful teacher leaders.

The apprentice pathway, the fast track into the classroom, can target teachers for high-needs areas. As such, it is valuable to districts facing serious teacher shortages. Because program participants become teachers of record after a brief summer training, the program is, by necessity, practice-driven. The problems of practice that participants face every day in the classrooms become the vehicle for learning. The apprentice pathway is also designed to recruit top talent because of the appeal of earning a teacher's salary with a minor investment. Built into the design is the assumption that some teachers will be a bad fit. Counseling some to leave is part of the program design, which gives districts the opportunity to keep the bar high and make difficult decisions. Apprentice programs are often run by local or national organizations that have strong experience and expertise in teacher preparation and induction. Districts can hire them to lead the work and then step back, which is particularly helpful if the district has limited capacity.

Induction and Tenure

What's Broken?

Currently, certification, induction, and tenure are treated discretely and with little intentionality. Certification is awarded before induction, based on completion of a program, courses passed, the attainment of (often minimal) scores on standardized tests, and a minimal number of hours for practice teaching. It is the rubber stamp at the end of preparation programs, which makes it difficult for districts to use certification as anything other than a low bar for entry. It does not reflect any assessment of teaching effectiveness.

Many districts have begun to focus on induction. Organizations such as the New Teacher Center have helped districts develop induction support aligned to standards of teaching and differentiated based on new teacher needs. Yet, in many districts, induction is a series of unconnected professional development sessions that cover a wide array of topics without supporting new teachers to successfully address any of them effectively. The expectations of what new teachers should know and do as a result of induction support and the measurement and use of the resulting data are often never addressed or are quite murky. There is little or no relationship between teachers' performance (or even participation) in induction and the provision of tenure.

Tenure is when a district commits to a teacher for as long as he or she chooses to teach, barring any extreme performance issues or egregious acts. For most districts, tenure has become something awarded on the first or last day of the third year of teaching, timing generally mandated in state statutes. It is quite common for teachers to be awarded tenure by default because the deadline arrives and no one has made a conscious, proactive decision about whether the teacher has earned it or not. In such circumstances, tenure becomes an administrative matter, rather than a high-stakes, high-bar assessment of teaching effectiveness and a celebration of excellence and entrance into a profession. As noted earlier, this decision costs $3 million over the lifetime of a teacher, a stunning reality considering how casually that decision is often made.

The results of this haphazard approach to certification, induction, and tenure are striking. The attrition rate remains high, and research suggests that some top performers leave because of poor organizational conditions, including lack of support and professional culture.[6] For those who remain, the tenure rate is high, yet it has no connection to teaching effectiveness, often leaving districts owning tenured teachers who are ineffective. Given these realities, we have to question the purposes of certification, induction, and tenure. How might they be better designed and integrated to ensure teacher effectiveness?

How Can We Fix It?

Certification is a state policy over which districts have little authority. Districts may lobby for changes in certification policies, but it's not clear that is the best use of their limited resources, unless the policies contradict district values and reduce teaching quality. The framework doesn't address certification, focusing instead on induction and tenure to ensure that policies and practices for teachers in their beginning years ameliorate the inadequacies of certification and ensure that those who earn tenure are well qualified and effective (see figure 8.3).

In the framework, the guiding principles that inform induction and tenure are:

Standards-based. Both induction and tenure review are driven by standards of effective teaching, which reflect a school system's values and research on the instructional practices that lead to increased student learning. Induction focuses on building teachers' skills in these areas; tenure review is the point at which decisions are made about teacher performance against standards. As chapter 1 outlines, the development of these standards is the work of school systems.

Figure 8.3   Induction and tenure

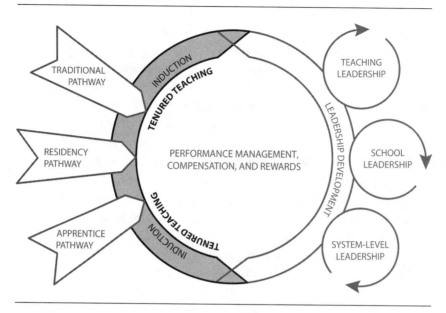

Integration. Induction and tenure review represent a coherent pathway to a career in teaching. The performance benchmarks at each step are articulated, and achievement of them leads to tenure.

Differentiation. While the standards provide a clear image of effective performance, induction support is differentiated in response to an individual teacher's needs. Through measures of teachers' impact on student learning, classroom observation data, self-evaluation, and feedback from others, the competence of new teachers is assessed regularly against the standards during the induction process. As chapter 5 explains, the results of this assessment guide new teachers' career progression and their individual development plans, which are focused on the standards, differentiated based on skills, and amended regularly to drive continuous improvement. High performers are identified, and their development and performance is tracked and accelerated.

Induction can be differentiated based on the preparation pathway that teachers choose. The induction of traditionally trained teachers builds on their preparation, using program exit assessments that are mapped to the system's teaching standards. From this assessment, teachers and their supervisors develop individual plans with performance benchmarks building to the tenure process. The district sets the standards, tracks new teachers' progress toward them, and supports and makes suggestions to principals in the design of induction efforts. Induction resources are devolved to schools, leaving the principal to build a school-designed support structure or to take advantage of centrally designed support.

Residency-trained teachers are often placed in a school as a cluster of new teachers. This ensures a built-in support network and collegiality. It also allows the residency program to work with a manageable number of receiving schools to organize induction support according to the standards and practices of observation, reflection, collaboration, and skill building taught in the residency. Clustering can also be a way to build a critical mass of new teachers to leverage improvement in schools. Because residency-trained teachers are deeply integrated into all aspects of schools in their residency year, they are well positioned to influence whole-school improvement once they become fully-fledged teachers. To make this viable, clusters of new teachers need to be partnered with groups of experienced, effective teachers to ensure strong induction support and to reach critical mass that creates a tipping point for improvement in schools.

For teachers who pursue the apprentice pathway, induction is equivalent to on-the-job preparation. The reduced teaching load in the first year allows for regular intensive training. Their induction focuses on just-in-time knowledge and skill building based on the content they are teaching, the students they are teaching, and the immediate problems of their practice. This support is designed to both respond and align to the standards of effective teaching that guide tenure decisions.

Regardless of the approach to induction, tenure represents a capstone decision to usher a new teacher into the profession. The standards for tenure are high, and the process is rigorous. Elements of the tenure review include student performance, as measured through value-added assessments; observations of practice by a mix of peers and administrators; and participation in the school's professional community, measured by collaboration with peers, participation in school initiatives, and general professionalism (which can include 360-degree feedback from peers, parents, and administrators). The timing for the tenure review can either be fixed at the same moment in every teacher's career or occur within a certain window, e.g., between years three and five, based on teacher readiness. High-potential employees identified early in the induction process are placed on a fast track, with the goal of enabling them to achieve tenure within two or three years. This recognizes and rewards their performance and quickly puts them in a position to pursue leadership opportunities. Chapter 5 makes the case for a two- to three-year window for tenure and then putting teachers whose performance is acceptable but not tenure-worthy on a nontenure track. Another approach is to expect all new teachers to either achieve tenure or leave the profession by the end of their fifth year. This approach provides time for teachers who take longer than three years to reach the tenure performance bar, but it leaves open the question of what to do with teachers in high-needs areas who are performing adequately but who are not worthy of tenure.

The accountability for those involved in the tenure decision is high. Principals who oversee the tenure decisions are evaluated in part based on the performance of the teachers they recommend. Teachers involved in peers' tenure review must decide whom they will work side by side with for years and who will contribute to or detract from the learning of children in their school. In addition, if the system uses group performance incentives, a bad tenure decision may cost teachers money.

This reconceptualization of tenure would contribute powerfully to building a culture of performance and professionalism. Standards are high, colleagues make professional judgments, and the achievement of tenure has significant implications for teachers' futures. Tenure comes with a significant salary increase and is the gateway to opportunities for leadership at the classroom, school, or system level.

Leadership: Teaching, Schools, and System

What's Broken?

Leadership opportunities for teachers have expanded in the last decade. Pursuing the principalship is no longer the only option. Mentor teaching, instructional coaching, data management, and curriculum development are just a few of the leadership opportunities for teachers if they want to remain in or connected to the classroom. With this growth have come some challenges. The opportunities can be quite transient; they are often among the first things cut in tough economic times, or they rely heavily on external funding, which is less predictable. The level of strategic thinking and design of these efforts tends to be quite varied. Sometimes teachers with great potential are thrown into difficult roles without the right support, leading to high attrition and/or limited success. Furthermore, the opportunities tend to be created in a vacuum, with little organization and coordination of the roles into a leadership pathway for teachers. It is often unclear how the different roles relate to one another and how pursuing one will position teachers for further advances. And they are seldom organized to provide a systemic approach to school or system improvement.

Who is eligible for these opportunities and how teachers earn them tend to vary from district to district. Some require a designation of lead or master teacher, something the system confers. The criteria for conferring that status are often vague and not well aligned to teacher effectiveness in supporting student learning and teacher collegiality. The mix of skills a teacher leader needs to be successful in particular roles is often not well understood or considered, and districts rarely screen teachers for these abilities or provide sufficient support to enable teachers to succeed in these roles. A common example is a teacher who demonstrates tremendous effectiveness in helping students learn and is given a position as lead teacher. She is expected to talk about her own practice, share her expertise, and facilitate adult learning, but she is given little preparation to develop these skills. As a result, a teacher often struggles to make the transition into these roles, perhaps getting some training and support on the job, working to stay one step ahead of the demands of the position. At best, the result is a stressful transition for teacher leaders and compromised effectiveness early on. At worst, the investment in these positions is wasted, people with potential leave out of frustration, and the system settles for mediocre performance.

How Can We Fix It?

The proposed framework introduces several key principles of effective teacher leadership development:

1. *Leveraging talent.* Identifying and targeting high-potential employees—those teachers who in their first few years distinguish themselves as very talented—is a strategy for retaining top talent. As discussed in chapter 7, focusing on this select group accelerates their growth and development, moves them as quickly as possible into roles that leverage their talents, increases their value to the organization, and compensates them through opportunities, prestige, and differentiated pay.

2. *Competency-driven.* Clear competencies and criteria for leadership roles and performance measures are used to assess applicants to ensure quality. Training is aligned to the competencies, and the competencies can be used before, during, and after training to assess teachers' readiness and can serve as the foundation for supervision and evaluation once on the job.

3. *Strategic and systemic.* The development and deployment of teacher leaders provides an ongoing resource that enables the district to address its highest priorities. The district makes long-range plans to identify, prepare and tap teacher leadership to address anticipated needs. By doing so, the district gives teachers a sense of the progression of leadership opportunities over time. It provides them with dynamic images of what choosing to stay in teaching offers—a sharp contrast to the traditional image in which the first day on their twentieth year of teaching looks remarkably similar to the first day of their second year.

4. *Ongoing development.* Training for aspiring teacher leaders before they assume roles accelerates their effectiveness once on the job and improves their job satisfaction. Such training builds their readiness for the roles and forces the district to anticipate and address likely implementation issues that could compromise the teacher leaders' effectiveness. Providing ongoing training once teachers are on the job—focused on skill building and implementation problem solving—creates a culture of continuous learning that supports their ongoing development.

The proposed framework outlines three leadership pathways—teaching, school, and system—which are also reflected in examples of differentiated roles in chapter 7 (see figure 8.4). The rationale behind these pathways is that effective teachers can contribute through their work in the classroom, through leadership in the school, or through system improvement efforts. The variety of options responds to the different interests of high performers, ensures their job satisfaction, and improves retention.

Classroom leadership can take many forms. Assuming responsibility for the learning of a larger or more challenging than normal group of students is one option. Another is opening one's classroom to other teachers— aspiring, new, experienced, and struggling—to share promising instructional practices. A third is to create new ways of organizing instruction

Figure 8.4 Leadership: teaching, schools, and systems

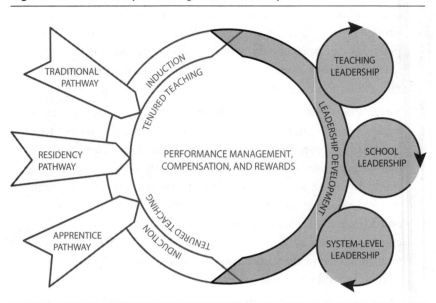

to address stubborn learning challenges, such as through team teaching, looping, or leveraging technology to fundamentally redesign instruction. Another option is piloting curriculum or pedagogical innovations.

School leadership opportunities expand teachers' sphere of influence beyond the classroom, allowing them to have schoolwide impact. They provide teachers the chance to learn how schools function as organizations and how to drive school improvement. Analyzing data is one example; such work gives teachers the chance to assess school improvement progress, identify instructional priorities at the grade and school levels, and strategize how to use data effectively. Serving on a school leadership team or improvement planning team is another example that affords teachers the chance to see the school holistically and understand the building blocks of effective schools.

System-level leadership leverages teacher talent to influence how the system functions. These opportunities build teachers' understanding of the system's role in guiding school improvement and the interplay between the levels of the organization—classroom, school, central office—and allow them to contribute to systemic improvement. Systemic opportunities include developing or piloting new curriculum and assessments, designing and implementing a peer assistance and review program, and defining effective teaching standards and the metrics used to assess performance.

This mix of leadership opportunities will make teaching a dynamic and rewarding career. Such a mix is possible because these pathways are simultaneously distinct, related, and permeable. Imagine the career trajectory of a top-performing third grade teacher who has a particular interest and expertise in literacy. During her career as a teacher, she might move through various roles: model literacy teacher, literacy coach, turnaround teacher assigned to a low-performing school and responsible for facilitating the third grade team, founding teacher of a new school, member of district literacy curriculum (or assessment) design team, member of a school improvement planning team, and central-office literacy curriculum coordinator.

There is no single linear progression through these roles. They are simply opportunities toward which teachers can grow and from which they can choose over the course of their careers, based on their interests. They allow teachers to stay in the classroom, if that is their preference, while creating more permeable boundaries between classrooms, schools, and the system, for teachers who aspire to move between those levels of the district.

Performance Management, Compensation, and Rewards

What's Broken?

Performance management is a term used in other sectors to encompass supervision, evaluation, training, and development, all of which are integrated. As discussed in chapter 3, supervision is an ongoing process, punctuated by an annual or biannual summative evaluation. Training and development are aligned to performance, as is compensation. The traditional practice in education looks almost nothing like that. Teacher training and development are seldom connected to supervision and evaluation, except possibly in the case of poor performers. Yet while training is tied to compensation, as pursuing course work is one of the ways teachers increase their salary, compensation is divorced from supervision and evaluation. The lack of coherence of these levers, the lack of their integration to drive improvement, and the perverse incentives built into the system create a performance management, compensation, and rewards system that does not promote effective teaching.

Looking closely at the current conditions related to the individual components of this element of the framework makes the problems much clearer. Embedded in the idea of supervision and evaluation is the belief that professionals need ongoing support and feedback, as well as regular summative assessments of their performance, to support their improvement. Yet in reality, teachers seldom have regular opportunities to talk about their practice or get differentiated support to improve their performance. Instead, assessment of teacher performance happens every one to three years, a process that is sometimes reduced to a single twenty- to forty-minute classroom observation and a rating of satisfactory or unsatisfactory, with little additional information to guide improvement.

Training also is disconnected from performance. Whereas in other sectors, an employee and his or her supervisor would jointly develop a training plan based on an evaluation of practice, in education, teachers can choose from a diverse menu of training options that may not have anything to do with their needs for ongoing development. Moreover, the quality of training varies, its alignment to standards for professional development and standards for teaching practice is inconsistent, and it is often designed in a scattershot way that is too far removed from the practice of teaching to be effective. The primary incentive to participate in training is that the accrual of graduate credits leads to salary increases.

Teacher compensation is likewise uncoupled from performance. Teachers earn higher pay based on course credits and years of service, not their effectiveness in improving student learning. The emphasis on these variables communicates the belief that years on the job and continuing education are what matter the most. Yet there is little data supporting them as important contributors to teaching effectiveness. While there are clear challenges associated with aligning compensation to performance, the conversation in education has only recently shifted from dismissing the idea to exploring how to make it fair and manageable.

How Can We Fix It?

Performance management, compensation, and rewards serve as the centerpiece of our proposed framework because they affect all teachers and therefore have the potential to be key drivers to improve performance (see figure 8.5).

There are two guiding principles that drive this element of the framework:

1. *Aligned, integrated, and cyclical.* Training and compensation are aligned to teacher performance. High performers are recognized for

Figure 8.5   Performance management, compensation, and rewards

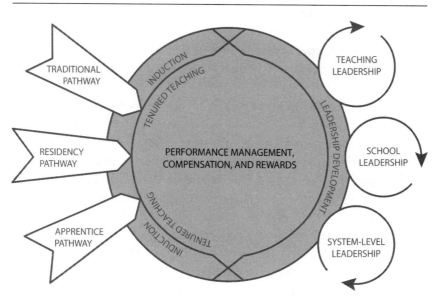

their efforts, and low performers are incentivized to improve and given support and plans for improvement. There is a regular cycle of performance management to support continuous improvement.

2. *Right incentives.* Compensation and rewards systems signal the district's commitment to improving student learning. They create incentives to focus on highly effective teaching, improved student learning, continuous improvement, and collaboration, rather than seat time and the accrual of course credits.

Performance management forms a cycle of improvement. Teachers and their supervisors assess their performance based on student achievement results, observational data, and other artifacts of practice, collegiality, and professionalism. From that analysis, each teacher, working in partnership with a supervisor, develops an individual learning plan, which outlines the supports needed and how they will be provided, along with a time line and benchmarks. The problems teachers face in their practice drive training and development, as advocated in chapter 5. Training and development are facilitated through a variety of vehicles: grade level/department teams; teacher collaboration on curriculum planning, instructional strategies, and assessment; action research that lets teachers use their classroom as a laboratory for learning; classroom observations; and pursuit of new knowledge and skills through book studies and course work. The supervisor supports the implementation of the plan by helping teachers identify resources (e.g., other teachers to observe or partner with, course work, action research, readings).

Once implementation of the plan is underway, the supervisor regularly observes the teachers, provides feedback on progress, and talks with them in order to support continued development. The supervisor and teachers review student performance data to assess progress, refine plans, and set new learning goals as needed. The supervisor then reflects on all supervision data and makes a summative evaluation of teachers' performance. This assessment considers observations, student performance data, and other sources of data on teacher performance.

Compensation focuses on rewarding performance, retaining talent, and recognizing leadership. Tenure is accompanied by a significant boost (10 percent to 20 percent of salary) in compensation. Thereafter, compensation is based on the summative evaluations of teacher performance, which include measures of student learning growth, standards-based observations, and teacher professionalism and collegiality. As discussed in chapter 1, compensation rewards can be calculated at the level of the individual teacher, teachers by grade level or subject areas, or for all teachers in a school collectively, based on overall school performance. These approaches reflect different values, strategies to motivate performance, and ways to address the system's highest needs (e.g., placing high-performing teachers in the neediest schools, retaining math and science teachers). In addition, teachers who demonstrate exceptional performance and take on leadership opportunities can earn increased compensation based on the leadership roles they pursue. Sometimes they assume additional responsibilities for which they are paid. Other times they are compensated for pursuing harder teaching assignments and achieving results.

While compensation is the predictable way to recognize performance, nonmonetary rewards can be powerful motivators. Rewards can range from something as simple as additional classroom materials or a coveted parking spot to plaques and certificates recognizing a teacher as an educator of distinction. This distinction can carry privileges, including targeted training and development, a voice in school and system improvement efforts, and the opportunity to propose and/or pilot new instructional innovations. The beauty of nonmonetary rewards is that they are generally only constrained by the limits of our imagination.

The Larger Context

This human capital framework does not stand alone, but must be considered within the context of school and district cultures, policies, and practices. The first four chapters focus on the role of the district and principals, because they determine how the framework is interpreted, how the ideas are reflected in schools, and the extent to which structures, systems, support, and accountability are created that bring it to life.

At the school level, the principal's disposition and skills greatly influence the school environment, teachers' work conditions, and the approach to human capital management. Does the principal have an earn-your-stripes mentality or does she intentionally nurture young talent? Does she see career growth as something earned through seat time or a reward driven by performance? Can she coach teachers and engage in in-depth discussions of instructional practice or does she take a hands-off approach to instruction?

The culture of the school—be it toxic, deeply focused on and supportive of teacher collaboration and continuous improvement, or somewhere in between—has an impact on the extent to which human capital management is a priority. Student and teacher demographics, performance results, and mobility all influence how well positioned a school is to address human capital issues and how the school can most effectively take them on. A school with a stable population of students and teachers and a track record of strong student achievement has different needs and is positioned very differently to address human capital than one that has a turnover of students and staff and a history of failure. Resources also influence the approach to human capital. Does the school have extra resources in the form of time, people, and money to devote to working conditions and human capital priorities? Does it need to rely heavily on nonmonetary rewards to recognize performance because it is struggling to simply stay afloat?

At the district level, issues of scale, infrastructure, improvement strategy, and governance all influence how the framework can be implemented. Its application in a district of 5,000 students and 400 teachers will be fundamentally different from its application in a district of 400,000 students, 600 schools, and 25,000 teachers. The needs, resources, scale, and capacity to partner are inevitably different in those two situations. A system's level of infrastructure in the areas of human resources, training, and information management has tremendous implications for the approach to human capital management and the logical entry points. A system's approach to improving schools and student achievement also has an influence. A system that mandates the curriculum, instructional practices, and assessments that teachers use has different human capital needs than one that has devolved all decisions to the principal and has a strong accountability system. District governance also informs this work. The history of the school board's role in personnel matters influences the pursuit of human capital management, the amount of change in practice, the political implications of the work, and the best starting points.

Finally, the larger environment of districts deeply affects the implementation of human capital management. Union relationships, state policy and statutes, the labor market, and community resources all influence human capital management. There are contractual implications for bringing the framework to life that affect how systems whose teachers are union members pursue this work compared to districts that function in right-to-work states. State requirements for teacher certification and tenure statutes either drive human capital or require political action to be changed to reflect the district's human capital values. Labor market issues are a key consideration as well. A community that has sustained enormous job losses in the changing economy has a potential teaching pool that other communities lack. A community with rich higher education resources has different options than a community that has a single higher education institution or none at all. Finally, community politics affect the kinds of partnerships and resources available for human capital work. Community organizations and foundations can supplement the opportunities districts provide for high-performing teachers, for example. These opportunities vary from one district to another, based on districts' varying relationships with such organizations.

Touchstones

Given the complexity of the contextual issues and the significant shifts in beliefs and practices represented in the proposed framework, districts need to build a robust human capital management system slowly and incrementally. They cannot change everything at once. Districts have to build their capacity and prioritize their needs. The decisions of where to start the work and how it evolves are contextual and secondary to a commitment to build from that starting place to a comprehensive system. Yet the potential to ultimately transform the quality of teaching and student achievement can be realized through a series of incremental steps. There are a few key ideas to remember.

Human capital management is about improving student achievement.

Human capital improvements are a means, albeit powerful; the end is improved student achievement. Every human capital improvement made must be accompanied by a measure of its effect on student learning. Early efforts will surely be imperfect, but they must be pursued and refined so that everyone in the organization and beyond is clear about the purpose.

Human capital management is made up of interconnected pieces that must be considered together.

Addressing one element of the framework inevitably has implications for other elements. Rethinking pathways into teaching invariably surfaces misalignments of induction and tenure. Starting to identify high-potential employees creates the need to build a system of teacher leadership opportunities. Understanding these interrelationships and anticipating this reality at the outset will make the work easier and will deepen and accelerate impact. It allows districts to anticipate the next challenge and opportunity and to think in advance about the resources and capacity that it needs to develop, the contractual and policy implications, and how to set the stage.

There are particular levers that offer the greatest opportunity to improve teaching quality.

Given the vast landscape of human capital management, making strategic decisions about what to focus on is essential. The choice of levers is contextual. Chapter 1 highlights the five levers districts can pull that have the greatest impact on teaching quality. Districts can choose from these based on their values, priorities, capacity, available resources, and political considerations. Analyzing meaningful data about student achievement and the teaching work force, balancing quick wins and longer-term improvements, and assessing capacity and resources available to support the work help inform the choice of levers.

New ways of doing business must be considered.

People outside of education are often simultaneously fascinated and horrified by certain practices (or lack thereof) in the education sector. The list includes the lack of clear ways to measure teacher effectiveness; not tying teacher effectiveness to compensation; the lack of differentiation among employees based on performance; tenure, which people outside education interpret as a near guarantee of lifetime employment; and the reality that teachers who leave teaching before they fully vest in the retirement system (usually after ten years of employment) leave behind all the money they were required to contribute to the system. It is important to imagine other ways of doing business. Without imagining, we will never muster the courage, capacity, and political will to realize improvements that could have a dramatic effect on student learning. Other sectors and charter management organizations can provide concrete images of other ways of doing business that can inspire and guide us.

Doing things differently will require new capacity, the renegotiation of roles, and new relationships.

Pointing fingers at districts, unions, or higher education will not solve the human capital problem. Each had a significant role to play in creating current conditions, and each too can play an important role in improving them. This requires redefining priorities, building new capacity, and being driven, first and foremost, by a commitment to student achievement and a belief that the quality of teaching is the most important contributor to that achievement. Engaging other partners introduces new capacity and can break long-standing logjams. Nonprofits with expertise in particular aspects of the human capital framework or community-based organizations that can navigate and mediate the district–higher education–union labyrinth can be powerful contributors, strategically exerting pressure for improvement and brokering new relationships. The school board (and mayor in communities where the mayor champions education) sets the tone. Extricating the board from the micromanagement of personnel issues to champion strategic issues of human capital management is essential. The board's alignment of resources, other supports, information management, and accountability makes human capital improvements possible and signals their importance to the district and the community.

The promise of human capital efforts is tremendous. They have the potential to make teaching a dynamic and compelling career that draws and retains top talent. Teachers would feel respected, supported, and accountable, and know that they are the critical factor in determining their students' achievement. Ultimately, the power of human capital efforts will be measured by districts' ability to raise student achievement, close persistent achievement gaps, and graduate all students who start high school with the opportunity to choose from the options of higher education, job training, or work. At the end of the day, addressing the adult human capital issues in schools is the best way to ensure we develop the human capital of students.

Conclusion

Creating the Conditions for Success

Rachel E. Curtis

Years ago, when I was training aspiring principals in one of the first residency-based principal-preparation programs, one of the students, unable to contain himself, interrupted the conversation by exclaiming, "It's all about the teachers. I finally get it. All we're talking about—improving schools, good instruction, parent engagement, better outcomes for kids— at the end of the day, it's about the teachers. They're who I need to focus on." People in the room grew silent, almost reverential. What wasn't clear in that moment was what was more compelling: the passion of his proclamation or its simple, elegant truth.

The premise of this book is that improving student achievement and opportunities demands that we improve teaching quality. The focus on teachers reflects their preeminent role in raising student achievement. Each of the preceding chapters has endeavored to uncover the implications of that simple truth for the work of districts and principals and to imagine a system of preparation, support, opportunity, and recognition that recruits talent into teaching and retains it. Reconceptualizing public education as a human capital enterprise represents a profound shift in thinking that requires an equally intense reconsideration of the role of districts and the people who work in them.

Throughout the book, the authors have proposed what needs to be done and given images of how to do it, often focusing on a particular intervention or element of the framework. When the framework is considered in its entirety and the breadth of what needs to be done to create a comprehensive human capital management system sinks in, the lingering, nagging question is: *How do you do all of this?*

There is no existence proof, no single district that has successfully tackled each of the elements of the framework and woven them together into a comprehensive human capital system for teachers. But there are districts working toward that, having engaged deeply in this work and made tremendous progress. We can learn much from the approach these districts have taken to pursue this work to greatest effect. Two lessons stand out. First, these districts have placed teacher human capital efforts in the larger context of a human capital management effort that addresses all employees. Second, they have developed a systemic human capital strategy with clear priorities and outcomes and have partnered with external resources to execute the strategy. They have cast their role as a strategic one—setting direction, leveraging resources, building the coherence of the overall system, and tracking results.

A Larger Context

The decision to expand a human capital management system that targets teaching quality to include all employees reflects several critical understandings. First, the system's ability to effectively support teachers and principals in their work of improving student learning is defined by the quality of the work force that surrounds them. Second, by definition, and for maximum effect, a robust human capital management system must serve an organization's entire work force.

Tackling the teaching quality issue is surely the most important aspect of human capital management in school systems. Yet it is only one of several elements to which systems must attend. A system can't function at its highest potential for children without a quality work force throughout the district and systems in place to ensure its continued growth and development. The human capital issue permeates every level of the organization. Classroom aides who have not been carefully screened and trained sometimes create more work for teachers than they do support. Human resource staff who have been directed to enforce rules rather than solve problems are unlikely to know how to partner with principals to address their most challenging HR dilemmas. Custodians who don't understand their role in supporting student learning make different choices about how they do their work and how they interact with students than those who understand they are an integral part of the student support system. Budget coordinators who know numbers and spreadsheets but don't understand schools can't help principals think creatively about how to use their limited resources to maximum effect for children.

The human capital challenges that districts face with their nonteaching staff are very similar to those they face with teachers: lack of a strategy to recruit, develop, and retain talent, particularly in critical central office management roles; minimal focus on performance, including a common lack of performance standards tied to job responsibilities; few ways to distinguish different levels of performance and differentiate support and opportunities; and a lack of a career trajectory for high performers. Much of what this book advocates for in building teaching quality can and eventually must be translated to the nonteaching work force in school systems. Doing so is a prerequisite to building a robust human capital management system and ensuring the system functions at its highest potential for children.

A good place to start is with the district central office. Central office departments exert enormous influence in schools. They can support effective teaching or create barriers to it. They have tremendous authority and influence as they control multimillion-dollar budgets, often serve as the conduit of resources to schools, and include staff who can either build pathways to enable innovations or erect roadblocks to stop them. Ensuring the talent of the people in those positions and their ability to work in ways that emphasize support and performance over compliance is the cornerstone to school and system improvement. Differentiating treatment of teachers, distributing leadership, and redefining the role of principals are just a few of the ideas raised in this book that implicate central office. They require different kinds of management systems (people and information). They push for more flexible ways of thinking about roles and the traditional orientation toward the principal as the single authority in schools through which all things must run. These ideas cannot succeed without the support of a central office that deeply understands that its job is to support schools and strives every day to find new ways to do that effectively.

Few school systems have a strategy to recruit, support, and retain talented central office staff. Central offices are often largely populated by people who once worked in schools and who usually obtained their positions in one of two ways. Some were identified as promising talent and were promoted to the central office. This targeting of high-performing employees is a promising human capital move. Yet districts seldom couple it with clarity about the knowledge and skills required for success on the job, recruitment and screening based on them, and support and accountability aligned to those abilities. The issues of managing the shift from a classroom or school-based orientation to a system perspective, which is a challenge for most people making this career move, are seldom explicitly addressed. As a result, people who were chosen because of their talent are often left to succeed or fail based on their own resourcefulness. The lack of attention to ensuring their success has the potential to limit their performance and retention, just as it does with teachers.

Others came to the central office because their performance in schools was so poor that they were sent "downtown" to limit the damage they could do to children. Then, once away from children, they are often ignored and allowed to further languish, serving as a drag on the system. There is, in effect, no performance management system for them. There is seldom a proactive strategy to support these employees to either improve their performance or exit the system.

Both examples reflect what is often a fairly low-level, insular approach to central office human capital in districts. The result is a wide variation in competence and job satisfaction. Performance is judged on a relative basis—is one person performing better than another?—rather than against clear standards for effectiveness; "good enough" seems to be acceptable. Districts generally don't understand how to set up systems that raise the performance level of employees and seem unaware of its profound importance. This stance leads to haphazard approaches to recruitment, selection, support, performance management, and differentiation. The resulting lack of a human capital management infrastructure makes it particularly hard for districts to compete for central office management talent and even unaware of what that requires. Yet that is the level of the organization where ensuring and nurturing talent could have an instrumental effect on central office functioning and on creating the conditions in schools that support student learning.

Districts that have made it a priority to bring business and management talent into their central offices, through targeted recruitment or participation in programs such as the Broad Residency, which supports professional with advanced degrees (MBAs, JD, and so on) with demonstrated leadership and management success, quickly learn that recruiting the talent is a key first step—just as it is with teachers. People coming into the roles from other sectors often bring with them expectations about human capital management. They anticipate having clear job responsibilities and training to execute them. Six to twelve months into their new roles, they expect feedback, what their next career move will be should they continue to excel, and their trajectory in the organization over the next three to five years. Most often, they get none of this. They are left to figure out their work and the organizational culture. When they ask about their performance, they are told they're doing a great job, with no evidence to support the claim.[1]

These are all the same issues high-potential teachers face, and there is much to be learned from the work of teacher human capital management that can inform the design of a system for high-potential central office staff. In the same way that nurturing teaching talent holds the potential to improve teaching at scale, nurturing central office leaders who have management expertise and can think in creative ways about how to support schools has the potential to transform the central office, focusing it squarely on supporting the work of schools.

Districts that have begun to address human capital management beyond the teaching force often start with the performance management system. They tie central office performance to clear metrics. These metrics are tied to goals for departmental work, and, whenever possible, they include indicators that show concretely how well the department is serving teachers, principals, and schools. Customer service data—such as the time that elapses between a principal's requests for support and receipt of it, and the principal's satisfaction with that support—are included to underscore central offices' responsibility to principals. These metrics are often made public, and department heads are held accountable for them. Department work and improvement plans are expected to address them, and the data are collected in a consistent manner so that performance can be tracked over time.

Recruiting and nurturing talent is the other area districts focus on to accelerate systemic improvement. The superintendent who spends 50 percent of his time on human capital issues gets personally involved in recruiting for key central office positions. He knows his success is tied to the capacity of his senior leadership team and other leaders of significant departments and initiatives. Superintendents who think this way search for talent in other sectors. They sell their district and think creatively about how to define key roles to make them appealing to talented candidates. They have a strategy for building their management bench, and they know that recruiting strong people is the first step toward improving the quality of the central office. They then create the right mix of training and development opportunities, assignments that stretch high performers and keep them growing and developing, and the promise of continuous career growth to retain them. In that way, districts can keep high-performing individuals on board and leverage their talents to strengthen the support they provide to schools.

Strategy, Partnership, and the Role of the School System

Beyond its effects on the individuals who work there and the support they provide to schools, a comprehensive human capital management system can transform how a school system operates. Addressing human capital management can be a powerful wedge to influence broader systemic improvement: a strategic orientation, data-driven management, high standards, and an orientation toward teachers, principals, and schools as the central office's customers. It can be the catalyst for major changes, such as building a data warehouse and an information management system or defining standards of effective teaching and organizing support based on them. If the system has the commitment to drive this level of transformation, the results can extend beyond the human capital realm to fundamentally redefine the system and its functions—and, ultimately, its students' results.

When considering the scope of the work to drive human capital improvements, though, the logical question is: *Who is going to do all this work?* The reality is that effecting systemic change in a bureaucracy is daunting and takes tremendous expertise, stamina, and political acumen. Building internal capacity through the strategies described is one way of addressing the challenge. But should all the human capital capacity rest within the district? Do school systems need to develop their own teaching standards? Should each school district work through its own requirements and process for tenure review? Must every district develop its own leadership development program for high-potential employees? There are different schools of thought. Some vehemently respond, "Yes. That is *the* work of school systems." Others are just as passionate in saying, "No, school systems are not well-positioned to do this work, and it will likely generate weak results." There isn't a right answer to this question. It depends in part on context and capacity. Yet it is worth deliberating on to ensure an approach that will realize student learning results in an efficient and sustainable way.

Many of the districts that have made the greatest progress on human capital management have strategically partnered with private organizations to tap external expertise and capacity to drive results. These partnerships have enhanced the system's capacity to respond to human capital needs and, in most instances, ensured high-quality work. When districts develop partnerships to support functions that are fundamental to the success of the organization, their role is to set up the partnership and manage it for success. Collaborating with partners to define the purpose, goals, expectations, and outcomes for partnerships; to develop a process for partnering; and to create a system of mutual accountability sets the stage for an effective partnership.

To ensure effectiveness, districts must be clear about the purpose of the partnership. Do they want to off-load a key human capital management function (e.g., teacher preparation, hiring) to achieve results quickly and eliminate dysfunctional systems and practices in the district? Or do they want to build the system's capacity to function differently or do new work? These are two points on a continuum of possibilities. Partnerships evolve over time and are much more nuanced than this characterization might suggest. Often districts hire partners to do something the district doesn't have the capacity for, and over time the partnership evolves as the district and the partner learn from one another.

For example, consider a district that hired a partner to train all principals and other staff in a rigorous, standards-based process of teacher supervision and evaluation. This partnership is the centerpiece to the district's strategy to begin to address the performance management of teachers. The partner was hired because of its expertise in this area, and the initial contract was to teach a series of courses in teacher supervision and evaluation and provide in-school support as principals applied the skills. The district and the partner had the foresight to set up a management team for the project that included the chief academic officer, several principal supervisors, the project manager, and the lead consultants from the partner organization. This team met quarterly to measure progress, solve problems, and set strategic direction for the work. It took several years to train the hundreds of teacher supervisors in this methodology. During that time, the partner and the district learned a lot about the conditions required to institutionalize this new approach to teacher supervision and evaluation. Because they were in regular conversation with one another, they were able to make strategic decisions based on their learning that strengthen the work.

At first, the team addressed basic questions such as: What do we do when a principal doesn't meet the performance expectations required for successfully completing the course? What can principals' supervisors do to support principals and hold them accountable for using the skills they have learned? Over time, the issues expanded and evolved. The partner identified deficiencies in the current teacher evaluation instrument that compromised the impact of principals' evaluations on teacher effectiveness. The team revised the evaluation instrument accordingly, and the district negotiated the change with the teachers' union. Then, once a common foundation of knowledge and skills had been developed among principals and other teacher supervisors in the evaluation process, the team turned its attention to building further capacity in the district. It decided to target principals who excelled in the course for further training and then established them as coaches to support their colleagues in implementing the evaluation model and managing difficult cases. The team decided to organize this support using the system's geographic clustering of schools as a way to bolster that system and build more support.

In this example, the expertise of the partner was leveraged to drive systemic improvement, and the district used its own capacity and authority to deepen the impact of the work. The partnership evolved over time in big and small ways to respond to district needs and the partner's capacity.

Chapter 6's exploration of Boston's and Chicago's approaches to urban teacher residencies (UTRs) provides two more images of how partnerships evolve. In Boston, BTR has one foot inside the district and the other outside. It takes direction from the district based on staffing projections, while maintaining the independence needed to design and execute its program. BTR works collaboratively with the system on developing elements of the human capital management system, specifically those that have an impact on the effectiveness and job satisfaction of their program's graduates—teaching standards and induction support. BTR contributes its expertise to build district infrastructure and capacity that serves all teachers, making the reach of the program broader than its program participants. In Chicago, meanwhile, AUSL started its partnership with the Chicago

Public Schools as a preparer of teachers for the district. Over time, its partnership with the system evolved into that of both a preparer of teachers and a manager of low-performing schools. This shift allowed AUSL to target its resources to a group of high-needs schools and struggling learners.

As different as these examples are, they make one thing very clear: partnerships are not static. They evolve over time based on results, learning, needs, and capacity. The plan to train principals in teacher evaluation didn't initially include redesigning the teacher evaluation instrument. AUSL didn't start out managing schools; it grew into that work in response to its learning and the system's needs. BTR didn't set out to define effective teaching standards in the Boston Public Schools. Yet as it developed standards for its own program, which places all its graduates in the system, partnering with the district on standards rather than risking conflicting messages to graduates made sense. Districts and partners can't initially know how a partnership will evolve. What matters is that they have the awareness that it inevitably will evolve, watch for signs of the evolution, and then think strategically to make good decisions that propel the overall human capital agenda.

This level of intentionality about the work of partners and the evolution of these relationships is what provides districts the greatest external leverage for improvement. Districts improve by having close relationships with partners through which they understand the partners' experience in the system, the partners' ideas about ways to further build capacity to address human capital needs, and the supports they need to be successful. While working in this collaborative way with partners, districts think systemically and strategically about the full scope of the human capital endeavor. By considering the work of individual partners, across partnerships and internally, the district looks across the entire human capital landscape, asking key questions: What are the data telling us about how we're doing? For what elements of the framework do we have a pretty good strategy? What is the next piece of the framework that we need to take on? On what evidence are we basing that decision? Where are we making progress internally, and where do we need more external support? Where are the gaps in the system? The role of the district is to design and manage the human capital strategy, thinking about all the different pieces, their interrelationship, and how to combine them to realize the greatest effect.

As districts simultaneously build internal capacity and draw on external resources, there is a tremendous opportunity to use the external partners to support and sometimes drive internal capacity building. Sometimes this is very explicit: bring in organization X to teach the human resources recruiting and screening team how to do Y. But this is a place where subtle, strategic partnering can be invaluable in building an internal vision for the work and the policies and practices that support it. Bringing together partners and internal departments that are all working on the same or related elements of the human capital framework to share information, calibrate efforts, measure and report progress, collaboratively solve problems, and set strategic direction can deeply influence how the district does business.

One district's experiment with a new teacher support system work group is an example of this dynamic. The group was established as momentum was growing in the district for new teacher hiring and support. Several internal departments were taking responsibility for pieces of the work, an external partner had been surveying new teachers about their experiences for several years and reporting findings, and a local foundation was underwriting an expansion of the new teacher support efforts. Participants in the group included the director of human resources, the two staff people in HR responsible for managing the "on-boarding" process for new teachers, the external partner who surveyed new teachers, the director of new teacher induction, and the director of teacher professional development (and occasionally, a representative from the foundation). The assistant superintendent responsible for teacher and principal training and development facilitated the monthly meetings of the group, signaling the importance of its work.

At first, the meetings focused on information sharing to build group members' understanding of what each other was doing in the realm of new teacher support. The meetings built the capacity of individual team members and the team collectively, as participants shared ideas, considered best practices, and began to think about new teacher support holistically. Over time, the team developed a sense of its efficacy and began to problem solve and work collaboratively to decide the best way to provide a coherent and comprehensive support system for new teachers. The partner's survey data provided initial metrics to measure the effectiveness of the efforts and ensure the conversations and work were data-driven. The partner's understanding of the new teacher support issues gleaned over several years of surveying and analysis were instrumental in defining the problems to address. The conversations in the meeting influenced the work in participants' individual departments and organizations, and there was a shared sense of responsibility and accountability for the team's work.

As this example illustrates, forming partnerships to address human capital needs transforms districts from the traditional command-and-control structure to a much more fluid and dynamic entity that has both strong internal capacity and the ability to tap expertise to augment that capacity. Districts and their partners continually learn from one another and build their capacities together. The result is a new kind of district where the boundaries are permeable, expectations are high, and everyone knows his or her job is to support student learning.

APPENDIX A

Further Resources

The resources listed provide additional information on each of the elements of the framework as well as the role of districts and principals in developing and supporting human capital management. The list can guide your continued learning but is not intended to be comprehensive.

Pathways into Teaching

Grossman, Pamela, and Susanna Loeb. *Alternative Routes to Teaching: Mapping the New Landscape of Teacher Education.* Cambridge: Harvard Education Press, 2008.

Hess, Frederick, Andrew Rotherham, and Kate Walsh. *A Qualified Teacher in Every Classroom: Appraising Old Answers and New Ideas.* Washington, DC: AEI Press, 2004.

Johnson, S. M., and S. E. Birkeland. "Pursuing a 'Sense of Success': New Teachers Explain their Career Decisions." *American Educational Research Journal* 40, no. 3 (2003): 581–617.

Kane, Tom J. "Photo Finish, Certification Doesn't Guarantee a Winner." *Education Next* 7, no. 1 (2007): 60–67. http://media.hoover.org/documents/ednext_20071_60.pdf.

Peske, H. G., E. Liu, S. M. Johnson, D. Kauffman, and M. Kardos. "The Next Generation of Teachers: Changing Conceptions of a Career in Teaching." *Phi Delta Kappan* 83, no. 4 (2001): 304–311.

Walsh, Kate, and Christopher Tracy. *Increasing the Odds: How Good Qualities Can Yield Better Teachers.* Washington, DC: National Council on Teaching Quality, 2005. http://www.nctq.org/p/publications/docs/nctq_io_20071129024229.pdf.

Induction and Tenure

Alliance for Excellent Education. "Tapping the Potential: Retaining and Developing High-Quality New Teachers." 2004. http://www.all4ed.org/files/TappingThePotential.pdf.

Baldacci, Leslie, Susan Moore Johnson, and the Project on the Next Generation of Teachers. "Why New Teachers Leave . . . and Why New Teachers Stay." *American Educator,* 2006. http://www.aft.org/pubsreports/american_educator/issues/summer06/intro.htm.

Breaux, Annette, and Harry Wong. *New Teacher Induction: How to Train, Support and Retain New Teachers.* Mountain View, CA: Harry K. Wong Publications, Inc., 2003.

Britton, Ted, Lynn Paine, Senta A. Raizen, and David Pimm. *Comprehensive Teacher Induction: Systems for Early Career Learning.* San Francisco: WestEd, 2004. http://www.wested.org/cs/we/view/rs/692.

Darling, Marilyn. "Learning in the Thick of It." *Harvard Business Review,* July-August 2005. http://harvardbusinessonline.hbsp.harvard.edu/b01/en/common/item_detail.jhtml?referral=7855&id=R0507G&_requestid=35231.

Donaldson, Morgaen L. "What Do Teachers Need, What Do Teachers Get, What is the Gap?" Harvard Graduate School of Education, 2007. http://www.aspeninstitute.org/sites/default/files/content/upload/Teachersupportgap_donaldson.pdf.

Feiman-Nemser, Sharon. "What New Teachers Need to Learn." *Educational Leadership* 60, no. 8 (2003): 25–29.

Ingersoll, Richard M., and Thomas M. Smith. "Do Teacher Induction and Mentoring Matter?" *NASSP Bulletin* 88, no. 638 (2004): 28–40. http://www.cpre.org/index.php?option=com_content&task=view&id=201&Itemid=116.

Ingersoll, Richard, and Jeffrey Kralik. *The Impact of Mentoring on Teacher Retention: What the Research Says.* Denver: Education Commission of the States, 2004.

Ingersoll, Richard, and Thomas Smith. "Reducing Teacher Turnover: What Are the Components of Effective Induction?" American Educational Research Association, Annual Meeting, Chicago, IL, 2003.

Johnson, Susan Moore. *Finders and Keepers: Helping New Teachers Survive and Thrive in Our Schools.* San Francisco: Jossey-Bass Publishers, 2004.

Moir, Ellen. "Launching the Next Generation of Teachers Through Quality Induction." National Commission on Teaching and America's Future, Annual Commissioners and Partner States' Symposium, 2003. http://www.nctaf.org/documents/Moir2.doc.

Rennie Center for Education and Research Policy. "Ready for the Next Challenge: Improving the Retention and Distribution of Excellent Teachers in Urban Schools." *A Proposal by Teachers,* 2009. http://www.teach-plus.org/pdf/RENNC1-35035_FPO.pdf.

Villar, Anthony. "Measuring the Benefits and Costs of Mentor-Based Induction: A Value-Added Assessment of New Teacher Effectiveness Linked to Student Achievement." The American Educational Research Association Annual Conference, San Diego, CA, 2004.

Leadership Opportunities

Darling Hammond, Linda, Ruth Chung Wei, Alethea Andree, Nikole Richardson, and Stelios Orphanos. "Professional Learning in the Learning Profession: A Status Report on Teacher Development in the United States and Abroad." The National Staff Development Council, 2009. http://www.nsdc.org/news/NSDCstudy2009.pdf.

Hall, Pete, and Alisa Simeral. *Building Teachers' Capacity for Success.* Alexandria, VA: Association for Supervision and Curriculum Development, 2008.

Kimmelman, P. "Building Teacher Leaders." PAEC Digital Workshops, 2006. http://www.paec.org/teacher2teacher/bldgteacherleaders.html.

Paliakos, Kathleen. "Creating a System of Educator Development." *Transforming Education: Delivering on our Promise to Every Child* (2009): 29–36. http://www.ccsso.org/content/pdfs/Transforming%20Education%20-%20CCSSO%20discussion%20document.pdf.

Spillane, James P. "Distributed Leadership: What's All the Hoopla?" Institute for Policy Research, 2004. http://www.northwestern.edu/ipr/publications/papers/Spillane_Distrib Lead.pdf.

Teacher Advancement Program. 1999. http://www.tapsystem.org/. (for more on extensive, practitioner-focused resources).

Performance Management, Compensation, and Rewards

Center for Teaching Quality. "Performance Pay for Teachers: Designing a System that Students Deserve," 2007. http://www.teacherleaders.org/teachersolutions/index.php.

Denver Public Schools. Teacher ProComp. http://denverprocomp.dpsk12.org.

Donaldson, Morgaen. "So Long, Lake Wobegon." Center for American Progress, 2009. http://www.americanprogress.org/issues/2009/06/pdf/teacher_evaluation.pdf.

Gordon, Robert, Thomas J. Kane, and Douglas O. Staiger. "Identifying Effective Teachers Using Performance on the Job." *The Hamilton Project* (2006): 5–6. http://www.brookings.edu/views/papers/200604hamilton_1.htm.

Heneman, Herbert G., and Steve Kimball. "How to Design Teacher Salary Structures." Consortium for Policy Research in Education, 2009. http://www.smhc-cpre.org/resources/.

Jerald, Craig. "Aligned By Design: How Teacher Compensation Reform Can Support and Reinforce Other Educational Reforms." Center for American Progress, 2009. http://www.americanprogress.org/issues/2009/07/pdf/teacher_alignment.pdf.

Milanowski, Anthony. "How to Pay Teachers for Student Performance Outcomes." Consortium for Policy Research in Education, 2009. http://www.smhc-cpre.org/resources/.

Odden, Allan. "New Teacher Pay Structures: The Compensation Side of the Strategic Management of Human Capital." Consortium for Policy Research in Education, 2009. http://www.smhc-cpre.org/resources/.

Project on the Next Generation of Teachers. "A User's Guide to Peer Assistance and Review." http://www.gse.harvard.edu/~ngt/par/parinfo/.

Silva, Elena. "The Benwood Plan: A Lesson in Comprehensive Teacher Reform." Education Sector, 2008. http://www.educationsector.org/usr_doc/TheBenwood Plan.pdf.

Singapore Ministry of Education. "Singapore Staff Appraisal (Education Service)," 2006. http://www.aspeninstitute.org/site/c.huLWJeMRKpH/b.2282637/k.FDAF/Materials_provided_by_Meeting_participants.htm.

Slotnik, William J. "It's More Than Money: Making Performance-Based Compensation Work." Center for American Progress, 2009. http://www.americanprogress.org/issues/2009/07/pdf/making_performance_work.pdf.

Toch, T., and R. Rothman. *Rush to Judgment: Teacher Evaluation in Public Education.* Education Sector, 2008. http://www.educationsector.org/usr_doc/RushToJudgment _ES_Jan08.pdf.

Resources for Multiple Elements of the Framework

Barber, Michael and Mona Mourshed. "How the World's Best School Systems Come out on Top." McKinsey & Co., 2007. http://www.mckinsey.com/clientservice/socialsector /resources/pdf/Worlds_School_systems_final.pdf.

Baron, James N., and David M. Kreps. "The Five Factors." *Strategic Human Resources Management*, 16–37. New York: John Wiley, 1999.

Clark, Rosemary, Fabrizio Antonelli, Donna Lacavera, David W. Livingstone, Katina Pollack, Harry Smaller, Jim Strachan, and Paul Tarc. *Beyond PD Days: Teachers' Work and Learning and Canada.* Toronto: Ontario Teachers' Federation, 2007.

Levin, Ben, Avis Glaze, and Michael Fullan. "Results Without Rancor or Ranking: Ontario's Success Story," *Phi Delta Kappa International* 90, no. 4 (2008): 273–280. http://www.michaelfullan.ca/home_articles/08_Dec_PDK_ResultsWithoutRancor .pdf.

McKinsey & Co. "Creating a World Class Education System in Ohio." Prepared for Achieve Inc. (2006): 17–21, 29–41. http://www.achieve.org/Ohio_report.

Olson, Lynn. "Teaching Policy to Improve Student Learning: Lessons from Abroad." The Aspen Institute, 2006. http://www.aspeninstitute.org/sites/default/files/content /docs/education%20and%20society%20program/Ed_Lessons_from_Abroad .pdf.

Sclafani, Susan, and Edmund Lim. "Rethinking Human Capital in Education: Singapore As A Model for Teacher Development." The Aspen Institute, 2008. http://www.aspeninstitute.org/sites/default/files/content/docs/education%20and %20society%20program/SingaporeEDU.pdf.

The Role of the District in Human Capital Management

Campbell, Christine, Michael DeArmond, and Abigail Schumwinger. "From Bystander to Ally: Transforming the District Human Resources Department." Seattle, WA: Center on Reinventing Public Education, 2004. http://www.crpe.org/cs/crpe/download/csr _files/pub_crpe_bystander_apr04.pdf.

Carpenter, Guy, and Oliver Wyman. "Transforming HR to Drive Organizational Success: Lessons Learned Through Project Home Run at the New York City Department of Education," Mercer LLC, 2008.

Heneman, Herbert G., and Anthony T. Milanowski. "Alignment of Human Resource Practices and Teacher Performance Competency." *Peabody Journal of Education* 79, no. 4 (2004): 108–125.

Hightower, Amy M., Michael S. Knapp, Julie A. Marsh, and Milbrey W. McLaughlin. *School Districts and Instructional Renewal.* New York: Teachers College Press, 2002.

Lawler, Edward. *Talent: Making People Your Competitive Advantage.* San Francisco: Jossey-Bass, 2008.

Levin, Jessica, and Meredith Quinn. "Missed Opportunities: How We Keep High-Quality Teachers Out of Urban Classrooms." The New Teacher Project, 2003. http://www .tntp.org/files/MissedOpportunities.pdf.

Liu, Edward, and Susan Moore Johnson. "New Teachers' Experiences of Hiring: Late, Rushed and Information-Poor." *Educational Administration Quarterly* 42, no. 3 (2006): 324–360. http://eaq.sagepub.com/cgi/content/abstract/42/3/324.

O'Reilly, Charles. "New United Motors Manufacturing, Inc." Stanford Graduate School of Business, 2004. http://harvardbusinessonline.hbsp.harvard.edu/b02/en/common /item_detail.jhtml?id=HR11&referral=2340.

Strategic Management of Human Capital. http://www.smhc-cpre.org/resources/.

Weisberg, Daniel, Susan Sexton, Jennifer Mulhern, and David Keeling. "The Widget Effect: Our National Failure to Acknowledge and Act on Differences in Teacher Effectiveness." The New Teacher Project, 2009. http://widgeteffect.org/downloads/The WidgetEffect.pdf.

Principals as Human Capital Managers and Leaders of Learning

Amrein-Beardsley, Audrey. "Recruiting Expert Teachers in Hard-to-Staff Schools." *Phi Delta Kappan* 89, no. 1 (2007): 64–67.

Army Leadership. "Be, Know, Do." *Leader to Leader Journal* 26, 2002. http://www.leader toleader.org/knowledgecenter/journal.aspx?ArticleID=126.

Brown, Kathleen M., and Susan R. Wynn. "Finding, Supporting, and Keeping: The Role of the Principal in Teacher Retention Issues." *Leadership and Policy in Schools* 8, no. 1 (2009): 37–63.

Bryk, Anthony S., and Barbara Schneider. *Trust in Schools: A Core Resource for Improvement.* New York: Russell Sage Foundation, 2002.

Center for Comprehensive School Reform and Improvement. "Improving Teacher Retention with Supportive Workplace Conditions," 2007. http://www.centerforcsri.org/ index.php?option=com_content&task=view&id=466&Itemid=5.

Charan, Ram, Stephen Drotter, and James Noel. *The Leadership Pipeline: How to Build the Leadership Powered Company.* San Francisco: Jossey-Bass, 2001.

Easley, Jacob. "Alternative Route Urban Teacher Retention and Implications for Principals' Moral Leadership." *Educational Studies* 32, no. 3 (2006): 241–249.

Hope, Warren C. "Principals' Orientation and Induction Activities as Factors in Teacher Retention." *Clearing House* 73, no. 1 (1999): 54–56.

Johnson, Susan Moore, and Sarah Birkeland. "The Schools That Teachers Choose." *Educational Leadership* 60, no. 8 (2003): 20–24.

Kane, Kate. "Anthropologists Go Native in the Corporate Village." *Fast Company,* 2007. http://www.fastcompany.com/magazine/05/anthro.html.

Leithwood, Kenneth, Karen Louis, Stephen Anderson, and Kyla Wahlstrom. *How Leadership Influences Student Learning: Review of Research.* New York: Wallace Foundation, 2003.

Ouchi, William G., and L. G. Segal. *Making Schools Work: A Revolutionary Plan to Get Your Children the Education They Need.* New York: Simon & Schuster, 2003.

Waters, Tim, Robert J. Marzano, and Brian McNulty. *Balanced Leadership: What 30 Years of Research Tells Us About the Effect of Leadership on Student Achievement.* Aurora, CO: Mid-Continent Educational Research Laboratory, 2003.

4. S. Miller, "Kimberly-Clark Corporation," *HR Magazine* 51, no. 11(November 2006): 64–68; D. Bradford Neary, "Creating a Company-Wide, On-Line Performance Management System at TRW," *Human Resource Management* 41, no. 4 (Winter 2002): 491-498.

5. Carrie Olesen, David White, and Iris Lemmer, "Career Models and Culture Change at Microsoft," *Organization Development Journal* 25, no. 2 (Summer 2007): 31–36.

6. T. Judge, C. Higgins, and D. Cable, "The Employment Interview: A Review of Recent Research and Recommendations for Future Research," *Human Resource Management Review* 10, no. 4 (2000): 38–406.

7. Linda Aldred, "Texas Children's Hospital Makes Leadership Development a Core Business Strategy," *Global Business and Organizational Excellence* 26, no. 3 (March/April 2007): 22–34.

8. M. Frase-Blunt, "Peering into an Interview," *HR Magazine* 46, no.12 (December 2001): 71–75.

9. Gerard Seijts and Dan Crim, "What Engages Employees the Most, or the Ten C's of Employee Engagement," *Ivey Business Journal* 70, no. 4 (March/April 2006), http://www.iveybusinessjournal.com/view_article.asp?intArticle_ID=616; Robert J. Vance, *Employee Engagement and Commitment: A Guide to Understanding, Measuring and Increasing Engagement in Your Organization* (Alexandria, VA: Society for Human Resource Management Foundation, 2006).

10. J. Sammer, "Calibrating Consistency," *HR Magazine* 53, no. 1 (January 2008): 73–75; Miller, "Kimberly-Clark Corporation."

11. Barnett Berry and Tammy King, *Recruiting and Retaining National Board Certified Teachers for Hard-To-Staff, Low-Performing Schools: Silver Bullets or Smart Solutions* (Chapel Hill, NC: Southeast Center for Teaching Quality, May 2005), http://www.teachingquality.org/pdfs/RecruitRetainHTSS.pdf; Susan Moore Johnson and Sarah Birkeland, "The Schools That Teachers Choose," *Educational Leadership* 60, no. 8 (May 2003): 20–24.

12. Robert Frigo and Robert Janson, "GE's Financial Services Operation Achieves Quality Results Through 'Work Out' Process," *National Productivity Review* 13, no. 1 (Winter 1993): 53–61.

13. E. White, "Theory & Practice: How Surveying Workers Can Pay Off: Companies Are Finding Engaged Employees Become More Motivated," *Wall Street Journal*, June 18, 2007; Ken Carrig and Patrick M. Wright, *Building Profit through Building People: Making Your Workforce the Strongest Link in the Value-Profit Chain* (Alexandria, VA: Society for Human Resource Management, 2006).

14. Steven P. Kirn, Anthony J. Rucci, Mark A. Huselid, and Brian E. Becker, "Strategic Human Resource Management at Sears," *Human Resource Management* 38, no. 4 (Winter 1999): 329–335.

15. Audrey Williams-Lee, "Accelerated Leadership Development Tops the Talent Menu at McDonald's," *Global Business and Organizational Excellence* 27, no. 4 (May/June 2008): 15–31; Donald P. Cushman and Sarah S. King, *Communication Best Practices at Dell, General Electric, Microsoft, and Monsanto* (Albany, NY: SUNY Press, 2003), 31–44.

16. Phillip Hallinger and Ronald H. Heck, "Exploring the Principal's Contribution to School Effectiveness," *School Effectiveness and School Improvement* 9, no. 2, (1998):

157–191; Kenneth Leithwood, Karen Seashore Louis, Stephen Anderson, and Kyla Wahlstrom, *Review of Research: How Leadership Influences Student Learning* (New York: The Wallace Foundation, 2004).

17. Linda Darling-Hammond, Michelle LaPointe, Deborah Meyerson, Margaret T. Orr, and Carol Cohen, *Preparing School Leaders for a Changing World: Lessons from Exemplary Leadership Development Programs* (Stanford, CA: Stanford Educational Leadership Institute, Stanford University, 2007), http://seli.stanford.edu/research /documents/sls_tech_report.pdf.

18. Jessica Levin and Meredith Quinn, *Missed Opportunities: How We Keep High-Quality Teachers Out of Urban Classrooms* (New York: The New Teacher Project, 2003); Jessica Levin, Jennifer Mulhern, and Joan Schunck, *Unintended Consequences: The Case for Reforming the Staffing Rules in Urban Teachers Union Contracts* (New York: The New Teacher Project, 2005).

19. Christina A. Samuels, "Focus On: Leadership & Management: Managers Help Principals Balance Time," *Education Week* 27, no. 23 (February 13, 2008): 1, 18–19.

20. Christine Campbell, Margaret DeArmond, and Abigail Schumwinger, *From Bystander to Ally: Transforming the District Human Resources Department* (Seattle: Center on Reinventing Public Education, 2004).

21. See, for example, David A. Thomas and C. King, "Reinventing Human Resources at the School District of Philadelphia" (Public Education Leadership Project Case, PEL-029, 2005); Susan Moore Johnson and Jennifer M. Suesse, "Staffing the Boston Public Schools" (Public Education Leadership Project Case, PEL-024, 2005), http:// www.hbs.edu/pelp/casestudies.html.

22. For more on HR department performance metrics, see Brian E. Becker, Mark A. Huselid, and Dave Ulrich, *The HR Scorecard: Linking People, Strategy, and Performance* (Boston: Harvard Business School Press, 2001).

Chapter 4

1. Richard Elmore, "Building a New Structure for School Leadership" (Washington DC: Albert Shanker Institute, 2000).

2. For more on "leading for learning," a term that is being used in place of instructional leadership in some circles to frame this shift, see Center for the Study of Teaching and Policy, "Leading for Learning Sourcebook: Concepts and Examples," (Seattle: Center for the Study of Teaching and Policy, 2003).

3. Roland Barth, *Learning by Heart* (San Francisco: Jossey-Bass, 2004).

4. Peter Senge, *The Fifth Discipline: The Art and Practice of the Learning Organization* (New York: Doubleday, 1990).

5. John Marvel, Deanna M. Lyter, Pia Peltola, Gregory A. Strizek, and Beth A. Morton, "Teacher Attrition and Mobility: Results from the 2004–05 Teacher Follow-up Survey" (NCES 2007–307; U.S. Department of Education, National Center for Education Statistics; Washington DC: U.S. Government Printing Office, 2007); Alliance for Excellent Education, "What Keeps Good Teachers in the Classroom? Understanding and Reducing Teacher Turnover" (Washington, DC: Alliance for Excellent Education, 2008); Morgaen L. Donaldson, Susan Moore Johnson, Cheryl L. Kirkpatrick, Wil-

liam H. Marinell, Jennifer Lynn Steele, and Stacy Agee Szczesiul, "Angling for Access, Bartering for Change: How Second-Stage Teachers Experience Differentiated Roles In Schools," *Teachers College Record* (New York: Teachers College Press, 2008).

6. James P. Spillane, Richard Halverson, and John B. Diamond, "Investigating School Leadership Practice: A Distributive Approach," *Educational Researcher* 30, no. 3 (2001): 23–28.

7. Stephen R. Covey, *The Seven Habits of Highly Effective People* (New York: Simon and Schuster, 1989).

8. Other possible questions include: How does the teacher engage the students? How does she develop their academic vocabulary? What new words does the text introduce? How does the teacher get students to use the new vocabulary words? What do the students think the purpose of the lesson is? What does the teacher think the role of her own emotions should be vis-à-vis her learning goals for her students?

9. In the case of an incompetent teacher for whom improvement is not possible in a reasonable amount of time, principals have to be committed enough to student learning that they will follow the necessary protocols for dismissal. Different from the principal's primary developmental role in teacher learning, in the case of an incompetent teacher, the principal's responsibility is to gather the necessary and often substantial documentation in order to fire the teacher. As with any firing, when principals identify an incompetent staff member, they need to anticipate potentially unpleasant relations with the union leadership, other teachers, or the ineffective teacher him- or herself. In education institutions, the difficulty of firing ineffective staff members can carry additional layers of doubt; while effective educators never give up on children, school leaders do at times have to give up on adults on behalf of children. Additionally, some school leaders fear that if they remove an incompetent teacher, they may not be able to fill the vacancy with someone more talented.

10. Senge, *The Fifth Discipline.*

11. Liz Gewirtzman and Elaine Fink, "Realigning Policies and Resources" (Chicago: Cross City Campaign for Urban School Reform, 1998).

12. S. Davis, L. Darling-Hammond, M. LaPointe, and D. Meyerson, *School Leadership Study: Developing Successful Principals* (Stanford, CA: Stanford Educational Leadership Institute, Stanford University, 2005); L. Darling-Hammond, M. LaPointe, D. Meyerson, and M. Orr, *Preparing School Leaders for a Changing World* (Stanford, CA: Stanford Educational Leadership Institute, Stanford University, 2007).

13. Sandra Stein and Elizabeth Gewirtzman, *Principal Training on the Ground: Ensuring Highly Qualified Leadership* (Portsmouth, NH: Heinemann, 2004).

14. See, for example, W. N. Grubb and J. J. Flessa, "A Job Too Big for One: Multiple Principals and Other Nontraditional Approaches to School Leadership," *Educational Administration Quarterly* 42, no. 4 (2006): 518–550.

15. Atlanta's efforts to "flip the script" between the principals and the central office personnel and New York City's restructuring midlevel district management into a market of nongeographic school support organizations that principals choose are two current examples of district efforts to shift the roles of central office staff to support the principals' instructional work.

16. Dave Ulrich, Steve Kerr, and Ron Ashkenas, *The GE Work-Out: How to Implement GE's Revolutionary Method for Busting Bureaucracy & Attacking Organizational Problems—Fast!* (New York: McGraw-Hill, 2002).

17. Holly Holland, "Out of the Office and into the Classroom: An Initiative to Help Principals Focus on Instruction," Center for the Study of Teaching and Policy, The University of Washington, 2008, http://www.wallacefoundation.org/SiteCollectionDocuments /WF/Knowledge%20Center/Attachments/PDF/stories-from-field-out-of-the-office. pdf; Jan Walker, "Superheroes or SAMs? A Change in Practice for a New Kind of Educational Leader," National Council of Professors of Educational Administration, 2008, http://www.jefferson.k12.ky.us/Departments/AdminRecruit Develop/ard-sams /superheros_or_sams.pdf.

Chapter 5

1. For more on optimizing teacher ability, see Richard Ingersoll, *Is There Really a Teacher Shortage?* (Seattle: Center for the Study of Teaching and Policy, University of Washington, 2003).

2. The Editor's Desk, "Youngest Boomers: 10.8 Jobs from Ages 18–42," Bureau of Labor Statistics, 2008, www.bls.gov/opub/ted/2008/jun/wk5/art01.htm.

3. National Commission on Teaching and America's Future, *Unraveling the "Teacher Shortage" Problem: Teacher Retention is the Key. A Symposium of the National Commission on Teaching and America's Future*, and NCTAF State Partners (Washington DC: National Commission on Teaching and America's Future, 2002).

4. S. Birkeland and Rachel Curtis, Ensuring the Support and Development of New Teachers in the Boston Public Schools: A Proposal to Improve Teacher Quality and Retention (Boston: Boston Public Schools, 2006).

5. Alliance for Excellent Education, *Teacher Attrition: A Costly Loss to the Nation and the States* (Washington, DC: Alliance for Excellent Education, 2005).

6. Richard J. Murnane and Barbara R. Phillips, "Learning by Doing, Vintage, and Selection: Three Pieces of the Puzzle Relating Teaching Experience and Teaching Performance," *Economics of Education Review* 1, no. 4 (1981): 453–465; Jonah E. Rockoff, "The Impact of Individual Teachers on Student Achievement: Evidence from Panel Data," *American Economic Review* 94, no. 2 (2004): 247–252.

7. See Steven G. Rivkin, Eric A. Hanushek, and John F. Kain, "Teachers, Schools, and Academic Achievement," *Econometrica* 73, no. 2 (2005): 417–458.

8. Ulrich Boser, "A Picture of the Teacher Pipeline: Baccalaureate and Beyond," *Education Week* 19, no. 18 (2000): 16–17.

9. Jonathan Rochkind, Amber Ott, John Immerwahr, John Doble, and Jean Johnson, *Lessons Learned: New Teachers Talk about their Jobs, Challenges and Long-Range Plans. Issue No. 3: Teaching in Changing Times* (New York: Public Agenda, 2008), http:// www.publicagenda.org/files/pdf/lessons_learned_3.pdf.

10. Jonathan Rochkind, Amber Ott, John Immerwahr, John Doble, and Jean Johnson, *Lessons Learned: New Teachers Talk about their Jobs, Challenges and Long-Range Plans. Issue No. 2: Working Without a Net: How New Teachers from Three Prominent Alternative Route Programs Describe their First Year on the Job* (New York: Public Agenda, 2007), http://www.publicagenda.org/files/pdf/lessons_learned_2.pdf.

11. Daniel Weisberg, Susan Sexton, Jennifer Mulhern, and David Keeling, *The Widget Effect: Our National Failure to Acknowledge and Act on Differences in Teacher Effectiveness* (New York: The New Teacher Project, 2009); for more on teacher effectiveness, see National Center on Teacher Quality, *State Teacher Policy Yearbook 2008* (Washington, DC: National Centre on Teacher Quality, 2008).

12. Jennifer King Rice, *Teacher Quality: Understanding the Effectiveness of Teacher Attributes* (Washington, DC: Economic Policy Institute, 2003); Andrew J. Wayne and Peter Youngs, "Teacher Characteristics and Student Achievement Gains: A Review," *Review of Educational Research* 73, no. 1 (2003): 89–122.

13. Patrick O'Brien and Richard Goddard, "Beginning Teachers: Easing the Transition to the Classroom," *The Australian Educational Leader* 28, no. 1 (2006): 28–31, 48. For more on combining cognitive and noncognitive teacher predictors of effectiveness, see Jonah E. Rockoff, Brian A. Jacob, Thomas J. Kane, and Douglas O. Staiger, "Can You Recognize an Effective Teacher When You Recruit One?" (NBER Working Paper 14485; Cambridge, MA: National Bureau of Economic Research, November 2008).

14. Thomas J. Kane, Jonah E. Rockoff, and Douglas O. Staiger, "What Does Certification Tell Us About Teacher Effectiveness? Evidence from New York City," *Economics of Education Review* 27, no. 6 (2008): 615–631.

15. For more on Science Applications International Corporation, see Robin Athey, "It's 2008: Do You Know Where Your Talent Is? Why Acquisition and Retention Strategies Don't Work," Deloitte Research, 2004 http://www.deloitte.com/dtt/cda/doc/content/TM_Do_you.pdf; Morgan McCall, Michael Lombardo, and Ann Morrison, The Lessons of Experience: How Successful Executives Develop on the Job (New York: Free Press, 1988).

16. Lynn Olson, *Teaching Policy to Improve Student Learning: Lessons from Abroad* (Washington, DC: Aspen Institute, 2006).

17. But the jury is still out on the true impact of comprehensive induction. A recent study found that two comprehensive programs—ETS and the New Teacher Center—did not improve student achievement, rates of teacher retention, or teacher practices after one year of implementation. See Steven Glazerman, Sarah Dolfin, Martha Bleeker, Amy Johnson, Eric Isenberg, Julieta Lugo-Gil, Mary Grider, and Edward Britton, *Impacts of Comprehensive Teacher Induction: Results from the First Year of a Randomized Controlled Study* (Washington, DC: U.S. Department of Education, Institute for Education Sciences, 2008). Further research will determine if there are effects after two or three years.

18. For more information on PAR, see *The Project on the Next Generation of Teachers: A User's Guide to Peer Assistance and Review*, http://www.gse.harvard.edu/~ngt/par/.

Chapter 6

1. All of the quotes and details about the Boston Teacher Residency and the Academy of Urban School Leadership were gathered as part of a study of the two programs conducted in 2009 by the chapter authors. Quotes are not attributed to ensure confidentiality.

2. For more on Boston Public Schools' Dimensions of Effective Teaching, see http://boston.k12.ma.us/teach/Dimensions.pdf.

3. The dual mission of AUSL to prepare and support teachers in its Urban Teacher Residency Program while also staffing and managing CPS turnaround schools results in a very different budget structure that integrates these two areas of work.

4. At the time of this writing, the TEACH Act Discussion Draft provides ten federal grants that would provide current or new UTR programs with $5 million over three years.

5. Nicole Y. Ireland, Regis Shields, and Karen Hawley Miles, *Finding Resources to Pay for High Quality New Teacher Support* (Boston: Education Resource Strategies, 2008).

6. Martha Alt and Robin Henke, *To Teach or Not to Teach? Teaching Experience and Preparation Among 1992–93 Bachelor's Degree Recipients 10 Years After College* (Washington, DC: National Center for Education Statistics, 2007), http://nces.ed.gov/pubs2007/2007163.pdf.

7. Eric Hirsch and Scott Emerick, *Teacher Working Conditions in Turnaround Team High Schools* (Hillsborough, NC: Center for Teaching Quality, June 2006); Barnett Berry and Ed Fuller, *Stemming the Tide of Teacher Attrition: How Working Conditions Influence Teacher Career Intentions and Other Key Outcomes in Arizona* (Hillsborough, NC: Center for Teaching Quality, November 2007).

Chapter 7

1. Morgaen L.Donaldson, Susan Moore Johnson, Cheryl L. Kirkpatrick, William Marinell, Stacy Szcesiul, and Jennifer Steele, 2008. "Angling for Access, Bartering for Change: How Second-stage Teachers Experience Differentiated Roles in Schools." *Teachers College Record* 111, no. 5 (2008).

2. Daniel Weisberg, Susan Sexton, Jennifer Mulhern, and David Keeling, *The Widget Effect: Our National Failure to Acknowledge and Act on Differences in Teacher Effectiveness* (New York: The New Teacher Project, 2009).

3. This is a "back of the envelope" calculation of estimated career earnings: (30 • 60,000) + (30 • 40,000) = 3,000,000; 60,000 is average salary and benefits (not counting the pension contribution), and 40,000 is 67 percent salary and benefits, a safe estimate for the value of the pension package.

4. Weisberg et al., *The Widget Effect*.

5. John Marvel et al., "Teacher Attrition and Mobility: Results from the 2004–05 Teacher Follow-up Survey," NCES 2007–307, 2007, http://nces.ed.gov/pubs 2007/2007307.pdf.

6. Donald J. Boyd et al., "Who Leaves? Teacher Attrition and Student Achievement" (CALDER Working Paper 23; Washington, D.C.: National Center for Analysis of Longitudinal Data in Education Research, 2009); Dan Goldhaber, Betheny Gross, and Daniel Player, "Are Public Schools Really Losing Their Best? Assessing the Career Transitions of Teachers and Their Implications for the Quality of the Teacher Workforce" (CALDER Working Paper 12; Washington, DC: National Center for Analysis of Longitudinal Data in Education Research, 2007); Eric A. Hanushek et al., "The Market for Teacher Quality" (NBER Working Paper 11154; Cambridge, MA: National Bureau of Economic Research, 2005).

7. Florida Department of Education, "Teacher Exit Interview 2006-07," Series 2008-10B, Statistical Brief (Tallahassee, FL: Bureau of Education Information and Accountability

Services, Florida Department of Education, 2008), http://www.myfloridaeducation.com/eias)/

8. Robert M. Costrell, Richard W. Johnson, and Michael J. Podgursky, "Modernizing Teacher Retirement Benefit Systems," in *Creating a New Teaching Profession*, eds. Dan Goldhaber and Jane Hannaway (Washington, DC: Urban Institute Press, forthcoming, 2009). Also, see Richard J. Murnane and Randy Olsen, "The Effects of Salaries and Opportunity Costs on Length of Stay in Teaching: Evidence from North Carolina," *Journal of Human Resources* 25, no. 1 (1990): 106.

9. See Marvel et al., "Teacher Attrition and Mobility."

10. Sari Levy, Van Schoales, and Tony Lewis, DPS Employee Compensation: the Role of Pension Benefits (Denver: The Piton Foundation and the Donnell Kay Foundation, 2008).

11. Murnane and Olsen, "The Effects of Salaries and Opportunity Costs on Length of Stay in Teaching.

12. Marvel et al., "Teacher Attrition and Mobility."

13. See studies from The Project on The Next Generation of Teachers, http://www.gse.harvard.edu/~ngt/papers.htm.

14. Susan Moore Johnson, "Second-Stage Teachers and Coaching: Building School Capacity and a Teaching Career" (NGT Working Paper; Cambridge, MA: Next Generation of Teachers Project, 2009).

15. Stacy Agee Szczesiul, "Safe to Say, It's Not Like It Used to Be": Second-Stage Teacher Responses to External Accountability Policies and Reforms (NGT Working Paper; Cambridge, MA: Next Generation of Teachers Project, Cambridge, 2009).

16. Sarah E. Fiarman, "It's Hard to Go Back: Career Decisions of Second-stage Teacher Leaders" (NGT Working Paper; Cambridge, MA: Next Generation of Teachers Project, 2009).

17. Ann Duffett et al., *Waiting to be Won Over: Teachers Speak on the Profession, Unions, and Reform* (Washington, DC: Education Sector, 2008).

18. Richard F. Elmore, *Building a New Structure for School Leadership* (Washington, DC: The Albert Shanker Institute, 2000), 2.

19. J. York-Barr, and K. Duke, "What Do We Know About Teacher Leadership? Findings from Two Decades of Scholarship," *Review of Educational Research* 74, no. 3 (2004): 255–316.

20. There may be fewer barriers to advance this agenda than most realize. A review of the teacher collective bargaining database on the National Council on Teacher Quality's Web site revealed no explicit prohibitions against early career development or talent management initiatives. Although many teacher collective bargaining agreements implicitly or explicitly prohibit the use of student performance data for the purpose of evaluating teachers, if talent identification functions are not explicitly linked to teacher evaluation systems, then those barriers can also be jumped. This is not simply a gesture of tactical policy finesse. At present, teachers are often advanced to leadership programs without the use of such data. Just like admission criteria for a university-based principal development program, the decision to incorporate teacher effectiveness data may well be something wholly in the purview of the program's designers. It would be just as easy

to include it. Finally, decisions to create compensation incentives could be derived from extra-pay provisions in the collective bargaining agreement, which usually permit compensation for professional development. A local teacher union affiliate may easily want to participate in the design of such a leadership development program, and therefore would not be limited from discussing how it would be implemented, either.

21. Fiarman, "It's Hard to Go Back."

Chapter 8

1. Arthur Levine, "Educating School Teachers" (New York: The Education Schools Project, 2006), http://www.edschools.org/pdf/Educating_Teachers_Report.pdf. See also Aspen Institute Datasheet, "The Teaching Workforce" (The Aspen Institute 2007), Table 2, http://www.aspeninstitute.org/sites/default/files/content/docs/education%20and%20society%20program/Ed_AspenTeacherWorkforceDatasheet.pdf.

2. Richard M. Ingersoll, *CPRE Policy Briefs: Misdiagnosing the Teacher Quality Problem* (Philadelphia: Consortium on Policy Research in Education, 2007).

3. National Commission on Teaching and America's Future, *No Dream Denied: A Pledge to America's Children* (Washington, DC: 2003), Figure 5, http://www.nctaf.org/documents/no-dream-denied_full-report.pdf.

4. Richard M. Ingersoll, *Is There Really a Teacher Shortage?* (Seattle: Center for the Study of Teaching and Policy, University of Washington, 2003).

5. Thomas E. Kane, Jonah E. Rockoff, and Douglas O. Staiger, "What Does Certification Tell Us About Teacher Effectiveness? Evidence from New York City" (Working Paper 11844; Cambridge: National Bureau of Economic Research, 2006).

6. Ingersoll, *Is There Really a Teacher Shortage?*; S. M. Johnson and The Project on the Next Generation of Teachers, *Finders and Keepers: Helping New Teachers Survive and Thrive in Our Schools* (San Francisco: Jossey-Bass, 2004); Eric Hirsch, Casia Freitas, Keri Church, and Anthony Villar, *Massachusetts Teaching, Learning and Leading Survey: Creating School Conditions Where Teachers Stay and Students Thrive* (Santa Cruz, CA: New Teacher Center, 2009); Susan M. Kardos and Susan Moore Johnson, "On Their Own and Presumed Expert: New Teachers' Experience with Their Colleagues," *Teachers College Record* 109, no. 9 (2007): 2083–2106; Morgaen L. Donaldson, "Teach For America Teachers' Careers: Whether, When, and Why They Leave Low-Income Schools and the Teaching Profession" (paper presented at the American Educational Research Association 2008 annual meeting, New York).

Conclusion

1. Based on interviews with Broad Residents conducted by Rachel Curtis in Fall 2006.

About the Editors

Rachel E. Curtis works with school systems, foundations, higher education, and education policy organizations on district improvement strategy; leadership development; and efforts to make teaching a compelling and rewarding career. Her clients include the Aspen Institute, the Broad Center for the Management of School Systems, the Executive Leadership Program for Educators at Harvard University, and a variety of traditional and charter school systems. Curtis worked for the Boston Public Schools for eleven years, during which time she devised the district's instructional coaching model for literacy and math, developed a data-driven school planning process, founded the School Leadership Institute, developed teaching standards and a new teacher induction program, and oversaw professional development for all teachers and school administrators. Her publications include: *Strategy in Action: How School Systems Can Support Powerful Learning and Teaching* (Harvard Education Press, 2009), *The Skillful Leader II: Confronting Conditions that Undermine Learning* (Ready About Press, 2008), *Ensuring the Support and Development of New Teachers in the Boston Public Schools* (Boston Public Schools, 2006), *Preparing Non-Principal Administrators to Foster Whole-School Improvement in Boston* (Boston Public Schools, 2005), and *Professional Development Spending in the Boston Public Schools* (Boston Public Schools, 2005). She holds a master's degree from the Harvard Graduate School of Education.

Judy Wurtzel was, at the time she coedited this volume, the codirector of the Aspen Institute education and society program, which provides a forum for education practitioners, researchers, and policy leaders to reflect on efforts to improve student achievement and to consider how public policy changes can affect progress. In May 2009, she was named deputy assistant secretary for planning, evaluation, and policy development at the U.S. Department of Education. The Office of Planning, Evaluation, and Policy Development (OPEPD) coordinates the department's policy and budget activities. Prior to joining the Aspen Institute, Wurtzel was executive director of the Learning First Alliance, a permanent partnership of twelve national education associations with more than 10 million members. Wurtzel also served as a senior adviser at the U.S. Department of Education during the Clinton administration, working on a wide range of elementary and secondary education issues, including the reauthorizations of the Elementary and Secondary Education Act and the Individuals with Disabilities Education Act. Wurtzel started her career as an attorney, working as a law clerk to Dolores Sloviter, judge in the U.S. Court of Appeals for the Third Circuit and to Barbara Crabb, chief judge for the Western District of Wisconsin, and then in private practice. She also taught English in a Moroccan high school as a Peace Corps volunteer. She holds a JD from New York University.

About the Contributors

Barnett Berry is the president and CEO of the Center for Teaching Quality, Inc., a research-based advocacy organization dedicated to cultivating teacher leadership and conducting research that can transform the teaching profession. In 2003, he created the Teacher Leaders Network—a dynamic virtual community—whose purpose is to elevate the voices of expert teachers in policy debates regarding their profession and the students they serve. A former high school teacher, Berry also has worked as a social scientist at the Rand Corporation, served as a senior executive with the South Carolina State Department of Education and directed an education policy center while he was a professor at the University of South Carolina. He has a PhD in educational administration and policy studies from the University of North Carolina at Chapel Hill.

Jane Hannaway is senior fellow and founding director of the Education Policy Center at the Urban Institute, where she oversees the work of the center and is a member of the institute's senior management team. She is also director of CALDER (National Center for the Analysis of Longitudinal Data in Education Research), a federally funded national research and development center. Hannaway is an organizational sociologist whose work focuses on educational organizations, in particular, the effects of education reforms on school policies and practices and ultimately on student outcomes. Her current research is heavily focused on effects of various accountability policies and issues associated with teacher labor markets using state-level longitudinal administrative databases. Hannaway previously served on the faculty of Columbia, Princeton, and Stanford universities. She was also a senior researcher with the Consortium for Policy Research in Education (CPRE). Hannaway has authored, coauthored, or edited seven books and numerous papers in education and management journals. She has a PhD from the Stanford University Graduate School of Education.

Mindy Hernandez is working with Princeton University on applying recent findings in the behavioral sciences to improve a wide range of programs and policies that have an impact on low-income people—from rethinking college scholarship programs to creating smarter automatic savings opportunities. From 2007 to 2008, she served as the research director of the Aspen education program. Before joining Aspen, Hernandez worked with the education division at the Carnegie Corporation of New York, where her work focused on high school reform, including a large reform initiative, Schools for a New Society. Prior to joining Carnegie, Hernandez managed the literacy initiative of For Love of Children's (FLOC) Neighborhood Tutoring Program, an organization that serves at-risk children in Washington, D.C. Her background includes a stint in the AmeriCorps VISTA program where she designed an English-language after-school program for children in low-income Puerto Rican communities; work in Kolkata, India, where she conducted research on the gap between sex-trafficking legislation and its implementation; and in the office of U.S. Representative Barney Frank (D-MA). Hernandez holds a master's degree in public affairs domestic and social policy from the Woodrow Wilson School of Public and International Affairs at Princeton University.

Brad Jupp is a senior program adviser in the office of U.S. Secretary of Education Arne Duncan. He is on loan to the secretary from the Denver Public Schools, where for the past twenty-four years, he has been a teacher, union leader, and senior administrator. His most recent assignment was senior academic policy adviser to Superintendent Michael Bennet. In that role, he shaped district direction in a wide range of areas, including individual, school, and district performance management and accountability; school choice, new school development and school portfolio management; and the management of educator human capital. Prior to that assignment, Jupp spent nineteen years as a middle school language arts teacher, lead teacher of the DPS Alternative Middle School, and an activist and chief negotiator for Denver's teacher union, the Denver Classroom Teachers Association (DCTA). From 1999 to 2005, he led the joint district–union effort to develop and implement the Professional Compensation System for Teachers, ProComp, a nationally recognized, path-clearing effort to reform the way teachers are paid. He is the coauthor of *Pay-for-Performance Teacher Compensation* (Harvard Education Press, 2007). Jupp holds BA from the University of Texas. Jupp's work on the book began during his tenure in Denver and continued outside of his work obligations with the U.S. DOE.

Steven Kimball is an assistant scientist with the Consortium for Policy Research in Education (CPRE) and the Strategic Management of Human Capital project at the Wisconsin Center for Education Research and the University of Wisconsin-Madison. His work includes research on standards-based teacher evaluation and compensation reforms. Kimball was also the coinvestigator of a study funded by the Institute for Educational Sciences on principal performance evaluation, and is principal investigator for the evaluation of the Chicago Community Trust Education Program. Before joining CPRE, Kimball held legislative analyst positions in the U.S. House of Representatives, the U.S. Senate, and the Texas State Office in Washington, D.C. Kimball holds a PhD from the University of Wisconsin-Madison, Department of Educational Leadership and Policy Analysis.

Kavita Kapadia Matsko is an assistant clinical professor on the Committee of Education and the founding director of the Urban Teacher Education Program at the University of Chicago's Urban Education Institute. Her research, often conducted with the Consortium on Chicago School Research, focuses on urban schools, preservice preparation, and new teacher induction. She has been a classroom teacher in a variety of settings, including Chicago Public Schools, a demonstration-classroom teacher, a literacy teacher-leader, a mentor teacher, and adjunct faculty at Northwestern and National-Louis universities. In 1998, she cofounded New Teachers Network, a teacher induction program sponsored by the University of Chicago Center for Urban School Improvement that is now part of the Chicago New Teacher Center. Matsko holds a master's degree in education and administrative certification, and a doctorate in sociology from the University of Chicago.

Tony Milanowski is an assistant scientist with the Wisconsin Center for Education Research at the University of Wisconsin-Madison. He has been doing research on teacher compensation, teacher evaluation, and other aspects of human resource management in education since 1997. From 1999 to 2007, he coordinated research on standards-based teacher evaluation and teacher performance pay for the Consortium for Policy Research in Education's Teacher Compensation Project. He was also co-principal investigator of a study of principal performance evaluation. Current projects include a study of school-level human resource management practices and a review of teacher performance assessment systems. He is also on the technical assistance staff of the Center for Educator Compensation Reform, which provides support to the U.S. Department of Education's Teacher Incentive Fund grantees. Before coming to the Wisconsin Center for Education Research, he worked as a human resource management professional for sixteen years. Milanowski received a PhD in industrial relations and an MA in public policy from the University of Wisconsin-Madison.

Diana Montgomery was a senior research associate for the Center for Teaching Quality when she contributed to this volume. At CTQ, Diana served as project director for research and evaluations, focusing on policies and practices related to the preparation, support, and retention of teachers. Her work included programs to develop models of mentoring; research on establishing professional learning communities to enhance retention of quality teachers; evaluations of higher education institutes funded by Teachers for a New Era, an initiative of the Carnegie Corporation of New York; development of quality indicators for assessing and improving teaching quality in K–12 schools; and studies of effective use of teachers certified by the National Board for Professional Teaching Standards and quality and effectiveness of alternative certification programs. With a background in science and mathematics research, evaluation, and policy analysis, Montgomery has extensive experience in the design and implementation of large-scale evaluation studies; has led the design and implementation of online resources and research instruments; and has experience with all levels of the education system, including classroom teaching, professional development for teachers, preservice teacher education, and systemic reforms at state and district levels. She has a PhD in curriculum and instruction from the University of North Carolina.

Jane Ngo is a research/project associate for the Aspen Education and Society Program where she works to support its ongoing project on Rethinking Human Capital in K–12 Education to identify better ways to recruit, support, develop, and advance teaching excellence and school leadership. She has served as a research analyst for the Corporate Executive Board where she studied best practices in corporate communications, including corporate philanthropy, and crisis communications. She also studied contract language, labor-management relationships, and English language learner issues in her work at the American Federation of Teachers. In addition, she served at the Charlottesville, Virginia, Department of Social Services, providing support and supervision for at-risk youth, and assisted in the launch of a new rural program, which included community partnership development. As an AmeriCorps member for City Year San Jose/Silicon Valley, Ngo designed and delivered enrichment and support programs for middle school students and English language adult learners, and wrote and delivered curriculum in reading, math, and social justice. Ngo holds a master's in education from the Harvard Graduate School of Education.

Robert Schwartz has, since 1996, been a faculty member at Harvard Graduate School of Education, where he currently serves as Academic Dean and Professor of Practice. From 1997 to 2002, he also served as president of Achieve, Inc., a national nonprofit established by governors and corporate leaders to help states strengthen academic performance. He previously served in a variety of roles in education and government, including high school teacher in California and principal in Oregon; education adviser to Boston mayor Kevin White and Massachusetts governor Michael Dukakis; executive director of the Boston Compact; and education program director at the Pew Charitable Trusts. He currently cochairs the Aspen Institute's education program and serves on the boards of the Education Trust, the Noyce Foundation, and the Rennie Center for Education Research and Policy. Schwartz has an MA from Brandeis University.

Jon D. Snyder is dean of the graduate school of education at the Bank Street College of Education. His practitioner background includes working as public elementary school teacher and curriculum and staff developer. Snyder's academic interests include teacher learning, conditions that support teacher learning, and relationships between teacher learning and student learning. He has an EdD from Teachers College, Columbia University.

Laurence B. Stanton provides planning and performance management consulting to clients in education and work force development. He helps clients build consensus and establish goals, develop and communicate strategies and plans, identify measures for tracking progress, and create and implement systems to support continuous improvement and learning. Clients include the New Teacher Center, the National Education Association, the National Association of Charter School Authorizers, the Public Education Leadership Project at Harvard University, and several districts and charter management organizations. From 2003 to 2008, Stanton served as strategy and planning officer for the Chicago Public Schools. In that role, he was responsible for developing, managing, and communicating the district's three core improvement strategies, leading development of school and district scorecards and dashboards and building new department and school planning processes. He has a MPA from the Harvard Kennedy School and a JD from Loyola University Chicago.

Sandra J. Stein is an internationally recognized expert in school leadership development, well known for her rigorous, experiential approach to developing strong instructional leaders. As the CEO of the New York City Leadership Academy, an alternative principal preparation and support program serving the largest school district in the nation, Stein has applied her visionary method of teaching using problem-based, real-world simulations and job-embedded learning to contribute to the development and success of hundreds of current and prospective principals in New York City.

Before joining the Leadership Academy, Stein was an associate professor at Baruch College, School of Public Affairs, and founding director of its Aspiring Leaders Program (ALPs). She has written comprehensively on the issue of preparing the nation's educational leaders. She is the author of *The Culture of Education Policy* (Teachers College Press, 2004) and *Principal Training on the Ground: Ensuring Highly Qualified Leadership* (coauthored with Liz Gewirtzman, Heinemann, 2003). In addition, she was the codirector and producer (with David Loewenstein) of *Creating Counterparts*, a video-documentary about the power of urban and rural youth to transcend distance and embrace difference through artistic collaboration, and was codirector of the mural project on which the documentary is based. Stein received a PhD in education administration and policy analysis from Stanford University and holds two MA degrees from Stanford in political science and international and comparative education.

Index